A
WHOSOEVER
CHURCH

A
WHOSOEVER
CHURCH

Welcoming Lesbians and Gay Men
into African American Congregations

Gary David Comstock

Westminster John Knox Press
LOUISVILLE
LONDON·LEIDEN

©2001 Gary David Comstock

Unless otherwise indicated, scripture quotations are from the New Revised Standard Version of the Bible, copyright © 1989 by the Division of Christian Education of the National Council of the Churches of Christ in the U.S.A. and are used by permission.

Book design by Sharon Adams
Cover design by Lisa Buckley
Cover illustration: Jacob Lawrence, There are many churches in Harlem. The people are very religious. *1943, transparent and opaque watercolor on paper, 15½ x 22½ in., 1987.94, Amon Carter Museum, Forth Worth, Texas, copyright controlled by Francine Seders Gallery.*

First edition
Published by Westminster John Knox Press
Louisville, Kentucky

This book is printed on acid-free paper that meets the American National Standards Institute Z39.48 standard. ♾

PRINTED IN THE UNITED STATES OF AMERICA

01 02 03 04 05 06 07 08 09 10 — 10 9 8 7 6 5 4 3 2 1

Library of Congress Cataloging-in-Publication Data

Comstock, Gary David, 1945–
  A whosoever church : welcoming lesbians and gay men into African American congregations / Gary David Comstock.— 1st ed.
    p. cm.
  ISBN 0-664-22280-3 (alk. paper)
  1. Church work with African American gays. 2. Homosexuality—Religious aspects—Christianity. 3. African American clery—Interviews. I. Title.

BV4468.2.A34 C65 2001
261.8'35766—dc21
                                                                00-050458

Contents

Acknowledgments

I am grateful to my editor, Nick Street, for his enthusiasm when I proposed this project and for his support and wisdom throughout its completion.

I thank Rhonda Kissinger for transcribing the interviews with the promptness, patience, accuracy, and attention to detail that have characterized her help with this and my other work.

I dedicate this work to my partner, Ted Stein, who has loved and supported me throughout my research and writing projects.

And I offer these interviews in memory of James Baldwin who once said, "I think that the inability to love *is* the central problem, because that inability masks a certain terror, and that terror is the terror of being touched. And if you can't be touched, you can't be changed. And if you can't be changed, you can't be alive."[1]

Introduction

A Listening Issue

"Acknowledging the active and committed presence of lesbians and gay men in Black churches is an important listening issue," says ethicist Garth Baker-Fletcher. Because "we are living through a pivotal chapter in the history of Christianity where questions about sexuality and gender roles are in a state of transformation and flux," we "cannot afford to shut out anyone in this freedom struggle, even though such 'out of the closet' theologizing and ethical reflection has usually been ignored by Black Christians."[1]

In my previous research, I provided a forum in which lesbian/bisexual/gay people within organized religion could speak and be listened to. I learned that most lesbians and gay men seek acceptance but experience animosity and rejection in their churches, and gay African Americans in particular emphasize the importance of religion in their family, community, and history and say that much of the pain and sadness in their lives has centered around the Black church.[2] Many Black lesbians and gay men say that their sadness is made heavier when the Black church's leading role in "all progressive changes in civil rights since the days of slavery" is contrasted with its "silent or abusive" regard for the human rights of gay people. One person told me that rejection by the Black church is "especially devastating because this institution has been, and continues to be, the only place where we can take real refuge from the racism we experience in the society."[3]

To conclude, however, that Black churches are more homophobic than white churches would be a mistake, even though some Black religious leaders do not hesitate to make that claim.[4] Peter Gomes, professor of Christian morals and minister of Memorial Chapel at Harvard University, for example, says, "We're at least a generation behind. We're so used to being victims ourselves that we cannot contemplate that anybody else can share in that. We're just not used to talking in any other category than race."[5] Some leaders point out that predominantly white denominations vigorously debate the inclusion of homosexuals, while Black churches refuse even to talk about the issue. Others claim that Black churches historically have provided a haven for gay people but have clothed their tolerance and acceptance in silence and denial.[6] Yet, the first clergyman in the United States to organize a ministry to homosexuals was Rev. A. Cecil Williams, the African American pastor of San Francisco's Glide Memorial Church in 1962;[7] and no nationally recognized member of the clergy is better known for his pro-gay stances than the Rev. Jesse Jackson.[8] Statistically, too, Black Christians are not distinctively homophobic. When compared with the general population and other religious groupings, their rates of accepting homosexuality, gay rights, and same-sex marriage fall right in the middle.[9]

Recently, more Black pastors and congregations have acted publicly to support lesbians and gay men. A gay Black man in the United Methodist Church says that "what gives legitimacy and a boost to the gay and lesbian movement in the denomination is to have people of color stand up and say, 'I've studied the scriptures and studied my own heart, and I've come to the conclusion that gay and lesbian people can be people of faith of good standing.' The first time I saw it, I found it very amazing; the second time I saw it, I just accepted it. From talking with my African American friends in the church, I think that somehow they can get it that gay people ought to be treated fairly."[10]

If, as the earlier quote by Baker-Fletcher claims, we "cannot afford to shut out anyone" as we address questions of sexuality and gender, these pro-gay clergy must also be recognized and listened to. Having listened to lesbians and gay men, I seek now to listen to Black religious leaders who welcome and affirm lesbians and gay men. I turn to Black religious leaders also because pro-gay white clergy have already been recognized and received extensive coverage in the national news media. Some of the more notable are Rev. Dr. William S. Coffin of the United Church of Christ,[11] Bishop John Shelby Spong of the Episcopal Church,[12] Bishop Thomas Gumbleton of the Roman Catholic Church,[13] Rev. Dr. Tex Sample of the United Methodist Church,[14] Rev. Jane Adams Spahr of the Presbyterian Church (U.S.A.)[15], Rev. Dr. Michael K. Kinnamon of the Disciples of Christ,[16] and Rabbi Paul Menitoff of the Central Conference of American Rabbis.[17] With the exception of Rev. Jesse Jackson, a comparable group of Black clergy has not been

identified, even though many have been or have become outspoken supporters of gay people.

A Gathering of Voices

In this volume, then, I gather the voices of African American religious
leaders who are integrating lesbians, gay men, bisexuals, and transgendered people into their congregations, seminaries, and universities.
Although the twenty people whose interviews appear here cannot be said
to represent the Black church in its entirety, as a group they are not without representational qualities. Ten are women; ten are men. Their work
takes place in a variety of cities—Tampa, Atlanta, Nashville, Los
Angeles, Pasadena, San Francisco, Omaha, Chicago, Milwaukee, Kansas
City, Washington, D.C., New York, Cambridge, and Burlington. They are
affiliated with twelve denominations—the African Methodist Episcopal
Church, African Methodist Episcopal Zion Church, National Baptist
Convention U.S.A., American Baptist Churches in the U.S.A., independent Baptist churches, Original United Holy Church of America, storefront
Pentecostal churches, Roman Catholic Church, United Church of Christ,
Unitarian Universalist Association, Presbyterian Church (U.S.A.), and
Episcopal Church. Their ages range from thirty-five to seventy, with
some who "marched with Martin Luther King Jr." to others who were
born during the Civil Rights movement. The interviews were conducted
from June 1998 to October 1999.

   All of the people interviewed are pro-gay, but their experience, view-
points, visions, and hope vary. The interviews focus on each person's particular work and perspective. Each talks about his or her own personal
experience in coming to terms with and advocating for lesbians and gay
men. They speak candidly about their personal struggles with homophobia as well the problems and successes they have had in making the
church and society safe and welcoming for gay people. They acknowledge and take on the worst and best of their own religious traditions to
chart a pro-gay path that is biblically and theologically sound. They criticize the Black church for not being more openly welcoming, but they
also recognize its traditional role in having been a conditional haven for
gay people. Some discuss the courting of Black conservatives by the
Christian Right to mount an anti-gay political campaign. Each maps out
her or his own vision for greater acceptance of gay people and offers
advice to lesbians and gay men who want to remain and become more
visible in the church.

A "Whosoever" Church

The title of this book, *A Whosoever Church,* is taken from one of the interviews. Rev. Ed Sanders refers to his congregation in Nashville as a "whosoever" church because "we try to be inclusive of all and alienating to none." The term "whosoever" is from the Gospel according to John 3:16–17: "For God so loved the world, that he gave his only begotten Son, that whosoever believeth in him should not perish, but have everlasting life" (KJV). For Rev. Sanders, this passage means that "you need to get beyond difference and engage the person in a way that is transforming for them." As his and the other interviews show, the process of engaging, including, and changing people is complicated and difficult.

Although the interviews address similar topics and the interviewees often share similar points of view, I have organized the interviews according to their emphasis and focus. Their distinguishing characteristics allow me to organize the interviews into four parts, each part representing a different aspect or task in the process of creating churches that welcome and affirm lesbians and gay men.

The interviews in Part I, "Paving the Way," discuss the problems and resistance that clergy encounter when they try to make their churches more inclusive. Part II, "Charting the Course," presents the approaches, strategies, and programs that religious leaders use to overcome problems and to advance inclusion. The interviews in Part III, "Making the Connections," are with pastors of large urban congregations in which gay people are openly integrated into the life of the church. In Part IV, "Reflection and Prophecy," four professors and one church administrator place in a theological context these efforts to welcome and affirm gay people and discuss the meaning of these efforts for the future of the church. Together, the four sections take you through the troubles, struggles, successes, and theologies of building a "whosoever" church.

A Few Words from the Interviewer

Initially, I had reservations about my qualifications as a white gay man to conduct these interviews. I found encouragement to proceed in the work of the African American poet and essayist Audre Lorde. She tries to counter our difficulty with and resistance to teaching or writing about those who are unlike us. Her advice is direct and clear: "We must each of us recognize our responsibility to seek those words out, to read them and share them and examine them in their pertinence to our lives. That we not hide behind the mockeries of separations that have been imposed upon on us and which so often we accept as our own." Not to do this work would be, in Lorde's words, another one of "the endless ways in which we rob ourselves of ourselves and each other."[18]

After my first interview, which was with Rev. Sanders, I asked if he thought I was someone who could or should continue to seek out other Black religious leaders and develop a collection of interviews into this project. He said, to paraphrase: "Of course. A Black researcher may end up with a different kind of project, but that in some ways is the point. We all need to be finding out about each other, and we'll probably do that in different ways." Subsequently, I went on to find a series of cooperative and enlightening people to interview, and I am very grateful for their willingness to give their time and to share their ideas and experience.

In turn, these people often expressed gratitude to me for conducting this research. As Rev. Tim McDonald of Atlanta said in his typically good-humored way, "I appreciate what you're doing and I know it's going to help. It's going to get some of us in trouble, too; but Jesus was always in trouble (*laughs*). I think what you are doing is very healthy, and it's going to hopefully free us up more, even. So, I want to thank you for doing this." And Rev. Chip Murray of First AME Church in Los Angeles provided me with a blessing that is both humbling and exalting: "God bless your work. Please, remember, this isn't Comstock, this is God working through Comstock. And in your fearful moments, remember, it's your ministry. It's your calling. It cannot fail; it will outlive you if it is done with integrity. You will be taking us into another zone. So, God bless you. We look forward to seeing your book soon."

Audre Lorde also says that because "we have *all* been programmed to respond to the human differences between us with fear and loathing . . . we have no patterns for relating across our human differences as equals."[19] I hope this collection of interviews may encourage and create the kind of pattern that will help build inclusive relationships and communities across our differences.

PART I

Paving the Way

Chapter 1

Rev. Timothy Mcdonald III

*T*imothy Mcdonald III is the founding pastor of First Iconium Baptist Church in Atlanta, Georgia. Since its founding in 1984, First Iconium has grown from forty to twelve hundred members. The church publicly declares that it "is concerned about the total person: mind, body, and soul. Our calling is to be a church in the world, but not of the world; to seek out the lost, to uplift the downtrodden; to embrace the rejected; to comfort the lonely; and to live out the power of God's love."[1]

Previously, Rev. Mcdonald was the assistant pastor of historic Ebenezer Baptist Church in Atlanta. He has also served as executive director of Concerned Black Clergy of Atlanta, as president of the Atlanta Million Man March Organizing Committee, as special assistant for community concerns to Mayor Maynard Jackson, as national director of Operation Breadbasket and Special Projects for the Southern Christian Leadership Conference (SCLC), and as a member of the board of People for the American Way. He is included in *Who's Who among Black Americans.*[2]

Rev. Mcdonald is an outspoken advocate for social causes and has initiated national and local projects around drugs, economic empowerment, homelessness, HIV/AIDS, racism, and hunger. He has appeared as a special guest on national TV talk shows and has traveled as part of a peace mission to South Africa, India, Japan, Nicaragua, the Middle East, and Central and South America.[3]

First Iconium is known for its mix of professionals and blue-collar workers? Did you intend for that to happen when you founded the church?

Absolutely. I preached "mass" church instead of "class" church. We have sought to open up the church to any and all and to make everybody relatively comfortable.

When did gay issues become important for you and the church?

In 1986 a member informed me that he had AIDS. He expressed that he was really afraid to call me, because he didn't know how I or the church was going to react. But this young man was our lead usher, very involved in the church, well liked by all the members. People, myself especially, loved him; and I assured him that I was going to be there for him and that I would see if the church would be. I didn't know. We have a community outreach committee that takes care of our sick and shut-in members, and when I told them that he was dying of AIDS—he had been sick for some time before he got up the courage to call me—they immediately went over to his apartment and started taking care of him. And this was when folks thought you could get AIDS by shaking hands. They cooked, washed, and cleaned for him, because they knew him as Claude. His name was Claude Sims. The AIDS part didn't matter to me, and I guess I communicated that it shouldn't matter to them. They were with him all the way up until he died. His mother came to see him and wanted to take him home. He was in his last stages, and he looked at her and said, "Mom, I am home. I want to die here with my friends, my other family." We had a memorial service and then his mom took him home to bury him, but he stayed with his church and his church stayed with him. That was the beginning. Since then other members and their family members and folk who were not members of our church have felt free enough to call me. So, since 1986 we've had a history of at least being a compassionate congregation.

Why do you think you and your congregation were able to step up to this issue in a way that other pastors and other congregations haven't been able to?

I think it really depends on the pastor. The pastor sets the tone. If the pastor is scared, homophobic, and sends out negative signals about gays and lesbians, it's going to spread throughout the congregation. We had retreats where I talked with my deacons about being there and caring. I believe the Lord sent us Claude, because before we knew Claude was gay, we knew him as Claude. Everybody loved Claude. He was just a nice guy. So, folks were able to get beyond the gay part and see the person. And that carried over into other relationships. But I think the pastor is the key.

Do you think that the work you've been doing since 1986 has made your church more friendly for people in general and for gay people in particular?

I certainly hope so. I have a number of associate ministers here, and some of them came from other churches and places; and we had to have a meeting or two because some of what they had said from the pulpit regarding gay men and lesbians didn't set well with me, so I know it didn't set well with some other folk. I spend a lot of time counseling folks. I've had members come to me and tell me nobody else knows they're gay. So, because I know they are in my congregation—and to be honest they are in most Black congregations—I told my associates I thought it was better to be more sensitive and caring and to watch what they say. I had to say that the preaching that comes from this pulpit has to embrace people, to heal rather than hurt people.

Have they been open to working through this issue?

They've been pretty open. I don't think any of them doesn't realize there are probably homosexuals right out there in the audience. My thing is, "Do we proclaim the gospel by putting everybody in hell and hurting people, or do we proclaim the gospel by being compassionate, open, and healing? What would Jesus do?" And they start up with, "Jesus would condemn this, this is a sin." I say, "Well, after he's condemned this, if I accept your premise, then what would he do?" Then they get quiet, "Okay, he would show compassion and love, and he would try to understand where and how and not be afraid to go there." What really gets them is one of the lines I use, "Most folks who are so fearful of homosexuals are not sure of their own sexuality." That gets their attention and quiets them down (*laughs*). "If you were sure of your own sexuality, you wouldn't have to be so vocal and afraid of folk who are different from you."

Do you see some changes having happened in your associates?

Oh, yes. Definitely. One who is still very, very conservative is much more open now on that issue. He has gone to a Bible college, and he has since come and told me, "You know, I had to take some of my other students to task." It's a very conservative little Bible school where they say all homosexuals are going to hell; and he actually stood up and said "I don't really believe that." So, now he's getting a little dose of what I've been getting over the years. And he's kind of proud of it.

It sounds as though you're doing some training of people who go out and do the work elsewhere.

I hope I'm doing some sharing of faith that recognizes all human beings as God's creation. That's my basic premise of ministry. All human beings are God's creation whether we like them or not, whether they are Black or white or racist or homosexuals. We got to work through that. And as long as we have an open heart and an open mind, God will help us to work through it. It's a slow, tedious process, because you always get this sin thing, sin, sin, sin. And I do believe in sin, but how does one begin to move from condemning the sinner and throwing out the sinner with everything we perceive to be sinful? I've talked with homosexuals, because I had questions about whether they chose or were born gay. I wrestled with that question and did a lot of reading and I haven't totally resolved it, but a gay man whom I really respected said to me, "Reverend, do you think with all the hell that I catch that I would choose the ostracism of my own family and coworkers and used-to-be friends, that I would choose this lifestyle? There's no way." Now, that was him, and I don't make that a general statement, but it shook me up. I don't say that all are born homosexual, and I definitely don't say that all choose; but because I know that some are born, then I treat the whole idea of homosexuality with that in mind.

Because of the way things are in our society and because of genes and chromosomes, it is very possible, very probable that there are people born like this; and if they are born like this, we have to treat them with respect and we have to have a gospel that acknowledges them as God's creation. Whether I like it or not, God created them. So, if I want to go to heaven, I've got to deal with them in a manner that is compassionate, open, and honest with all of my fears. I need to be in an environment—and the gay people I've spoken with have provided that for me—where I can express the questions and fears that I have. I still wrestle with it. I don't want you to think that I have solved this dilemma in my own heart and mind. I have not.

Some situations are more difficult than others, because even some gay men and lesbians are so defensive that the least little thing that you say is interpreted wrong, when you didn't mean it to be that way at all. So, I've seen some resistance and negativism on their part, too. And I've said, "You are making it real hard for me to open the church up with that kind of attitude. You've got to relax a little bit more and not be so defensive. I know it's easy to be defensive with everybody pouncing on you, labeling you, and stereotyping you, but when you come to me, let down your guard. I'm not like that. I have an open mind. I still struggle with it myself, but I'm not where I used to be. I'm not where I want to be either, but I'm definitely not where I think most people—particularly most Black pastors—are. So give me a chance. Help me. I want to help you, but I need you to help me, too."

Do you have other advice for lesbians and gay men who are trying to find or keep a place in the church?

I think they should go to the pastor privately. I think it helps a pastor tremendously when you have that one-on-one, eye-to-eye contact. Let your pastor know, "I want to stay in this church. You may disagree with my lifestyle, but I want to stay in this church. So, help me to be able to stay in this church, because I like this church; my family is here and I have friends here." That will open doors like nothing else and will help the minister to be a better minister. If they've been in that church and like that church, I think one of the first things they should do is get up enough courage to keep going. When a gay person said, "I want to stay in this church, I don't want to leave this church," that really changed my preaching, the way I teach, and my vocabulary. I have some white members, and that also changed my preaching, because I am very Black. Having those white members in my congregation changed my Afrocentric preaching and style. Now I don't say "white folk"; I say "some white folk."

After talking with gay men, how have your preaching and teaching changed?

I found myself staying out of the bedroom, because when you get into the bedroom, you start talking about adultery, fornication, and homosexuality. I think it's a bad place to be preaching from anyway, which is what I tell my associate ministers. There's a million other topics we can preach on. You don't have to go into anybody's bedroom. Stay out of there. When I was younger and didn't know better, I could always get folks' attention by talking about sex. Most ministers know when all else fails, just talk about sex and you get folks' attention. Well, I don't have to do that anymore. I discuss it. We've had seminars on sexuality and parenting, particularly with teenagers. I have folks come in from the health department to talk about HIV/AIDS. Folks are a little uncomfortable at first, but they get into it eventually. It has changed. I used to be where some of my colleagues are, that's why I understand them. I used to be hellfire-and-brimstone, "You're going to hell if you do this, if you do that, if you don't do this, if you don't do that." I thank God I've grown in grace, awareness, and knowledge. I think the Holy Spirit has enabled me to see that the word of God is not static. It's dynamic and inclusive. Yes, it cuts; yes, there's wrath and judgment, but God is a people person. Once you understand that God is a people person, then you have to deal with people, even people you may disagree with, don't like, or label. Being an African American I know how that feels. Why should I subject anybody else to that?

Do you see a time soon when gay people will feel comfortable and free to express their sexual identity openly in church?

I think that's coming. We're much further than we were in 1986. We're getting there as family members experience having other family members who are gay. Because they are having more contact and conversations within their own families and extended families, a kind of awareness is carrying over into the church. It's really about trying to break down ignorance. Historically and now, Blacks are very conservative and literal when it comes to biblical interpretation. Even among the clergy it's a very difficult subject to talk about, because you're going to have literalists and progressives go at each other with deep convictions from whichever side they are on.

How do you deal with the Bible when it comes to homosexuality?

I deal with Jesus, the compassion of Jesus, such as, "I can understand that you want to interpret the Bible that way, but don't you think Jesus, if he were here, would show and demonstrate compassion whether it's cancer, HIV, AIDS, sickle-cell anemia, or leukemia?" I try to put all of those in a common category, because the tendency of those who want to discard gays and lesbians is to isolate HIV/AIDS, like, "This one is different from everything else, and the Bible speaks specifically about this." And I say, "Well, the Bible speaks specifically about a lot of things, but what happens when you deal with compassion and with accepting?" My thing is: Jesus meets people where they are. That's the genius and the majesty of Jesus for me. He meets people where they are. It may not be where I am, but he meets them where they are; and everybody should have an opportunity to get to know Christ.

I get quite of bit of negativism. I don't have a lot of supporters when I talk about gays and lesbians.[4] I don't preach it a lot from the pulpit, very rarely now. I do it in teaching sessions where there can be questions and answers and dialogue. I found that it's not to my advantage to do it in a monologue setting from the pulpit because people will murmur afterwards, get the wrong interpretation, have questions they can't ask, get frustrated, and then start rumors from what they don't understand. I found it works better when I'm in a Bible study, retreat, seminar, discussion kind of session. And even then it can still be difficult, because we have some very conservative people and some very liberal and progressive-minded people here, which is what I want and desire. It definitely leads to lively discussion.

So, it's an issue that needs dialogue rather than monologue?

Yes, and where there has been dialogue, people have been much more receptive and understanding, because you can break down your fears and begin to deal with the person rather than a label. Once you know the person, the label doesn't matter. I really hate discrimination. I believe in the right of the Klan to march and speak, even though I deplore and hate what they do. I don't think gays and lesbians should be discriminated against, and I've come out more forcibly on their issues. I don't think anybody should be discriminated against for whatever reason, including their sexual preference, sexual orientation. I've gotten more support for being against anti-gay discrimination in the secular arena than for my theological acceptance of gays, because Black folk understand discrimination. When you can see when certain people are being singled out just because they are gay, most people say that is wrong. But from some of my colleagues, particularly in the more traditional, conservative wing, I catch hell. They've said I'm not Christian because I believe this, that I'm going to hell because I believe all people should be accepted.

How do they criticize you? Do they take you to task in public?

Some have—maybe not by name, but because I'm a public figure here a lot of folk know who they are talking about. I'm head of the Concerned Black Clergy, and some ministers say they're not members of Concerned Black Clergy because we don't condemn homosexuality. A number of pastors, particularly from some of the larger churches, say, "They don't have any religion over there. If they had religion, they would condemn this." But they don't belong, so we go on.

Are you ever tempted to back off from the issue?

I hope not (*laughs*).

Have you had experience with the white religious right's efforts to court Black pastors?

I'm on the board of People for the American Way, and I've been dealing with the religious right before I came on their board—all the way back to Jerry Falwell and when I was in seminary. Since the late '70s and early '80s, these folks have been pouncing; and now they're using homosexuality, what I call a wedge issue, in the Black community, because they know that Black people are basically biblically conservative and literal: "If you support homosexuality, you are not Christian; if you condemn them, you are." They have come into the Black community and said, "You know Concerned Black Clergy supports homosexuals, so you don't want to belong to them. Come and join us." So, I have no respect for the religious right. I even interpret their efforts biblically, that the battles that Jesus fought were not with the governors and mayors, but with the Pharisees, scribes, and Sadducees, the so-called "religious" leaders. His battle was against their religious bigotry, and I think the religious right is carrying on that same religious bigotry. They are the same kind of folk who had slaves, supported slavery, and used the scriptures, "Slave, obey your masters." But now they come back and say, "If you support homosexuals, then you are going to hell; and if you don't preach against it, then you are not following the word of God." And I say, "Who are you to tell me? You're the ones who kept my family enslaved. You're the ones trying to destroy affirmative action. So, I'm not going to listen to you." By using the issue of homosexuality, the religious right divides and does a disservice to the Black community.

You're well-educated and willing to read and study when you don't understand something. Is that part of what enables some pastors to face this issue in a way that's not reactionary?

Absolutely. Reading has helped me to broaden my perspective, but dialogue has helped me more. Not being afraid to talk to and about homosexuals. Believe me, that's a major step.

It would be helpful if you could tell other pastors who are probably afraid of the same thing why they don't need to be afraid of it. What's the fear and why is it not such a big deal?

I think the fear is of their own sexuality. That's at least part of it. It's fear of what they don't know and don't understand. I don't understand it and I don't claim to; and part of the reason why I've been able to dialogue with other ministers is because I share with them that I still wrestle with this. I am much further along now than I used to be; and if you want to grow as a pastor, then you've got to be willing to have an open mind and heart and to listen to and be in dialogue with people as people. I don't want to judge, which is another big thing for me. Judging belongs to God. I can't judge another person, whether it's lifestyle or sexual preference or faith commitment. I think it is wrong for me to judge. The Bible does speak about that, too. "Judge ye not, lest ye be judged. And with the same judgment you judge others, you should be judged likewise." I do make value judgments, yes; that's legitimate. But I don't think it is right to judge and condemn any person.

What is it about your background, your education, or just your personality that makes you somebody who is not homophobic?

I think Claude helped me more than anything not to be homophobic. I knew him before I knew he was homosexual. I knew him as one of the finest persons I have known. I think God put that experience in my life so that I could perhaps help other clergy not to be so homophobic. I was there when he was nothing but skin and bones. I saw him go from a healthy, robust, lively human being to just. . . . I mean I've never seen any other case as bad as his. He held on a long time. This was before all the medications were available. He just went slowly, slowly, slowly, daily. There wasn't a week that went by that I didn't go by to see and pray with him; and there wasn't a week that members of the church were not over there. I think that helped me a lot.

You said something about the pastors and your colleagues who criticize you. Have you also been able to make alliances with pastors because of this issue?

Oh, yes. You get some who are allies and who will stand in solidarity with you. The tendency is not to have a bullhorn proclaiming it but certainly to be supportive.

If a gay person were to say to you, "I do want to go public; I want to be known as gay in the congregation," how would you tell him to go about doing that?

I think it would be wise to test it out first. I would support them. What I've told them is, "Find some people in church you know and share it with them. See what kind of reaction you get, and then decide if you want to go public. But know that if you do go public, I will support you." What I think has happened is as they have discussed with others, they may have been encouraged not to go public because others have said, "You may not want to subject yourself to the reaction you'll get." But I say, "Get a feel from some of the folk you trust, whether they're in the choir, the ushers' board, or Sunday school—one or two you can share with privately. If you can't do that, maybe you're not ready to go public yet. If you do find support, it may lead you to want to go public."

Do you know families or people within your congregation you could count on to be supportive if someone were to go public with their sexual identity?

Yes. From our discussions over the years and from what people have said, such as, "If I had a gay person in my family I'd be supportive," I think we have some folks who would be supportive. It's not the majority of our congregation who are there. Even among my deacons, I know some aren't there, but some are. It's a lot easier for those who have homosexuals in their own families.

Often homosexuals are stereotyped as people who are bad. From your talks with gay men, have you found them to be people of good faith?

Yes, as I said, Claude was a case in point. There have been others in my church. There have been three whom the church knew of either when they got sick or when they shared with them.

What made them people of good faith?

They were just good people (*laughs*). They came to church, worked, served, were there when I or whatever auxiliary needed them. Apart from the fact that they had a different lifestyle, they weren't any different from anybody else. That's the thing that's hard to get my colleagues to understand: "If you didn't know that this person was homosexual, he would just be there in the workplace, in the military, or any other place. There have always been homosexuals, and you probably went to school with some. So why are you so hell-bent over this, like it's some new phenomenon? Why do we act like it's so new?" Another thing with the religious right is the family, family, family, like we just discovered the family and family values. Heck, we've always had family values. I say, "Don't present this like it's some new phenomenon and don't present homosexuality like it's new." I may have my feelings about it and I may even disagree about it at certain points, but my basic theological premise, which is what I always go back to, is that we are all children of God. This is my brother and this is my sister; I've got to relate to them and I've got to work through whatever feelings, fears, and inhibitions I might have, because this is my brother, this is my sister. We've got to live together in this house. Let's figure out how we're going to live together. Believe me, when you start with that you are going to run into trouble. Creation is a hell of a concept (*laughs*).

You think it's what challenges Christians the most?

Yes, I do. Even more than racism.

So, you think coming to terms with gay issues probably challenges us more theologically than racism?

Yes.

Because it bends us even more to being inclusive and compassionate?

Yes. It gets you at a core of your being—more heart than mind. I think racism is more head; homophobia/homosexuality is more heart. And people are easier to deal with cognitively than emotively. I've seen folk get very passionate about discussing homosexuality.

Do you want to say something about the particular situation of Black gay people?

For a long time the perception, not the reality, but the perception was that homosexuality was a white male thing. Even when AIDS first came out, it was seen as a gay white male disease. And we operated under that illusion for years, for over a decade. And it became increasingly known that it was indeed in the Black community, and now our children and our women increasingly are contracting HIV. Now there is a little more discussion, better than it was five years ago, because some of our college students are having to leave school and because HIV/AIDS is so prevalent, particularly in the state of Georgia. Those ministers who were hiding, ducking, and dodging are now having to confront and deal with it. I see that as a healthy thing, but again, as I said before, what we need is persons. Because homosexuality is so looked down at in the Black community and because Black ministers have been very hostile, Black gays are very, very reluctant to come out.

So, they're going to have to be a little braver?

Absolutely, but they need to know they get much more receptivity if they go privately, one-on-one. It's got to be that way. That's how you build confidence and relationships; and those relationships can turn into general theological principles, if dialogue takes place. It's not going to happen in every case. I have to admit that. There are some ministers who are going to believe the way they do, I don't care what they say, what you say, or who they meet. But my experience has been, as Concerned Black Clergy has made these dialogues available and as we've done in our church, that the outgrowth is that somebody is going to become more open.

And people becoming more open and inclusive is what you mean when you say that these relationships give birth to a general theological principle?

Absolutely.

Would you mind closing with your own advice about what Christians or the church needs to do concerning lesbian/gay issues?

I think the church needs to hold more discussions and to stop pretending as though the issue doesn't exist. Start with something that is considered safe, if you will. I mean, don't just start with homosexuality and lambasting gays and lesbians. Start with what I've found to be helpful: children with AIDS. Start with something that is not as controversial. Then you can build up to lesbian and gay issues. As you begin your discussions on how to minister to children with AIDS, then you say, "Okay, if you can deal that way with children with AIDS, why not gay men with AIDS?" And if they say, "Well, children didn't choose to get AIDS," then you have an opportunity to talk about sexual orientation as choice or creation and also to reach out to others with AIDS in your church, people who are known and loved, regardless of their sexual orientation. You build from one step to another step to another step, but start and stay with dialogue. Preaching and monologue won't advance their understanding. They need to ask questions and feel comfortable doing so. You can also share statistics and specific actual case studies of families, of folks you know, if it's okay with those folks, if they have talked to you and said they want you to use their stories.[5] Claude told me, "I want you to use my story, Reverend McDonald, to help other people. Use my story to help educate other people; tell them how this church responded to me."

Chapter 2

Rev. Larry C. Menyweather-Woods

*L*arry C. Menyweather-Woods is the senior pastor of Mount Moriah Missionary Baptist Church in Omaha, Nebraska. Mount Moriah has served the city for 110 years and continues to expand its ministry from a scriptural basis in Isaiah 43:18–19: "Do not remember the former things, or consider the things of old. I am about to do a new thing; now it springs forth, do you not perceive it?" With Rev. Menyweather-Woods as its pastor for ten years, the church's membership has grown from 125 (75 adults, 50 children) to 750. Before coming to Mount Moriah, he served parishes in Pennsylvania and Virginia. His denominational affiliation is with the National Baptist Convention USA.[1]

Rev. Menyweather-Woods holds executive positions in the Urban League of Nebraska, the National Association for the Advancement of Colored People, and the nonprofit North Omaha Renaissance Development Corporation. He has advocated for expanded housing and commercial development in neglected areas of the city, for better education in inner-city schools, for better police-community relations, for ending domestic violence, and for interracial and interfaith alliances. He is also an adjunct professor of theology at Creighton University and of Black studies at the University of Nebraska at Omaha.[2]

What do you think has been responsible for the growth at Mount Moriah?

People have come back, and it's been a great movement. Primarily, I think because we've been truthful and faithful as far as being consistent with the Word as well as our community outreach. We've been very active in the community and being part of the community. The Lord's anointing has been with us!

What kind of activities?

Just about everything dealing with justice issues.

You've also spoken out on behalf of lesbians and gay men.[3] Was that unusual for you or part of your basic theology and ministry?

Part of my liberation theology and belief.[4]

Was there a specific event that triggered your taking a public position?

What happened was that I was responding to the issue of one of the local United Methodist preachers marrying a gay couple, which was against his church bylaws. That's what sparked the controversy. The news media started questioning us preachers. And my position is I will not put one sin up against another. In other words, I don't say one is weightier than the other is. I believe that sin is sin, period. And when you use the text that homosexuality is an abomination before God, you should also look at what else is an abomination before God as well. It's like saying it's alright to be a whoremonger or whatever as long as you are straight— as long as you're doing it with someone of the opposite sex, then it's not an abomination to the Lord—but that's not true. It's like heterosexuals have an invitation to go ahead and do whatever and say, "At least I'm straight," and that's ridiculous.

Are there lesbians and gay men in your local congregation whom you know of?

There are some that I do know of. But there are many that I don't know of. Within the African American community that's been one of the hush-hush things, but they've always been there. Many have never identified themselves as such, and that's one reason why you really don't know who you're dealing with sometimes.

What happens when someone in your congregation identifies themselves to you as lesbian or gay?

Nothing as far as I'm concerned. I do not look at my responsibility as trying to force someone to change. My responsibility is to give folk a clear path to God and to challenge them to think and to put their faith into action, not to change them and try to make them change. I cannot force them to change. I do not enter into it from that perspective. I don't come into it saying, "That's okay, you come on in here and you will change." No. If you're going to change, it's between you and the Lord. My responsibility is to minister to you.

Has your congregation engaged in ministry to people with AIDS?

Yes, we have. We have done feedings, provided food, and participated in the National AIDS Month sponsored by The Balm in Gilead, Inc., out of New York.[5] I also began teaching about sexuality and dealing with the struggle of AIDS.

You've done this teaching from the pulpit?

On Wednesday night Bible study as well as on Sunday.

What has the reception been from the congregation?

The first week was very rough, very uncomfortable. After the first week it was better, because I told them I was going to try to move them from their comfort zone, and someone said I did succeed. But it was a battle. When you talk straight talk about certain things, it is a battle. But they have been more receptive since then.

What is the major stumbling block for people when discussing these issues?

I think the major stumbling block is the unwillingness to communicate. In certain parts of our American culture, talking about sex has not been a problem, but in many other parts people think that they aren't supposed to talk about it, that it's up to other folk to do it. That's bad. Parents cannot talk to their children. They feel a need to find someone else who can talk to their children for them and with them about the issue.

So, you brought it up at a meeting one week and then did follow-up meetings?

Yes. What we did to start was to look at what is love, and we did that by reading the Old Testament Song of Solomon for what it is, a love story, and the impact it has on human relationship—not just on the human-divine relationship, but on our feelings for each other in human relationships, using that story to reexamine, re-look-at our relationships. And we also looked at New Testament passages from First Corinthians, chapters six and seven,[6] to ask why is it that most young people want to get married. They want to get married because they want to have sex, because we've told them you can't do it until after you get married.

Have people been receptive to this discussion?

They are more receptive now. It's been going on for about a year. They know what I'm talking about; they understand why I'm doing it. Most of the controversy comes from outside of my church, not from within my church. In other words, I would be teaching my folk, they would tell their friends what I was teaching them, their friends would say something to their pastors or their friends, and the next thing you know their pastors and friends are saying I shouldn't be teaching that kind of stuff to them.

Would fellow pastors in the area approach you and criticize you?

I have been a recipient of that kind of criticism. But I'm sometimes considered to be a rebel anyway, because what I believe I do believe, and I'll stand by it regardless, and I believe the church needs to take a dramatically front-row seat on dealing with sexuality. We need to talk about it. I would rather for the church to talk about it than for the school to talk about it. But we have to be willing to really talk. That comes into the issue of dealing with homosexuality, too. What do you do when a male feels for another male or a female feels for another female? How do you treat that? What is it about? How do you deal with them? "Yes, alright, you say this is a sin. Okay, I understand why you may say that, but let's try to understand what those feelings are about."

Do you think that homosexuality is a sin?

Biblically, I think sin is anything that you put before God or that you end up doing against God's word. That applies to having sex that is against God, period.

How can a gay man or lesbian not be sinful? Do they have to abstain from having sex, or is there a way for them to lead a faithful life?

In reality, a good Baptist knows that people are going to sin even after they get saved. So, that's something we deal with. You would have to deal with it yourself. As we are discussing it among ourselves now, part of the gay lifestyle has to be about being accountable and responsible, just as part of a heterosexual lifestyle has to be about that. Going from house to house maybe could prove dangerous to you and you shouldn't do that. You need to talk about being faithful to your partner, whatever the situation may be. Just because people say that this is how they think your lifestyle is doesn't mean it has to be that way.

What would you say if a lesbian or a gay man approached you and said, "I feel very much that I am a Christian, I have a very good relationship with God, I have a very good relationship with my partner, but I don't feel comfortable coming to church"? What kind of advice would you give them?

I do have some who say that to me now, and I sit them down and ask them why. I tell them I can understand why they wouldn't feel comfortable, but I also find out more why they feel that way. I explore their reasons with them. If I find out that it's because someone is agitating them or teasing them, then I take care of that. I don't allow anyone, I don't care whether you're straight or gay, to deal with the membership like that. You don't have that right or authority. My ministry is one of trying to help heal the brokenhearted, to heal those who find themselves in the midst of a storm and are trying to overcome it.

You would approach the people who are criticizing and teasing them?

Oh yes. And I'd do it publicly, too. There is a way to do it publicly. I'm known for doing that. I had one member who used to work in a nightclub as a bartender. Some members knew her because they used to go to that bar, and they said something smart about it. She almost didn't come to church again, but she came to a Wednesday night Bible study and I made a comment about it. She's been coming ever since. I believe in defending my people. That's what I mean when I say that the issue with me is one of justice, of making sure you have the right to be able to do and fulfill what God wants you to do. The Lord must be the ultimate judge—about me and anyone else. I can fight for the rights of anybody, even if I think that what they may be doing might be considered traditionally sinful.

Do you think that African American lesbians and gay people see you as someone who will stand up for them?

I really don't know, and I'll tell you why I don't know. Sometimes people judge me based upon what they hear, and sometimes I can be so adamant in what I say that they don't understand that it's just the way I am. I have a very high compassion for people. And the only way to discover my compassion is when they come to me, and then they discover that I'm not a bear, just a teddy bear. I know that I try to live by the rule of treating everyone with the love that Jesus would have us love with—love in spite of, not love because of. I love people not because of but in spite of themselves and their situations.

Do you remember when you first realized that the issue of homosexuality was going to be something that the churches would have to deal with?

Oh yes, it was about fourteen or fifteen years ago when I was in seminary. I knew it was going to confront the Black church very much, very hard, because like I said, we know that there is a haven—that homosexuality exists—within the Black church, but yet we've never been willing to talk about it, to speak out on it. For us it just keeps saying it doesn't exist or a pastor will say, "We don't have none in my congregation." He's lying; he just doesn't realize it. So, in seminary is when I started looking at things differently.

What happened in seminary? Was there a particular event or people you met?

As I continued to study the Word, I discovered. It's not like I ran across one or two gay people and they had a profound effect on me. I treated them like I treated everybody. It's just that at seminary these issues came to me. I wanted to establish a special committee to look into dealing with sexuality. I wanted to be the first one to write a book on sexuality in the Black church, a down-to-earth record of it. All of a sudden I could see the topics that would be confronting us before the end of this century, such as women preachers, all the topics that are hot now.

Did you ever form the committee you talked about?

Yes, when I was pastor in a church in Pennsylvania. They considered themselves to like research, so I wanted to form a committee for them to look into this issue.

And did it happen?

No. They weren't brave enough.

Did you ever think about writing the book you mentioned?

No, someone else wrote one. Kelly Brown Douglas; she just came out with it.[7] I teach a course out here on womanist theology.[8] It has been a fascinating journey.

These are the courses you teach at the University of Nebraska at Omaha and Creighton University?

Yes, I also teach Introduction to Black Studies and Introduction to Black Church History.

For womanist theology, what are some of the resources that you recommend?

Well, Kelly Brown Douglas is one of them. Another would be Dolores Williams and then a young woman out of Washington, D.C., who is Catholic, Diana Hayes. And then there's Emilie Townes. At our state denominational meeting I'm using Emilie Townes, because we're discussing the issue of women preachers and women in ministry. Evelyn Higginbotham is also good. She's another woman who wrote about righteous indignation.[9]

It sounds as if you've been at the forefront of important issues dealing with women and sexuality in the church.

I've been blessed. I have four women preachers in my church, and my church was very traditional when I came here.

Four women preachers who are part of your church's ministry team?

Yes.

Is it unusual in your area for you to be receptive to women preachers?

Yes, definitely. This is one of the last strongholds.

Earlier you said that when you were in seminary you realized that the church needed to engage in a broader discussion of homosexuality. Do you think that discussion has gotten any broader, or do you think it's pretty narrow?

Still too narrow. That was my emphasis, my whole point, when the news reporters asked, "If you knew someone was a homosexual, would you make him a leader in the church?" And I said I couldn't just say no, because it doesn't work that way with me. That's not the right way to deal with anyone.[10]

What is the right way?

The right way is to pray and talk with them. You deal with them, you discuss with them. You discuss what you expect of them and if they can lead, then let them lead.

Have you found that they do make good leaders?

Oh, yes. A lot of folk might be surprised sometimes. Like I said, in the Black church we don't send the signals. There are men and women who you'd never guess are homosexuals. But yet they carry themselves in such a way whereby "my private life is my private life."

Are they central to the church family, the life of the church?

Yes.

Do you think that their faith may be stronger than other people's because they've had to deal with more difficult tests?

I think definitely so. You take a person who is homosexual, put on the fact that they're Black, then put on the fact that they are a woman, too, then you are in a lot of trouble, in the midst of a lot of struggle. I think once the church begins to open an honest dialogue and really to look at this issue, at the biblical passages and so forth, people will see the difference. I think there will be more ministry occurring.

Do you think pastors who have seminary training are better on the issue of homosexuality than those pastors who have not had formal education?

I don't think so. I have discovered that pastors who do not have seminary training but have studied on their own have more compassion. Unlike these older Black pastors, the young ones want to show how much they know.

So, they're more interested in showing they're right about an issue than showing compassion for the people who might be struggling with the issue?

Right. A lot of people think the Bible says, "Speak the truth." But that's not what it says. The Bible says, "Speak the truth in love," which means if you can't do it in love, shut your mouth. If it's not done in love, it doesn't matter.

Do you think that the older pastors have more of an understanding of compassion and that they lead with it?

There's no doubt in my mind. I remember when I got this young lady pregnant. I knew I had to go and tell my pastor. I was scared as I don't know what because he had already made me come before the church and apologize for dancing. So I knew he was going to run me up the ladder. I went to him, and he was the most compassionate man in the world. He said, "You were wrong. But God forgives and he has forgiven you." I went and married her anyway. Several years later I got a divorce. So, the old man was right. He was telling me to be responsible *for the child.* My baby now is 28 years old and she has a master's degree. Old ones can be more compassionate than the young ones can. The young ones don't know about compassion. They say the word "mercy," but they don't know what mercy is yet.

Where do the old ones learn it, through experience?

Life experience itself. Can you imagine trying to pastor a group of folk who have more education than you have, but yet you've got to show them that you're the leader? When they say they made it by grace and mercy, they know what they're talking about.

Do you still look to the older pastors when you want guidance?

Oh, yes. There are things that we disagree on, but yet we move on. I can disagree with my pastor today. He's eighty-seven years old, but there's one thing about it, he never stops loving me. We had homosexuals in our church back home.

How were they treated?

They were treated just like everyone else.

Where's back home?

Muskogee, Oklahoma.

The story you just told about going to your pastor for advice on having gotten the woman pregnant—it seems to me that it became your model for your ministry?

That's right. That was a life-changing event for me. He could've blown it that day, but by showing me compassion, he showed me the importance of "it's not up to me to judge anybody."

Do you think that on issues of sexuality, and especially homosexuality, the white religious right has preyed on Black churches to make alliances?

Oh, most definitely. They do that quite well.

How do they do it?

They do it primarily because they know the spirituality of most Blacks. They know which buttons to push, and they push those buttons well. They know how to push the button to say you ought to have prayer in school, etc. They know the things to say. And they make Black folks forget that they have their own kinfolk who are homosexuals. But Black folks know that's the way it is, the way it's been. They want the whites to feel that they are just as Christian as they are. That's sad.

On the other side of it, though, do you think that Black pastors like yourself when you speak on behalf of lesbians and gay men have a moral authority or are taken more seriously than white pastors?

I think sometimes I'm taken more seriously. I think they find it just so fascinating that a Black pastor can even talk, be articulate, that they don't know how to take that sometimes, especially someone who's able to stand up against someone else and dialogue without getting ignorant. They really don't know how to deal with that.

Some African American lesbians and gay men say that to leave the church, or to get kicked out of it, is to be "cut off from their people." It's an expression that I don't hear white gay people using. Can you say what's going on with that?

I think we model our churches as family, as community. The Black church has always been part of the Black community. Gayraud Wilmore used to say they are one and the same, and they were.[11] And that makes a difference. In other words, yes, we're the lifeblood of the community; we are that part of the community that gives the consistent moral imperative as well as the cultural imperative of who we are and whose we are. We're family; so, the Aunt Janes and Uncle Dans are part of it, and we are part of them. We are part of one another. We've always emphasized that individualism has not been part of the genre of the Black church. It's always about community.

Is that why lesbians and gay men are expected not to say something about their individual sexual identity?

They know what their sexual preference is, and it does not have to keep them from being part of the community. It's the idea of flaunting that would make it a problem. That does not define who you are. Your sexuality does not define you.

So, flaunting anything about oneself detracts from the community?

Right.

Is there anything that can be flaunted, like can you flaunt that you are a good parent or a good mother?

You always remember that it would not be except for others. You can't even take credit yourself because all of it's about the community. The community helped rear the child. You're not by yourself in the struggle.

That's the constant thing. You're not by yourself; you're part of this family. We are family; we pull together. The problem is that we isolate homosexuality and act like it's different from heterosexuality. My responsibility is to bring you into the family, show that you're loved in spite of whatever the case may be, and not to sit in judgment on you.

What kind of advice do you have for lesbians and gay men who want to stay or find a place in the church but feel that they might be driven out?

You know, our folk laugh because Black churches add by dividing. We're the only group that can add by dividing. We get teed off at the pastor, or get teed off at somebody, and we start our own church. I used to be one of those who said we've got too many churches in the community. But then something hit me one day. There's a church in the community for every personality. All you have to do is find it. Now, that shows how much God loves us.

So, you think that it's okay or even better for lesbians and gay men to form their own churches and to find their community that way?

I think they already have. I think there is already a church there for them; they just have to be willing to go ahead and find it. Maybe they've been in a big-size church for so long that they need to go to a mid-size church or another kind of church. But find a church where their personalities can match. In other words, the church takes on the personality of the pastor. That's the uniqueness of it all. However their pastor's personality is, if he is gregarious or whatever the case may be, that's what that church is going to become. If you just take note of how certain pastors act, then you'll find out how that church is. A lot of folk talk about the friendliness of my church—the fellowship period, the hugging and kissing and all that stuff—but that's how I am.

Chapter 3

Rev. Dr. Amos C. Brown

Amos C. Brown has been the senior pastor at Third Baptist Church in San Francisco since 1976. Founded in 1852 by two freed slaves, Third Baptist is "the oldest Black church west of the Mississippi" and has a history of direct social activism and service to the poor and needy. Under Rev. Brown's leadership, the thirty-two-hundred-member congregation has come to be seen as "a magnet church with a mission of restoring the inner city as a decent place to live."[1]

Rev. Dr. Brown received his Doctor of Ministry from United Theological Seminary, has served as the national chairman of the Youth and College Division of the NAACP, and currently serves as national chairman of the National Baptist Commission on Civil Rights. He is listed in *Who's Who among African Americans* and is on *Ebony* magazine's "Roll of Great Preachers."[2]

Since 1996 he has also been a member of the San Francisco Board of Supervisors. At the time of the interview in 1999, the Board was engaged in a controversy over granting a street-closing permit for the anniversary celebration of the Sisters of Perpetual Indulgence. The Sisters are a gay street-theater group whose members dress as nuns and use elements of Roman Catholic ritual in their performances. They also raise money for charities, do volunteer work in hospitals, and promote safe-sex education.[3]

In 1991 you and several other African American religious leaders spoke out in favor of the gay rights bill before California's legislature.[4] Why did you step up to the issue at that time?

It was a matter of principle. It was not politically expedient at all. It was just that I don't treat people wrongly just because they're different. I was taught as a child in Mississippi to respect people and not do to anyone else what I did not want to be done to me. And obviously Black people have been generalized on, stigmatized on, and treated wrongly because of the color of their skin; and I felt that these isms—such as racism, sexism, and anti-Semitism—are cousins, and we have to be consistent. Unfortunately, not many people have been consistent. I found it to be the case that, for example, white gays definitely promote their cause, and rightfully so, but when it comes to racial issues, they have exhibited some racial attitudes and bigotry. And I think we must be consistent on these areas. I think Black preachers must be consistent, not only when it becomes a question of how they treat gays but also women. The Black Baptist church in particular is one of the most male-chauvinistic institutions north of hell. I constantly try to remind my brothers that when white folks in the South told us to stay in our place because we were Black, we didn't like that; so, we shouldn't take the occasion to tell women you can't do something because you're a woman. I think it's a matter of a moral consistency, of treating people fairly and justly, and of not doing any violence or damage to the worth and dignity of all human personalities. That's why we have the problem going on over in Bosnia now. People did not learn how to live together in spite of their differences. Ethnic cleansing and getting rid of folk who are of a different race, different religion, a different ethnic background or gender or sexual orientation, that's what creates the pain and great difficulty in this world.

Why do you think you have a different perspective than some of your fellow clergymen?

As Tennyson says in *Ulysses,* "I'm a part of all that I have met"; and people by and large, even though there are some quirks in peculiar situations, are the products of their society. And many of these Black preachers, and I make no excuse for them, were exposed to Southern white Evangelism. They're from the Bible Belt. Basically, all they didn't know about the faith came from white folks. So, in great measure, whatever homophobia may have been in the Black community, I'd say for the most part came from the white persons who set the climate and called the cadence.

Why were you able to escape it? What was it about your upbringing and church that gave you the background to be open to these issues?

In terms of my development and orientation, I'm a product of the Civil Rights movement. I took very seriously my mission of ministry in the

Civil Rights movement to fight racism. I went to Morehouse College in Atlanta, which provided me with a liberal arts education, and I got a worldview there. I also went to Crozier Theological Seminary. That educational tradition drove us to be independent thinkers, to do critical thinking, and to be champions of social justice, equality, and fairness.

But many people out of that same tradition haven't taken a pro-gay position, as you have.

I think you then have to reduce it to the individual. Some individuals are fighting personal issues and insecurities that they have, and many times human beings do deal with their insecurities by looking down on or beating on somebody else in order to give themselves some kind of superficial affirmation.

What is it about your civil rights work that's key to your being open to other issues, other kinds of people?

Just respecting people, that's what the movement was about at its best. That's what Martin Luther King was about. I was one of his protégés. He taught me at Morehouse. We were in jail together. And that's the reason why in San Francisco I took a position that some didn't understand about the Sisters of Perpetual Indulgence. Martin Luther King challenged the status quo of the social order, but he did it with grace, dignity, and respect. He did not poke fun at anybody, even white folks.[5] He did not use caricatures and derision, which was what the Sisters of Perpetual Indulgence did by electing to celebrate their anniversary on Easter, a High Holy Day in Christendom. As justified as they may be in their pain and disenchantment with the Catholic Church, you can't generalize on all Christian churches, not even the whole Catholic Church, just as you can't generalize on me, a Black Baptist preacher, and say we've all been guilty of homophobia. That's not true. In the debate at the Board of Supervisors meeting about rescheduling their event, they tried to invoke the name and legacy of Martin Luther King, because it would fall on April 4, the anniversary of his assassination. But I reminded them Martin Luther King was not a mean-spirited person. He was a man of nonviolent, peaceful resistance. It did a disservice to use his name because of their history of parodying the sacraments of the Catholic Church by substituting the condom for the wafer and caricaturing the church by choosing vile and vicious names for each of the Sisters. There's a way to make your point and bring about change; and when you advance mean-spiritedness, it's like setting a forest fire. Once the fire starts going, you can't make the moral judgment of where it's going to stop.

When have you seen gay people, especially Black gay people, doing good acts within organized religion?

For the most part in the Black Baptist church, in the Black church in general, there has been an understanding, I guess, not to make an issue of one's sexual lifestyle. A lot of our musicians are gay, and ministers in the pulpit are gay. Some will say that as children they remember that nothing negative was said, but still the resentment was there, but the point I am making is that gay people for the most part in these churches have been accepted. Now, when the issue gets politicized and when people are "up in your face," as they put it, that's where you get a reaction from these smaller, less informed churches. But for the most part they have never gone on any witch-hunts. But I must also say parenthetically that there have been some ministers, such as E. V. Hill[6] and others, who have taken the occasion to do the unkind thing of lambasting gays and lesbians from the pulpit, which I think is wrong. He's one of the disciples of Jerry Falwell, Pat Robertson, and all.[7] That's his crowd. There are people of his ilk who do do the unkind thing, but in terms of the old, historic, established churches—where you tend to have more of a informed, enlightened laity—it was never a problem.

But now that gay people are out more, do you think Black churches will shift from a generally understood acceptance to a more outspoken welcoming of gay people?

They don't make an issue of it. You are who you are, and if you come to accept that, fine. But when it comes to the point of marriages, to be quite candid with you, in the main, Black people—though they may be affirming of a different lifestyle—are not ready for that. And why? Because historically the institution of marriage was so demeaned and put down for Black people. Families were broken up. So, in a sense we are playing catch-up. That's the cultural thing. I'm not justifying it, but I'm saying that is the historical reality. So they would say, "Hey, we haven't even had the occasion to have our families and rear our children as we ought."

You see, the Black family has been defined as dysfunctional. Moynihan presented to the Senate his study that said we were dysfunctional.[8] Now, if there's one thing that the unfortunate situation in Littleton, Colorado,[9] has taught us, it is that in a sense, to use the words of Malcolm X, "The chickens are coming home to roost." You see, for years white America and the white press, the establishment, have covered up the dysfunctional mainstream family. They have acted as if only Black families in the ghetto are dysfunctional. But now you have these white kids having spent all this time in that family, in that house, in an affluent suburban community, developing these bombs, being caught up in meanness and nonsense, and getting ready to go and blow up a whole school on Hitler's birthday—a calculated, protracted plan. And the authorities had spoken to the parents. The counselors had spoken to these kids. Dysfunctional kids. But the appearance always has been that the Black family was a pathological institution: we were messed up, we were not able to function at all. Consequently, there is a stigma on our families; so, I guess in a sense what some Blacks would say is, "Hey, give us our time to have our 'healthy' family in our community."

How do you help people understand gay marriage as something that doesn't threaten their own families?

I think through an educational process, a process of having quality relationships, and just through sharing with people, same as with the problem with racism. Once whites get to see Blacks as they are and Blacks get to see whites as they are, then all of these perceptions, generalizations, stereotypes just fall away.

Would you ever perform a gay marriage in your church?

To be quite candid, at this point in history, no.

How would a gay man or a lesbian know that they were welcome in your church?

For example, we've exchanged pulpits with Jim Mitulski at Metropolitan Community Church.[10] When his congregation comes over here, our people know they're gay and lesbian. We've had AIDS testings here, and publicly I've supported gay rights. But on the issue of marriage, I would not lead anyone to believe that I'm going to be able to correct instantly something that is felt so passionately about the family. I could say for myself personally, "Fine, if that's what people want to do, okay."

But I think here again, gays and lesbians are somewhat making too much of a challenge when they use traditional terms to affirm a nontraditional lifestyle. I think a red flag comes up when they use the term "marriage," because marriage in a traditional sense has been different than two men or two women forming a relationship. If they talk about a policy for "affirming relationships," fine, or "domestic partnerships," fine; but when you use that word "marriage," it elicits, it invites, it conjures up problems for people. Just as when the Sisters of Perpetual Indulgence used the communion service and Easter as an occasion to present their issues, it created a knee-jerk emotional reaction. The same thing goes here; it's a matter of language that's used.

What happens if one of your parishioners comes to you, identifies herself as lesbian, introduces you to her partner, says they want to spend the rest of their lives together and to make that good in the eyes of God. How do you help them do that?

They would have to define for themselves what their own ritual of confirming that is, the same as I do for other relationships in this church. I don't use the same ritual and ceremony for everyone. Each is done differently. But I'm saying that same-sex marriage would not fly that well in the wider context of the church, in the established churches.

When you're dealing with people in your church, what do you think remains the big stumbling block to accepting gay people?

As I said, it's about the matter of the family. That's the overriding issue.

What is it that most helps people to change, to become more accepting?

The climate that the pastoral and denominational leadership establishes.

Do your colleagues take issue with your pro-gay positions and stigmatize you?[11]

Well, they know me. I speak my mind; so they say, "That's just Amos." And yet, I do not ostracize them, I still relate to them, and with as much as I have to do, I go to the meeting of the Bay Area Ecumenical Pastors' Conference every Saturday. When I am in town, I'm there with them. So, they have sensed that though I differ with them on women in ministry—they don't believe in women preachers—and that I differ on literal interpretations of the Bible, they come to me and ask me for leadership. I'm chairman of the Conference; so, if they had that much antipathy toward me, they wouldn't have asked me to come to that position. But they asked me to come to that position because of my integrity and my leadership skills, and they know that I respect them and don't talk down to them. I know that they have some problems, some hang-ups that they are dealing with, and that's how I deal with it.

Do you think there's a growing group of Black clergy who are pro-gay?

No. You can count the congregations and pastors across the country that are actually pro-gay. Gardner Taylor at Concord in Brooklyn, who was named one of the top preachers in America. That would be years ago. Joseph Roberts at Ebenezer Church here. You have Jeremiah Wright at Trinity Church in Chicago, Jim Forbes at Riverside, Ratliffe at Brentwood in Houston. There are a number of others, too.

Do the pro-gay pastors come out of a similar tradition as your own?

Oh, yes, but the flip side of that is there are some who come out of this tradition, but because of whatever personal challenge they have had, they are still not open.

Do you think that when a Black pastor speaks in favor of gay rights, they have more credibility and moral authority than if a white pastor does it?

White folks don't pay attention to what Black folks say. People go around and pay attention to what Billy Graham says before they will to a Black person, like myself. A classic example of that is the problem we had—I don't know if you know about it—the Eugene Lumpkin situation.

The ousting of the Human Rights Commission member for anti-gay statements?[12]

Yes. The scenario is this. The white gay and lesbian communities and some Blacks went after Lumpkin, even though what he said initially was said in his pulpit as a literalist. But then he went on Channel 2 and got tripped up by Ross McGowen, who backed him into a corner about the

Leviticus 18:22, 20:13 passages.[13] Lumpkin mentioned that he didn't want to appear to his fundamentalist friends as not thinking the Bible was literally true. So, he just said he believed the whole book. Then Ross mentioned Leviticus and asked him if he believed it. Instead of Eugene saying, "No, I don't believe that; I follow Jesus, who said the greatest commandment is love," he said, "I believe the whole book, sure, that, too." Then all hell broke loose. The long-short of it is, he had to resign from the Commission. But when Billy Graham later came to town, he was in a full-scale press conference and the subject came up of the gay lifestyle. He said the same thing Lumpkin had said before he got tripped up by Ross. The first time Lumpkin basically said he believed in gay rights, but also that homosexuality is a sin as the Bible says. As a literalist he said, "I preach the Bible. What does the Bible say? Well, Paul's Letter to the Romans 1:18–32 says that homosexuality is a sin." Now, Billy Graham said the same thing, and I've got the article to prove it.[14] But what happened? The white lesbian and gay communities were very quiet. But I forced them into a corner. Just as I didn't support Lumpkin, I told them what's good for the goose is good for the gander; and if Billy Graham said that homosexuality is a sin, they all should have been just as indignant. They ought to have had as much protest, but they were quiet as a mouse until I embarrassed them.

It seems that you've actively supported gay rights, but when an issue comes up with which you disagree you've taken on the gay community. Is that right?

I'll take anybody on if I don't agree with them, not just the gay movement. I try to be consistent, rational, realistic, responsible, and relational in my responses.[15] What I'm saying is that "taking on" is not in any way being against gay rights, their positions, what they elect to do. If they want to have wedding ceremonies sanctioned by the city and blessed by the mayor—which can and did happen in San Francisco—that's fine.[16] But as a Christian pastor, I could not be a part of that. Why? Because in the first instance I don't perform civil marriages like that. Marriages here in this church are done in a context of a counseling process with the couples who are members of this community of faith. So, it wouldn't make sense for me to be out there in some kind of civil ceremony that says, "Here we are; affirm us." People affirm themselves in their private relationships. I'm not about to tell people what to do with their private relationships. That has to be their call.

What if two gay people come to you saying they want counseling about their decision to commit to each other as a couple?

If that's what they want to do, fine. I'll affirm that. But they do not need approval from me. For example, Howard Thurman, the great mystic, mentioned a couple he knew.[17] When they got married, they went out on the side of a mountain, and when the sun came up, they made their commitment to each other and then went about their business. Nobody had to stand up there and bless them.

Has both supporting and criticizing the gay community hurt you politically?

For me it doesn't matter, because I don't think you have to be perpetual enemies or perpetual friends. You should deal with an issue on its merits and fairness, and if anybody's going to differ with me on one particular issue when all of the other things are 99 percent, I think that is being unrealistic and is not living out the essence of what makes a democratic society work and what makes human community work. None of us gets all we want 99 percent. There's no utopia here. There's no perfect place. But I think the bottom-line issue is, as Scripture in all faith communities says, "Do unto others, as you would have them do unto you." That's what I try to live by.

From whom did you draw your support when you were elected to the Board of Supervisors?[18]

I get support from the gay communities, from the basic, solid people who have integrity and who are consistent, like the Alice B. Toklas Democratic Club. But from the Harvey Milk Democratic Club, which is a younger crowd that makes its point at any cost and any means, I don't get support. And neither did Mayor Willie Brown, as much as he did for them years ago. When he was up in Sacramento in the California Assembly, he was way out there for them. He even paved the way for them to come out of the closet. The other thing the gay and lesbian community has got to keep in mind is if it had not been for the fact that our heads were whupped and dogs set on us in the South, they wouldn't have come out of the closet. They came out on the heels of the Civil Rights movement, as did the women's movement and other movements.

What does what you just said mean for Black gay people? Can you say something about the needs of Black gay people compared to white gay people?

They need to find the strength to deal with racism plus expressions of homophobia in their own communities.

Sure, but some of the criticisms that you make of the gay community you couldn't make of gay Black people, right?

Yes, I can make it for some of them, in the sense that there are those who know of affirming churches, but they don't come to them. They don't bond with the community. They won't come and just be themselves, like I know many other gay and lesbian people in this church are. They're here, they're involved, they're serving on boards, giving leadership. But no big thing is made over it. I just licensed a young man to preach who obviously is known to be gay in this church. There are gay people on my deacon board, my trustee board, and the choir.

So, you're saying the welcoming part of being in your church is not about standing up and saying "I'm gay." It's being part of the community.

It's just like any other person whether they're from Mississippi or Alabama or Georgia, a literalist, a conservative reading from the King James translation or some other version of the Bible. We don't make an issue of that. The church is inclusive.

But something about your church brings lesbian and gay people there to do that.

First of all, my orientation is open, affirming, and liberal. For example, when I came here in 1976, a woman could not wear a pantsuit to church. But I took them through a process on that and dealt with Deuteronomy 22:5.[19] Cleaned that up. The next thing was that a woman couldn't be a trustee. I dealt with that. And the next thing was that they had this white, blue-eyed Christ up over the baptistry. I took them through a process and dealt with that. Then the other thing was the Interfaith Fellowship. I have exchanged the pulpit with Temple Emanu-El. There were some in the church who said we don't have dealings with Jews.[20] We dealt with that. And then I dealt with the gay and lesbian issues by bringing over here Jim

Mitulski to preach in this pulpit and also Yvette Flunder, a Black lesbian who pastors the City of Refuge church.[21] She's preached here several times. So, it's a matter of the leadership that I take; and yet as we take leadership on these issues, we don't push people into a corner to make them take sides. The other thing we had to deal with the other day was— would you believe it?—whether or not the church could have a spring ball in the name of the church.

Because of the dancing?

Yes. But I stood my ground, and when the matter was discussed and a consensus was called for, the people were with me. But you had about four or five folks who were telling me how ridiculous it is, that this is the way of the world and all that nonsense. So, I have been a change agent, but not in a way to make it a Pyrrhic victory where you end up just slaughtering people and downing every cross when it's not time for you to down that cross; instead, you pick your fights and your crosses as you move along, and you bring people from where they are to maybe where they ought to be.

Where do you think they ought to be right now on lesbian and gay issues?

I think we all—not just them—should be at the point of accepting people who are different from us. I even have a challenge to getting people to accept different music. All the young folks want to do is to add the beat and the volume and then rock, but they don't want to be reduced to any kind of disciplined effort of learning how to read music and to be musically literate. That's a challenge. You've got different people. So, what do I do? I make the point, "Okay, young folks, if you're going to do this, you've also got to have an ear to appreciate and respect an anthem or a Negro spiritual." But if I try to force it, I run them away. You can't just jump into those years of conditioning and emotions. We snatched music education out of the public schools. It's not the same world and social set as it was for me in the South. We were poor, yet we were rich in culture. We mastered an instrument, and we sang in the choir. But out here it's a different situation altogether. So, it's a matter of learning how to minister to people who are different and yet respecting them.

You've mentioned Jim Mitulski. What was he able to do that let people in your church listen to him? If the Sisters of Perpetual Indulgence set people off, what does Jim do that lets them listen to him?

First of all, Jim is a person of reason, conscience, and good will. But my first pro-gay efforts did not start with the pulpit exchange with him. For example, when I came in 1978–79, I was in the forefront of opposing Anita Bryant's anti-gay campaign.[22] I had just moved here from Minnesota.

What role did you take in that?

Saying that what she was doing and where she was going didn't make sense.

What did the people in your church think?

They didn't say anything. I preached a sermon titled "Alternatives to Despair" about why her disparaging and homophobic kind of statements should not be made and that there's an alternative. And the alternative is Jesus' great commandment of "loving one another, even as I've loved you." That was it.

Do you run into opposition in your church about gay issues?

No. No opposition at all.

What advice do you have for lesbians and gay men who are trying to find their place in the church?

I would say just as you go to a supermarket and shop for the meat and produce that meets your taste, shop around, find a congregation that suits you and become a part of it.

But what should we look for?

You look for an open fellowship that's driven by reason, respect, relationship, and reality, that's resourceful, and that brings to people hope and not harm.

You talked earlier about your seminary training. Can you link it to what you just said? What have you been doing consistently throughout all your years of ministry?

I've been an agent of liberation, hope, justice, and love. That's been it.

You've been in San Francisco quite awhile. Have you ever gotten tired of being here? Have you wanted to move on to something else or are you happy here?

I've given it some thought. I've been here twenty-three years. Unfortunately, the Black area has been gentrified. The utopian, perfect world has not come here yet, and our population base has been destroyed by gentrification and urban renewal. All the churches in this area have been. When I came here in 1976, on Easter and Mother's Day people overflowed the sanctuary and packed the gym. This past Easter and for the past ten years the sanctuary is just comfortably packed. I suppose the challenge would be for me to really establish a pluralistic, interracial, intercultural church, if we're going to maintain our numbers, because the Black population is just gone. We lost over twenty thousand Blacks from the city since 1970, and we're still losing them.

Does the pluralistic church interest you?

Yes, definitely.

Do you have anything you haven't said to lesbians and gay men before we close?

To know that they have a friend here who will stand for their rights to be respected, affirmed, and appreciated and who will expect them—as I expect of any other human being—to be civil, considerate, kind, and respectful of others.

Chapter 4

Rev. Dr. Mozella G. Mitchell

*M*ozella G. Mitchell is professor of religious studies at the University of South Florida. She received her Ph.D. from Emory University. Her primary areas of scholarship are the theology of Howard Thurman and Afro-American religious history. She has published four books, including *The Human Search: Howard Thurman and the Quest for Freedom,* and many articles in anthologies and professional journals.[1] Most recently Professor Mitchell conducted field research in Cuba on Afro-Cuban religion and culture.

She is also an ordained elder in the African Methodist Episcopal Zion (AME Zion) Church. She was the pastor for seven years at Mount Sinai AME Zion Church in Tampa, Florida, before founding the Love of Christ AME Zion Tabernacle in nearby Brandon.[2] Rev. Mitchell also serves on the Judicial Council of the denomination and as presiding elder of its Tampa District.

A longtime leader in community activities, she initiated and developed Women at the Well Inc., a single women's spiritual support ministry in the Tampa area.[3] She has also served as president of the Florida Council of Churches, president of the Society for the Study of Black Religion, and delegate to the Seventh Assembly of the World Council of Churches.

What led you to found a new local AME Zion church?

It was with the encouragement of the Bishop. Because some of our members had relocated and didn't have a church, the bishop wanted to develop one in St. Petersburg. He wanted me, as the presiding elder of the District, which is a supervisory and administrative position, to start a church over there. So I started it, and we met for a year at the Hampton Inn. We didn't have good results, so I got permission to relocate the church over here in Brandon near where I live. He agreed to that, so we bought property and located it here.

How were you able to purchase a building?

The national church stood for it; and it's in the name of the national church. Our local group just pays the mortgage.

Was there anything about the group of people with whom you started the church that gave it a distinguishing characteristic? Was there something the people wanted to do or something that identified them in any particular way?

When we relocated to Brandon, it was just my family and me, my daughter, and two granddaughters. That was the core of the church at first. Some other families joined us and friends of theirs came, but we have remained small. The name of the church is Love of Christ. I realized at the time we were starting that there were problematic situations in the wider church that led people to be exclusive, narrow, and prejudiced towards certain groups, so this church had a special mission to be inclusive, open, and encouraging to all groups of people.

One of the groups that has traditionally been neglected is single women. Both of my daughters are single; one had been married and has two children. And there are a number of different groups among single women—divorced, never married, single parents, widows—who don't get as much attention, love, caring, and consideration as they should. They are exploited, denied, and treated differently in the church than nuclear families. Single women tend to be seen as a threat to the families there. These women are very concerned about religion and want to be involved in the church, but they aren't trusted, opened up to, and received wholeheartedly by the church. They feel alienated. So that's one group, single women.

Married people are invited to share in developing inclusive ministry, of course. Single men are also a focus. Then, of course, there are gay people who are denied and mistreated by the churches and thought to be suspect. There are other groups, such as poor people, people on welfare, and disadvantaged people, who don't have the funds to contribute to the church. They feel discriminated against and not welcomed and helped. Then there are color problems. People who are fair-skinned in the Black church still tend to get better opportunities. In spite of the Civil Rights movement, the

Black power movement, and "Black is beautiful," color discrimination still exists. And there's class discrimination and, of course, AIDS discrimination. On and on, it just never seems to end. All these kinds of things do exist in the church.

That is the background for the name of the church that we founded, Love of Christ AME Zion Tabernacle. The motto of our church is "Where Everyone Counts and the Love of Christ Prevails." We have a scriptural foundation for the name, which we quote in the bulletin every Sunday. The founding scripture for our church, the expression of the love of Christ, says that everybody will be accepted, all groups.

People really feel at home here. The property we bought for the church is a big house with living space for the pastors. So, we have a parsonage and a huge recreation-type of room that we converted into a sanctuary area. It has an outside pool and a large lawn. It's a warm and homelike situation. The location and building tend to express the atmosphere of love and harmony that we like to have. As soon as we get large enough to outgrow this building, we'll get a regular-style church. But for a start, this is perfect. We're starting small, about twenty people. We've gained and lost people. People come and go. They're shopping around for a church, unhappy with their own, never quite happy with what they find, and keep coming and going.

When people do find a home with your church, what are the reasons they usually give for liking it?

They just like being accepted, that everybody is welcome and that they don't feel any alienation. They feel a part of everything that is going on. They don't see any people making differences between them because of who or what they are. We don't inquire into the background of people. We don't inquire into their private, personal, or family situation. You come as who you are, and our message is that whatever is wrong in your life is always addressed by the love of Christ, which works in people's lives to shape them into what God wants them to be. We do not interfere with and pass judgment on them, whatever their lives are like. We just let them be and pray with them.

We have an intercessory prayer at the close of each service asking for the intercession of God in the lives of people, in the world, in the problems in our society, and asking for the Spirit to use each of us in a group fashion and in individual ways to try to remedy the problems in our personal lives, in our family lives, and in our society as a whole.

We focus on several kinds of ministry—daycare, youth and children, assisting and welcoming people of advanced age. The foundation for this kind of ministry grows out of my teaching experience.

We have an interfaith type of ministry, which one of my students at the university has developed. I've published two books on Howard Thurman, and I wrote my doctoral dissertation on him.[4] I do a lot of teaching on mysticism, liberation theology, and all religions. All these courses deal with inclusiveness in society and oneness in mystical relations, the beauty of God's creation, the unity and oneness of faith, which in my background comes from Howard Thurman. This student, who's a senior now, started the interfaith group at the university and also joined the church and spear-headed an interfaith ministry here. Every first Sunday of the month we have interfaith worship.

Why do you think you were able to have a vision for inclusiveness, whereas other people in the church don't?

I think I drew from my own personal experience of being discrimi-nated against as a woman preacher, minister, and pastor in the church. I know what it means, extremely so. I was married and divorced. I've been discriminated against as a single woman—as a woman, period—trying to do ministerial pastoral work. I've been subjected to some of the most cruel discriminatory practices against women; and being an assertive, professional, career woman, I've always been able to adapt and succeed, although I've come through many hardships to make it where I am. And still people tend to feel that I shouldn't be in the positions I hold and be successful like I am. They don't seem to want to honor my calling and have done all kinds of things to undermine my ministry, because I'm a woman—that's the only reason, that and being a single woman. I've also been exposed to the racial type of discrimination and, as I advance in age, some age discrimination. I've been exposed to it all; it keeps coming. So, I realize the significance of getting rid of all those things. I don't want to engage in that kind of discrimination myself, and I want to try to get the church out of that kind of practice.[5]

Has some of the discrimination that you've experienced as a woman pas-tor been in hiring and promotion? It seems as though your current Bishop supports you.

Previous bishops have also been supportive of me in my ministry and pastoring, although they haven't advanced me equally with the men. Two of my bishops did promote me and pushed me as they did the men. Two of them did not. The one I have now seems very threatened by women ministers. He's been very tardy in being receptive to, supporting, and pushing me. He has sometimes been really destructive towards my work and status.

Is this through his communication with other people in the denomination?

It's more in this district, in the area over which he presides as bishop. I have status and a position in the national church. I'm on the Judicial Council, which is a very influential body with a strong power base in the church, and I think that's probably something else he doesn't take to readily. He feels threatened by that, perhaps, because we do have jurisdiction over bishops when they do not perform their duties correctly and charges are brought against them.

Tell me what the reaction is of fellow pastors to your being supportive of gays and lesbians.

I haven't really made a public display of my support anywhere but in this area. I have in the local community here, but not in the broader church. I am listed on the board of the local gay rights organization, the Human Rights Task Force. So, my name appears on the literature it publishes, I'm asked to speak up on behalf of gay rights on radio and TV programs, and I'm quoted in newspaper articles.[6] I speak against those in the Black community and Black church who try to deny gay rights or discriminate against gay people. Some local people made this known to our bishop, and he tried to subpoena me, which he didn't have the authority to do. They told him that I had appeared on these shows and identified myself as the presiding elder in the church, and that I should not have done that because people will be thinking that I'm speaking on behalf of the AME Zion Church. Another local pastor and his wife here are very anti-gay and are very vocal and outspoken against gays in their own church, but not in public. They're the ones who went to the bishop with that charge. It didn't work. So that got me in trouble with that church pastor, but I am the supervisor for this area. He's under my jurisdiction as presiding elder. He has to report to me every quarter. So, he resents my authority and suspects that I might be gay because I am supportive of gays. That has been the problem.

When they go to the Bible about gays, they find support there. Many people in the Black church are very literally oriented toward the Bible. So, these ministers and bishops have the Bible on their side and the people are also on their side. That's problematic for me and anybody else who stands up for gay rights. But, of course, the Bible is also on our side—or we're on the Bible's side—when we say that Christ's love is for everyone in God's creation, God created people as they are, and we have no right to judge them. Only God can judge and condemn, and God's grace and love is strong enough to cover anybody. Any kind of transgression against God's rules and law is under God's grace. So, the Spirit works with all people who accept Christ; and there is no way that we have a right to be destructive of people, to deny and exclude people, to try to do God's work for God.

It seems that in some ways you have gotten to a place where you do have power in your denomination. Do you think that other people see you as a powerful woman?

Yes *(laughs)*.

Do you think that some of the men are intimidated by that?

Yes *(laughs)*. Men are just naturally intimidated by a woman with a Ph.D., especially a single woman.

It also seems to me that you're not afraid to take a position.

No, I am not *(laughs)*.

Has that always been true?

Yes, that's kind of grown up in me. I've just been a person who believed in freedom and individual rights and group rights. I was very active in the liberation movement of the '70s.[7] I didn't get as much involved in the Civil Rights movement until after the assassination of Martin Luther King Jr., but I did become very active after that. I was a university professor and began to demonstrate, speak, and get involved in organizations, to be the advisor to the Black Student Union, which was a very active militant group at Norfolk State University where I was teaching at the time. I got into a lot of trouble there with the president. He was going to have me arrested because the students took over the administration building and locked the president in his office. A judge issued an order to vacate the kids and sent the police to remove them and to release the president. He blamed me, even though I didn't know anything about it beforehand. He said I was too militant, and others called me a witch. I've always believed that we should resist tyranny and injustices on the part of people in power over others.

Did any of that belief come out of your upbringing or your childhood church?

It didn't come out of church at all. I guess you might say it really came from my mother. In the 1950s, before the Civil Rights movement had begun, my mother was very independent, assertive, and always on the side of freedom. She pushed the females in her family to be independent, to go get an education, and to be on their own, because society was not supportive of women. It wasn't supportive enough of Black men for them to have the kind of economic power to take care of women. They were denied so much that women had to stand on their own, so Black men and women had to be independent, to be strong, and to assert themselves. My mother was always self-sufficient, and she pushed her daughters to be able to support themselves so that they could make a good life for their families and home. She pushed me strongly to get my education. I was the twelfth of thirteen children and the youngest daughter. And I was also the first one to finish high school and college. All the others dropped out in high school. They went back after I finished and got their education. One or two went to college. I was sort of a symbol and the one to lead the way, and I did so because my mother pushed me. I was so assertive that I even resisted my mother. She was a very religious and strict Baptist. I resisted her strictness and her attempt to control my life. I eloped and got married when I was fourteen, which was very upsetting to her. I came back home because my husband was in the military, and two years later I had my first child. I didn't even miss a grade in high school. I kept going to school while I was pregnant, had my child during December break, went back to school in January, and didn't miss any time. I was in tenth grade and just kept on going. My mother took care of my child. The only year I missed was my second year in college, when I had my second child. I just kept on going and she kept pushing me. She'd keep my children and have faith in me.

When did you realize the lesbian/gay issue should be a part of the liberation movement?

I can't think of anytime when I didn't think that it was a right issue. Whenever it came up, I knew it was the right thing to do, that all human beings had rights and that God was accepting and supportive of all God's creations. The first time I really saw it become a religious issue was when I was getting my master's degree at Colgate-Rochester Divinity School in the 1970s. It was a liberal school, and gays, lesbians, and women were embraced and accepted there. They were never denied anything, and people there realized that it was a human rights issue and that gays were a part of God's creation. There was a women's group and a Black liberation group, and we interacted with one another and we had our different issues. And being both Black and a woman, naturally I was caught up in both of them, although I catered more to the Black one and was more a part of it. A couple of the first women ordained—albeit "irregularly"—in the Episcopal Church by the rebel bishop[8] were at Colgate-Rochester when I was there from 1971 to '73. I was really happy when their ordination was officially recognized in the Episcopal Church. So, all of those issues flared up during that time.

Why do you think the lesbian and gay people in the area in which you live now see you as a friendly person? When they want someone to be on the board or to speak for them, why do they know that you'll be someone who will do that? Do you have a reputation in the area?

Yes, I think that is it. I have always supported liberal issues.

Do they know about you more from your work at the university or through the church?

From my work at the university and from my work in the community. Back in the 1980s I helped found HOPE—Hillsborough Organization for Progress and Equality—which is still very strong and growing, and many local churches are part of it. I've just always been involved in the community. The media also has consulted me regarding these various issues, so I've been on a number of news programs.

When they ask you why you, as a Black preacher, are supportive of lesbian and gay people, what do you usually say?

There was a TV program on the human rights amendment where I think I expressed my views most publicly. I was in a debate with a man from a so-called family-values group who was going around the Black community garnering opposition against the amendment, specifically against gay people. An AME [African Methodist Episcopal] Black preacher was on his side. The woman who is head of the Human Rights Task Force here asked me to be on the program. She and I were on one side supporting the amendment, and this Black preacher and white minister were on the other side. My position was that this white group that was trying to get support in the Black community was just as racist as they were anti-gay, and I found that there is no threat whatsoever from gays in our society and in the community, but the real threat in the Black community comes from those racists who are trying to get our support against gays. My position was that I've been hurt and damaged in society by such racists who are also trying to hurt and damage other people like gays and all kinds of other people.

Do you see AME Zion as being more liberal than AME?

No, I don't. Maybe in our acceptance of women, and historically we've had some very liberal movements and liberal persons in our body. For example, we claim Frederick Douglass, who was a local preacher in the AME Zion Church, and we claim Sojourner Truth and Harriet Tubman. In fact those are my historical mentors and role models who led me into the AME Zion Church. So, there's a liberal tradition there historically, but present day I can't say it's more liberal. It was a denomination that supported the Underground Railroad with Harriet Tubman. She was a member of Rochester Memorial AME Zion Church up in western New York, and she would hide the slaves in her church there. They have stained-glass windows with Susan B. Anthony and Harriet Tubman in them.[9]

Why do you think lesbian or gay men coming into your local church would feel welcome and comfortable? What is it about your church that would do that?

Because of our philosophy, our motto. Everyone is accepted. Everyone counts, and the love of Christ prevails in any situation. If we have anything that we cannot resolve, that means God and the love of Jesus take over. We have to bow to that love.

Do you know of lesbians and gay men who do attend your church?

I know informally that some of the women are in that category.

What do you say to Black lesbians and gay men who would like to be a part of the church but also feel that they cannot be open in it? What advice do you have for them?

My advice would be to go slowly, because coming out of the closet and pressing for rights in the Black church would be, I'd say, suicidal and destructive. I say that because you're going to have people come right back at them, oppose them fiercely, and make a big stink out of it. There are numerous gay people in the Black church who are still closeted, and people know that they are gay and aren't bothered by it. They love them and treat them well. But if they try to make a big issue out of it and try to force general church acceptance of them, right now the Black church hasn't yet reached that stage of understanding. Individually gay Black church members are embraced and accepted, but the church as a whole isn't ready to take an official position on formally recognizing and accepting gay people. There are musicians and preachers and others in the church who are gay and people know it, but nobody makes a big issue out of it.

If gay people want to have a confrontation, that's their decision, but it's going to be very disruptive of the Black church, of the harmony. Whatever harmony does exist in the Black church, that kind of confrontation is going to cause people to demonize one another and take sides. It just causes a big disharmony in God's church and it just shouldn't be there. The church is kind of on shaky ground anyway. The church in today's society is in disrepute. People just don't trust the church as much anymore, because the church has not been taking a stand and doing what it should do. There's so much corruption in the church that's causing people to distrust the church, like the Henry Lyons scandal[10] and so many other things that people are doing that are just not churchlike. So many leaders in the church are being found guilty of so many crimes.

So, you think that the church is at a point of not being stable enough to handle this kind of a confrontation?

Definitely.

What would happen if gay people wanted to celebrate their sexuality in your own local church? Would that create problems for people?

Yes, that would create an image which would cause people to say, "I don't want to come into that mess; there's a mess going on over there," because messes are happening in the churches all the time and people want to avoid a mess. They want to go to a place where they can be more at peace and get involved in work that is constructive to the community. And they don't want to involve themselves in a disruptive, destructive type of infighting.

Where do you think lesbians and gay men can find peace? Do you think they can find peace in the church?

I think they can. Some churches have a stronger foundation on which they can deal with these issues and disruptions. Others can't. But I still say that the whole church is not ready for a full confrontation on the part of gays and lesbians. I feel that they should work along in the society. Historically, whatever happens in secular society usually impacts the church, and that's unfortunate because the church should be impacting society. The church should be a leader, but unfortunately it's very conservative. It's both liberal and conservative, but that conservative element is still there. I think lesbians and gay men should work in the secular society to bring about changes there, and then hopefully the church will wake up (*laughs*).

In some ways, that's what you have been doing. You've been able to speak out in the media and in debates for lesbian and gay people in the secular realm, but as a scholar who is also a clergywoman.

Yes, I claim my rights to do that. In fact, I wrote the bishop a letter when he tried to confront me about my public image, and I told him that I was being consulted by the media and other people for my academic expertise, for my standpoint as a scholar in the area of religion. It was not because I was a member of the AME Zion Church, and it had nothing to do with it. So, I was able to establish my independence, and he didn't bother me anymore.

It seems that your power and effectiveness have been in utilizing both your positions—as a scholar in academia and as a pastor in the church.

Right. That puts me in a different category.

Based on your understanding of Thurman's theology and philosophy, what do you think he would have said about lesbians and gay men?

Thurman would be very receptive and inclusive. He'd be very much in favor of freedom for gays and lesbians.

Pretend I don't know anything about Thurman and explain that to me, please.

He said: I can go so deep within myself that when I come up, I come up inside of every other creature; I find unity and harmony within me, with all. He was very much against any type of exclusiveness. His whole position was one of inclusiveness. He was very much against any type of discrimination or harmfulness toward any other human being or animals. All creatures were under God's love—love, receptiveness, and understanding for all. He took what I would say is a divine perspective toward all things as expressive of God. God is within all; God is in each of us. That's what we get in touch with and in tune with. When we go within ourselves, we get in tune with God. God grounds, bottoms all creation, and that is where we get in tune with God and in tune with one another, within ourselves, within the God within us. Everything else in the external world, he sees as finding harmony in God. All disharmonious types of things that we encounter in the external world find their harmony ultimately in God. That's where we ought to resolve these issues.

That's very beautiful. How would you summarize what Thurman said?

When I look deep within myself, when I go deep within myself, I come up inside of every other human being or every other creature. Another thing he said was: I do unto others as I would have them do unto me, but also I do unto others as I do unto myself. It's like Jesus' saying, "Love your neighbor as yourself."

Chapter 5

Rev. Irene Monroe

*I*rene Monroe is a Ph.D. candidate in the Religion, Gender, and Culture Program at Harvard Divinity School. Her community activities in the Boston area have included Christian education ministry with Old Cambridge Baptist Church's high-school-age parishioners, assistant pastoring at United Baptist Church in Jamaica Plain, and serving on the advisory board of the Women's Theological Center. In 1997, *Boston Magazine* presented her as one of "The 50 Most Intriguing Women in Boston"; in 1998, she was selected to be a Grand Marshall of the Boston Gay Pride parade; in 1999, *OUT Magazine* named her as one of the 100 queer "People Who Rocked 1998" and PBS featured her in its gay newsmagazine *In the Life.*[1]

Several newspapers have covered her life and work. The *Boston Globe* described her infancy as follows:

> Irene Monroe does not have a birth certificate because . . . when she was probably 6 months old, someone "discarded" her—that is the word she uses, quite sadly—in a trash can in a park in Brooklyn.
>
> She was found—by chance, because that side of the park was not scheduled for cleanup that day—by city garbage men.
>
> After being rescued from the trash can, Monroe was taken to the New York Foundling Hospital, where she was put in the care of the woman who gave her a very personal name: Sister Irene, a fan of Marilyn Monroe. "It's a wonderful name," she says, "and I'd never change it as a lot of blacks have changed their white names, because by giving me a name, she made me who I am."[2]

She endured foster care settings with abusive, functionally illiterate foster parents and went on to graduate from Wellesley College and Union Theological Seminary.[3]

Rev. Monroe writes a column, "The Religion Thang," for the New

England gay newspaper *In Newsweekly,* and has also contributed articles to several journals, newspapers, and collections.[4] Her essay, "Louis Farrakhan's Ministry of Misogyny and Homophobia," is anthologized in *The Farrakhan Factor: African American Writers on Leadership, Nationhood, and Minister Louis Farrakhan;* she was guest editor of the *Journal of Women and Religion*'s special issue on "The Intersection of Racism and Sexism"; and she is included in *African American Quotations.*[5] She has conducted workshops and given addresses in schools and churches throughout the country and for such organizations as the National Conference of Christians and Jews, National Association of Social Workers, and National Black Gay and Lesbian Leadership Forum.

Say something about the recognition you've received in the news media.

Like the *Boston Magazine* article, right. Fifty of the "most intriguing" women . . . they should have said "bizarre" (*laughs*). That was because of a number of things, among them my being the first African American woman marshall for Boston Pride. I see my role, particularly as an out lesbian, as a public theologian. I feel that to acquire this kind of education and not to put it into practice is just talking among my elite colleagues. So, that's why I do a more public kind of ministry now, like writing the column and giving a lot of talks, to make things more accessible to a group of people who are desperately in need of information and affirmation.

You went right from getting your M. Div. at Union to the program at Harvard?

Yes, I'm an old, colored woman, so I don't have too much time (*laughs*).

How old are you?

Forty-four. I chose this particular doctoral program at Harvard because it's new and would allow me to study the relationship between gender identity and sexual orientation in a way that other doctoral programs wouldn't.

Somewhere along the line you got to pastor Presbyterian churches?

Yes, while at Union, but let me explain the glitch, because I don't want to in any way promote the Presbyterian Church as gay friendly. Race played a major factor in my getting to the Presbyterian Church. Urban Black Presbyterian churches are dying for the most part. Nobody—Black or white—wants to pastor them. The few Black men who get through the Presbyterian ordination process have the pick of the litter, and they're not going to go to these struggling, dying Presbyterian Churches. The thing about being a pastor in the Presbyterian church is you have to be schooled, unlike if you're Baptist, Methodist, or Pentecostal in the Black tradition; and Presbyterian really is a white denomination unlike what we call the Black denominations. So, the point of my getting to pastor is not that they're pro-queer at any level; it's because those churches were and still are dying. They need to fill them with Black clergy, because a lot of them don't want white ministers. They want a Black feel, Black owner-ship, a Black worship service.[6] And that's why I got those positions. Clearly I'm out—if you saw me or knew me, it's impossible for me not to be—but that's not what they're dealing with. They need to salvage as many of these dying Black churches as they can. So, I usually tell people I don't even talk about it, because under no circumstances do I want folks to think that the Presbyterian Church is queer friendly.

I also don't identify Presbyterian. I didn't grow up Presbyterian. I grew up at best as what you would call "Baptecostal." I come out of a tradition of storefront churches, which is what many African Americans come out of. A lot of these storefront Black churches call themselves Baptist, but they're really Pentecostal; and they're not part of what you'd call the mainline Black denominational churches, like AME [African Methodist Episcopal]. You can't be storefront and be AME, but you can be storefront and say you're Baptist. Saying you're Baptist as opposed to saying you're Pentecostal is a bit of class pretension. I really identify as a conglomerate of both of them, Baptist and Pentecostal.

When did you make the move out of the Pentecostal storefront tradition?

I would say that I never have, even when I was pastor at Bethany Presbyterian and at Soundview Presbyterian. One of the things I found as I was studying the Book of Order, Presbyterian policy, and hating it, was that I go to pastor these local churches and see that what you've really got is Black church housed in a Presbyterian edifice. It's Presbyterian by name, but it really is Black church. And the class distinction is very inter-esting. Soundview is in a more economically distressed area in the Bronx, where people don't own their homes, they live in housing projects and apartment buildings. They're renters. There you see what I call

Baptecostal tradition, very vibrant. But then when I was at Bethany Presbyterian in a Black middle-class area in Englewood, New Jersey, you don't see as much of that, but even Bethany doesn't get away from what we call Black religious tradition.

What's your view of queer Black people within organized religion?

I think for the most part those of us in the Black church are in at a tremendous cost, because most of us are in various ways cloaking our true identity. For example, if you are a gay male, there is a place for you in the Black church—in the choir or as choir masters. Really, we call gay males the choir queens. And that's sort of your entertainment aspect in the Black church. Music is very essential to Black church worship. King even said that you can't get good music unless you've got some gay boys up there in the choir. But even that visible role within the Black church—and everybody knows that the choir master or many of the boys in the choir are gay—is acknowledged by bifurcating their identity, like we forgive and love the sinner, we forgive the sin and thank God the sinner knows enough to come to church and serve God. Also, these positions are provisional or marginal within the church, because they have nothing to do with altering its administrative hierarchy, which is very gender specific and very patriarchal. These roles are essential and visible. They have prestige but no power to cause any kind of what I call a paradigm shift or systemic change within the body of the entire church. They will not improve or increase awareness about homophobia or about this group of people being oppressed.

Now for Black lesbians. I think when all of us who are queer go to Black church, we're all going in some form of drag; and the boys love it because they love the robes anyway (*laughs*). But part of the Black church is that the dress code is rigid, and you don't even have to voice it because it's instilled in the practice of each person who goes to church. It's passed on generationally that we have this rigid dress code. So, when I say we cloak our identity, the code says you can be lesbian but you make sure that you wear your dress. You wear dresses to Black churches, if you're female. Even if you are a butch woman who can't wear dresses as well as a real drag queen, the point is that you give the external surface of what is called proper clothing, proper decorum, which is heterosexual, of course. That's explicit as well as implicit. So, in that sense the doors of the church are open to you, but not for you to give voice, whether as a gay man or a lesbian woman or, God forbid, we won't even dare mention transgender. If you are gay or lesbian in the Black church, you don't have any key role in the church because if, God forbid, you should be superintendent of Sunday School, you'll give a wrong message to the children.

Also, there's a tremendous belief that we are an abomination to God because the Bible says it. I just want to say a little bit about our selective use of Biblical scripture. In the Genesis text we have the curse of Ham that legitimates slavery and then we have the Ephesians text where Apostle Paul says that slaves ought to be obedient to their slave masters. What we did with those damaging and damning texts was that we ignored them and took a Bible that was used to enslave us—not to make us better Christians, but to make us better slaves—and turned it around into a tool of liberation. It's always rather disheartening to know how we can be selective in developing a canon within a canon that gives us a sense of affirmation about who we are, but we can't understand or do that when it comes to women, as well as when it comes to lesbian/gay/bisexual/transgendered people. So, we're very literalist when it comes to other minorities, but certainly not when it comes to those damning and damaging passages about Black people.

Part of that has a lot to do with the way in which we construct Black identity and understand racism. The dominant belief in the African American community that racism is the only and ultimate oppression we face as Black people not only ignores the oppression of other groups of people, but it also ignores the oppression of sexism and homophobia within our community. It sets up what I call a hierarchy of oppressions which make people fight among themselves and believe that one oppression—only their oppression—is greater than any other oppression. So, for instance, if it is the belief that racism is far greater than sexism or homophobia or anti-Semitism, and you try to introduce and recognize any other forms of oppression that exist within your community, you are seen as threatening and trying to dilute the whole notion of solidarity toward liberation. Even though there are women and men, gay and straight, within the community, people are dismissive of how other groups within your community are oppressed. If racism is the ultimate oppression, it allows you to be dismissive of sexism; and if you're dismissive of sexism, then that allows you to be dismissive of women, straight or gay. It also allows you to be dismissive of homophobia and therefore of gay people within the community. So, what it leaves you with is straight Black men as the ones whose oppression counts.

The nonsense of this is that you really can't talk about a liberation movement or constructing a theology, ideology, or a politic that is inclusive because three quarters of your population is gone—dismissed—in this hierarchy of oppressions. In its simplest form, I call it Black patriarchy. When I give talks at Black churches or to Black groups, I do a graph so that people can visually get it. But even showing people, as we say, the light doesn't mean that they change, because there's something in place that benefits them to keep that kind of inequity in place: familiarity, comfort, simplicity, maybe even the security of knowing one's place or thinking that other people don't count as much.

I say we've got to move from a hierarchy of oppressions, which I show on rungs in a pyramid shape. At the top is racism and under it are various other rungs with different oppressions. We need to move toward what I call a wheel of oppressions on which each spoke represents a different kind of oppression and has equal weight. It allows everybody to speak from their particular oppression and is meant to open a dialogue in which everybody has a right to be heard. In the hierarchy of oppression with racism as the ultimate oppression, only two races—Blacks and whites—control the dialogue. Even though we don't like what we're saying to each other, those two groups control the dialogue, exclude Asians, Latinos, and other minorities, and don't try to understand in a more comprehensive way what racism is, particularly in the American context. Many people feel that lesbian, gay, bisexual, and transgender people can hide their oppressions, that the pain we feel for who we are we bring on ourselves. While many African Americans do not see a connection between the suffering of queers and themselves, because queerness is a "white disease," many white queers do not see their connection to the suffering of Blacks. But I try to point out that the struggle against racism is legitimate if we are also fighting anti-Semitism, sexism, classism, etc. All of these isms are merely tools of oppression that will continue to keep us fractured instead of united toward a common goal, a multicultural democracy. As Martin Luther King Jr. said, "It is not possible to be in favor of justice for some people and not be in favor of justice for all people. Justice cannot be divided."[7]

As one of a few openly queer Black clergy, where do you draw your strength from?

From a number of places and people, but I have to tell you what was my transforming moment. I wanted to go to ITC, which is the Interdenominational Theological Center down in Atlanta, or to Howard University Theological School in Washington, D.C. And I'll tell you why:

because I come out of the Black church, and my feeling was, "Who better to train me for ministry in the Black church than a Black seminary?" It just seemed to make sense to me. I'd gone to Wellesley and knew about elite white schools in the Northeast, and that was fine, but I said to myself, "If I'm going to be a Black Baptist minister, I'll go down to either D.C. or Atlanta and learn from professors who are schooling folks for the Black church."

I applied to both institutions and I got rejected because I am queer. And they openly told me that. I'll tell you briefly the story in Atlanta. The admissions woman called me and said, "I want to talk with you about your application and I'm worried." She said, "Academically you're strong," and she went on to give me some accolades about how strong I was compared to the rest of the applicant pool. And I'm thinking, "This is excellent. This probably means I'll get a lot of financial aid." "But," she said, "your faith statement is very problematic," and she referred to where I had talked about being a born-again Black lesbian Christian. I honestly had written about having been closeted and fearful of being Black and lesbian and also Christian, about letting go of that fear, about how I felt I embraced the wonder of God. She went on to say that the committee had tremendous trouble with that part of my application, and she told me I had two options: Right then as we were talking I was provisional, but that status could change if I would agree to be closeted in the program. If I wouldn't agree to be closeted, I would be rejected. I went on to explain that I couldn't believe that I would be the only lesbian there, and she just said, "Listen, what you need to understand is that you would have no support from the student body or faculty and that there wouldn't be a church in Atlanta that would take you for the field placement required of all students in the M.Div. program." I said, "What about King's church, what about Ebenezer Baptist Church?" She gave me this response like, "Girl, please!"

We talked some, and I was clearly upset. I said that I was very shocked that she even felt comfortable making this call, because wasn't Richard Allen and his folks not being able to worship in a white church what gave birth to the Black church?[8] That had to be a first. And there was a time when Black women couldn't enter seminary, so there had to be a first. And I even joked that I wouldn't mind being their "demo dyke" and assured her that being down there I'd find others in the school. She didn't find that humorous at all. But I had to make a decision, and I said to her that I really felt called to be who I really am, that this was one of those times when I didn't want to leave my identity at the threshold of the church. I wanted to bring it fully in. So she thanked me, and three days later I got my rejection letter. I cried for many months, feeling a whole bunch of stuff about the Black church and the call to justice it is not taking.

So, I went to Union two years later, not because it was my first choice, but my only choice. I had to look at Union as the opportunity to go where there was an open door, and that's how I got to the Presbyterian Church, because of Union's ties with it. It's not that I have any love for the Presbyterian Church or Black Presbyterians for that matter; it's because there was an open door. So, my charge to ministry came from some place not anticipated. I feel as though I've been on a journey without a road map, but I have managed to move forward. I really do think there's a door open somewhere and it will be revealed to me. It will not come in a way that I envision it, but it will come.

And one of my best educational experiences, I have to tell you, was Union Theological Seminary. I am who I am today because it placed its stamp on me and formed me. It gave me my voice, and I took it and ran with it. I feel blessed to have gone to Union. It's an ideological battlefield, as you well know. And you know what chapel is like at noon from Monday through Thursday. I used to call it "Showtime at the St. James," because of the various worshiping traditions students brought to Union. But it was a tremendous learning experience for me, and it really transformed me in some very wonderful ways. There's a queer student body as well as faculty, which are wonderful. Ethics professor Bev Harrison[9] was my advisor and sort of mentored me through the M.Div. program, because as a queer Black Christian I was having enormous difficulty with both the Black faculty and Black student body there. One Black professor blocked my getting a field placement at one of the prodigious Black churches in Brooklyn because I was lesbian.

Coming up here to Harvard was a change because it's conservative. We have no queer faculty. I am Professor Gomes's head teaching fellow and have been with him for five years.[10] The kind of affirmation and prophetic edge I got at Union calls me at this point to go out and take what I've learned to the community. So, where Harvard has not been for me the most supportive place, the queer community of Boston has been, Blacks as well as whites.

In the 1960s, African Americans pushed the doors open around integration and brought forth the prophetic call about race. We bring the prophetic call about sexual orientation. The struggle is very similar. Do you see the connection? They were the prophetic voice of the '50s and

'60s, and now we are the prophetic voice. Our struggle is a lot harder, because we have been spiritually abused by our faith tradition. What we have done is gone away from the church, and now we must push back into the church and transform it—at least those of us who can do it. We should not castigate those folks who can't come out, but we want to provide a way that should they come out they know it's okay. Those of us who can transform the church, whether inside or out, ought to do it. I'm doing it in my way now, as I said earlier, by moving from parish ministry to being a public theologian. I believe—and I know I sound crazy—that I along with you and others can change the world. I think we do it in our different ministries.

Somehow you're able to stand up and take the risk, while others aren't. Why do you think you're one who can be the prophetic voice?

I am one of many prophetic voices who stand up. I believe that no lie lives forever and that lies left unchallenged get more power. There's a time when we all were closeted. We remember that being in that closet had too much power over us. We missed some blessed opportunities by being in the closet and by not fully embracing who we are and, if called to ministry, who God calls us to be. I know it sounds kind of hokey, but I really do believe that.

But what gave you the strength and hope to see through the lie?

I was in the Stonewall riots in 1969. I was fourteen years old. It's a real hoot in terms of how many of the Black gangs got down there that first night. It had everything to do with, if you remember anything about the '60s, it being a very rebellious period in our history. Back then race relationships were very tense. We were spinning off the Black Power movement, and back then we called cops "pigs." In Brooklyn on one of those hot, lazy kind of nights when people are just hanging from fire escapes and sitting on stoops, we get this message—and messages travel in various ways in these Black enclaves and street gangs—that the pigs are beating up on our fags down in the Village. Now, mind you, as with most folks—but especially if you live in your Brooklyn enclave—you're very tribal, you don't really travel out of your enclave that much, and folks haven't heard of the Village, myself included. We're fourteen, fifteen, sixteen; we're rebellious anyway, and suddenly we had a reason to rebel, a context for rebellion. So folks got on the train, and of course we didn't pay, we just jumped the turnstile. And really to be honest with you, we're saying, "We gonna whip some cop's ass tonight. There's gonna be a fight tonight."

And we get down there, and it was a transforming moment for me, because I had some inklings that I was queer but I didn't have a name for it. The only face I had for it was what I call your diva queens who we would see in the neighborhood and who people jeered at. But I hadn't seen other forms of queerness, so that night was transformative. It was so moving just to fight anywhere, but here to fight for a cause was incredible—to really understand what this was all about and that these people had a right to be who they were. I understood it because of being Black and feeling I had a right to be who I was. In those days, we were saying, "Say it loud, I'm Black and I'm proud," and we were donning these big Angela Davis Afros. I swear to you I understood that moment. And I understood it not because I saw it in whiteface, but because I saw it in Blackface. I really got it that these human rights struggles tie us all to one another in a profound way. Those are the sort of things that keep me hopeful.

In your work, do you draw more from resources inside or outside of organized religion?

I do a balance of both. I don't want to lose the pulse of what's going on in the Black church. I'll keep going to a Black church, because I think my attempts to critique the Black church would be rather disingenuous if I didn't stay connected to it, as problematic and assaulting as it is when you hear the minister railing and ranting about homosexuality and a whole bunch of stuff and you say, "Jesus, help me through this." But I sit there because there's something, first of all, about his feeling called, and there's something that these people are hearing in a way that they find liberating and salvific. Even if it is through years of indoctrination, something else is going on for these people other than a moment of spewing bigotry.

So, you have stayed connected?

Yes, I have to. I also stay connected with the queer community, because I can't talk about this stuff and not be out on the street. Then I find ways to mix both. My column is one way. But I also hit more popular types of journals, as well as books—like the *Farrakhan Factor* is a commercial book as opposed to an academic book. I'm not only interested in talking to my colleagues. We're not really affecting change just by talking among ourselves. We may think we are in our head, but I'm talking about really affecting the lives of people. I think that only comes if you have pastored. Maybe if I hadn't pastored, I wouldn't know what changing lives and situations really involves. When you're down there in the trenches, you know. So, you've got to get out there.

African American lesbians and gay men talk about feeling cut off from their people when they can't go to their church as open queer folks. Can you say something about that?

Yes. The Black church has really been a spiritual and social institution within our community. E. Franklin Frazier describes the Black church as a "nation within a nation."[11] The Black church had a multiplicity of roles: social, educational, as well as spiritual. Even more when we were living more evidently in segregated America, everything centered around the Black church. That's where you went when you wanted to know what was going on in the world, what you should do to do right, as well as how you could move forward educationally or professionally. You got all that information from the Black church. It also cushioned you and was your refuge against racism. If you couldn't be anybody in the white world, in the Black church you were somebody. So, to be cut off from the Black church is really being cut off from the Black community, the Black family, because "ain't no place else" can you just by virtue of being Black be somebody. You're a child of God, you're someone with dignity, you're someone who holds the promise of a new world, of God's kingdom will be done. To be cut off from the Black church is to be cut off from your lifeline. It was the main organ that shaped the entire Black community. And it still does that. Not as much now though, since we moved into a period of integration, but it still—and somewhat in an anemic way, I must say—has a main function in the Black community.

Do you know of any out African American gay men or lesbians who remain in the church and still feel that connection?

No. What we've done—and I'm terribly troubled by it in some ways, because I understand it as a reactionary response to a void—is create Unity Fellowship Church, a Black queer denomination that has many local churches now throughout the country.[12] And Bishop Carl Bean of

Unity says he is providing an alternative for Black queers. They can come on Sunday morning and practice the religion that is such an important aspect of forming Black identity and sense of self. He's created—some would say "resurrected"—these Black churches, but the denominational structure and liturgy have not changed at all. So, in place of what I call the Black church's usual heterosexual patriarchy, you now have what I call homosexual patriarchy. You still have Black men in power, so nothing has changed and nothing really is salvific or liberating about those churches other than the fact that they provide an open door, but at a tremendous expense for women and transgendered people, depending on how you're transgendered.

What do you tell gay men or lesbians who are looking for a spiritual home or spiritual connection? What's the alternative?

I tell them two things: One is to get with like people, and two is that any journey you take is an arduous one because it's just not laid out there before you. The task is for forerunners—foresisters and forebrothers—to create the path rather than simply to find it laid out for you, because it isn't there—yet. The call, believe it or not, is for you to fill the void. A lot of people don't want to do that, but that's how I see it. There's a void. We all see it, speak about it, and want it to be filled, but that won't be done until we step up to the task and realize that we have to put it in place. That's what my ancestors did when they wanted freedom. They envisioned it. Harriet Tubman had a dream. She said, "I'm going to conduct a railroad out of here." People had different visions of it. But the point is that not to do anything does not cause any type of change. You have to do something. It does not exist unless we do it.

It reminds me of womanist theology,[13] which I'm so annoyed with because it doesn't address issues of sexual orientation,[14] even though some of the women constructing and shaping womanist theology are queer. They also don't address class issues. And I keep saying, "You know, I'm sick of it," but the point is that they're not going to change it. It's up to me and others like me to do it, and so I address the issue of sexual orientation and don't call myself "womanist." I've got to create something different so that those of us who feel alienated by the womanist discourse now have a place to begin to talk about how our voice ought to be incorporated into the feminist and Black theological discourses. Presently, it's not there. We have to create it ourselves. That's what the queer movement is about. It wasn't always a movement, not until at some point we had to say, "Look, we're sick of getting our ass whipped! We got to do something."

The article I'm writing now talks about the class and race division in the queer community. We have to educate white queer folks to the fact that, "Yes, you are oppressed because of your sexual orientation, but you have white-skin privilege. You have to put that in check in order to be able to talk to people of color." But then when I talk to people of color, I have to say to them, "We don't have a patent on oppression because we're Black." We all have to understand that when you have an attitude that impedes the possibility for discourse, you need to go about the business of changing things. I give two different types of talks to the different communities, but the point is that it's essential that we all find a way to work together.

You know what I like about the queer movement, although I see that we're light years away, is that it really is a profoundly prophetic movement, and you want to know why? Because it's global. Anywhere in the world you're going to find somebody queer. So, unlike the Civil Rights movement, which was particular to here, Black, and in some sense homogenous, the queer movement crosses race, class, ethnicity, all of those social barriers. And it's everywhere in the world.

PART II

Charting the Course

Chapter 6

Rev. Dr. Cecil "Chip" Murray

Since 1977, Cecil "Chip" Murray has been the senior pastor at First African Methodist Episcopal (First AME) Church, the oldest and largest Black congregation in the city of Los Angeles. During Rev. Murray's tenure, membership has grown from three hundred to seventeen thousand, ranging from the affluent, highly skilled, and educated to the poor, unskilled, and homeless. First AME has over forty community-outreach task forces with programs for health, HIV/AIDS, substance abuse, housing and homelessness, disabilities, tutoring and education, gang mediation, prison ministry, emergency food and clothing, senior citizens, job testing and placement, and pan-Africanism. President Bush named First AME as the 177th Point of Light for its community outreach services.[1]

Regarded as South Central L.A.'s most visible minister, Rev. Murray has been at the forefront of solving many social problems, such as reclaiming communities from drugs and gangs.[2] His reconciling role in the aftermath of the verdict in the 1992 Rodney King trial was nationally recognized and praised.[3] He was one of the earliest proponents of HIV/AIDS intervention and conducted a controversial condom handout program during Sunday services in 1991.[4] Rev. Dr. Murray received his doctoral degree in religion from the Claremont School of Theology, where he has also served as an adjunct professor. He is included in *Who's Who among African Americans* and is on *Ebony* magazine's "Role of Great Preachers."[5]

One of the questions I've asked other pastors is how and why they have been able to change from a less accepting to a more accepting position on lesbians and gay men. It's an important question, especially for others who want to change but are having difficulty doing so. Could you say something about your own experience on arriving at the position that you now have?

I think anyone who has been on the griddle knows what heat is. Coming from the Deep South of segregation, I have known the heat of being made to feel the outsider. If the fire doesn't sensitize a human being, then that human being borders on the hopeless. If one who has known what it is to be ostracized does not have a bridge of empathy to anyone else who is ostracized, then that person himself or herself is shut out. I think we tend to do that, because we have had it done to ourselves. When I feel shut out, I shut out others. When I feel inferior, I project that onto others. When I feel insecure, I pass the insecurity along. So, to ask why my arms would be outstretched, I would only be able to answer that my arms have felt the heat and the pain, and I am determined never, ever, ever to cause heat and pain to anyone else on the outside.

When did gay issues become important for you and your church?

I don't think there was a traumatic or dramatic moment. I have always observed that Black culture tends to be inclusive more than exclusive, that we pretty well receive whatever life or lifestyle is presented. I have found the Black church to be a microcosm of that larger concept of being inclusive. So, to ask if there was a dramatic moment where you ran the flag up, I would say no. If there was a time when because some people became proactive against gays and you reacted to that negativism, I suppose it came when the gay rights movement emerged as a self-conscious movement. So, sensitizing I don't think we needed, just concretizing was what was decidedly needed.

In your own lifetime what kind of changes have you seen taking place for lesbians and gay men within the church and as a pastor?

I have seen their emergence, as I said, from the closet—that they find less a need to be apologetic than a need just to assert there is-ness—and it is up to others how they are received. They seem to have taken the initiative and are saying, "I have the right to be who I am and you don't have the right to determine who I shall be." Over the last, let's say, two decades, but particularly the last ten years or so, I think there has been a decided change in those who were hidden and who are now revealed and are proud of the revelation.

Do you think that lesbians and gay men feel comfortable being open about their sexual identity in your church?

I think they feel quite comfortable, not as comfortable perhaps as they will be within another ten years, but our stance is known—without being flaunted—that we are not an exclusive church but an inclusive church. They understand and all understand that the word "religion" itself comes from *religare,* which means to bind, to tie together.

The question is, "What is the norm?" I suppose that most people would still agree that heterosexuality is the norm. Then the question becomes, "How can you be inclusive in dealing with that which is not the norm?" Then you deal with the question of ethics. It's simply ethics. I am not my brother's or sister's keeper, no; but I am my brother's or sister's brother. We are not to keep each other, no; but we are to love each other. And when we try to determine each other's way of being, then that is not loving, that is keeping. Ethics, I think, comes from *ethos,* which means "people." We are to be people-oriented, inclusive not exclusive.

How do you deal with people who have trouble with including lesbians and gay men? How do you work with them and help them not be reactive but to be welcoming?

We try to let them see that the church is an open door that enshrines, encloses, cherishes—that there must be these two aspects of religion. First, the church is an open door, and second, the church is a hospital for broken spirits, broken dreams, broken minorities. The church is a hospital for brokenness. Therefore, if a person who is different than you comes to you, you don't break them. You heal them if they are broken, and you let them heal you if you are broken. You have a decision to make: if you're going to be a hospital, you're going to accommodate brokenness; if you're going to stand at an open door, you're going to let everyone in. Now, you can't have it both ways: an open door that is shut, a hospital that only heals a certain category. So you have to decide, but the church doesn't have a decision. The decision was made for the church when the church advertised itself as a care package, not a care-less package.

What do you say to lesbians and gay men who want to stay in the church but have questions about how much rejection and difficulty they can take? How do you encourage them to be hopeful and to stay with it?

They're on the point of the spear. They're on the start of a revolution in values, and there is no revolution without a price to pay. There is no change without cataclysm. If they are willing to accept that charge, then they shall be a portion of the rewards that come. If they are not willing to accept the darts and the arrows, then they need to subdue themselves as was done in the '40s, '50s, and prior, and go into the closet again. Religion has to do with choices; movement has to do with choices; payday has to do with workday: no cross, no crown. You have a lifestyle that is different than the mainstream. You choose to be who you are because you have integrity. You understand that the mainstream will try to wash you downstream. God has made you a swimmer. Swim.

You must know that your position and your support of lesbians and gay men is unusual, whether you look at the Black church or the white church. Why do you think you've been able to be who you are? Do you think that your own religious tradition has an openness to this kind of inclusion?

I do not see myself in a unique category. I think the person who is unique would be the minister who would take the opposite stance. To say to gays and lesbians, "Welcome"—that would seem to be the standard. The nonstandard behavior would be to say to gays and lesbians, "You are not welcome." Now, everything of course depends upon whose yardstick we're using to measure the standard. Remember that little boy who said, "Mommy, oh Mommy, look, Mommy, I'm six feet tall." She said, "Son, who told you that you were six feet tall; how do you know?" He said, "I measured myself with this little ruler I made." And that is what people perhaps who are driven to put down gays and lesbians are judging themselves by: by that little ruler.

Now, they will say, "No, the ruler was designed by the Bible. Doesn't the Bible condemn lesbians and gays?" I think of that as simplistic reading, to which I would say, yes, the Bible does, but the Bible is value-driven; and the values are there clearly spelled out. Please, explain the values or portions of the Bible that favor war; then why are we struggling so hard to have peace? The Bible favors sexism. "Women," Paul says, "be quiet in church." And the opening chapters of the Bible place women in a subservient position derived from man, which is weird that a man is pregnant giving birth to a woman. After even a casual observance of the Bible, we would obviously see that the Bible is written against the background of its cultures, and cultures and values dialogue with each other. The Bible condones slavery, but you're not going to tell every thirteenth

American, "Go back into slavery," and yet that was the same rhetoric used in the Civil War and beyond to justify slavery and the rape of a continent. One hundred eighty million folks perhaps died on the continent, 18 million died in the mid-Atlantic passage to America, with the church baptizing slave ships as they passed through the inlet by dumping buckets of water on top of the slaves assembled on the deck in the name of the Lord.

So, when we say the Bible is value-driven, we must ask what values, whose values, and against what background. If you really want to read more literally rather than liberally your revelation to anyone, God says, "I'm doing a new thing—that we ought to change." The law was once blood revenge, *lex talionis.* Then Hammurabi comes along and softens it: not a life for an eye, but only an eye for an eye, a tooth for a tooth, a nail for a nail. And then Jesus comes along and absolutely radicalizes that, "An eye for an eye was good, because that limited it; but now I'm telling you even more. Turn the other cheek, don't return insult for insult, don't return eye for an eye." So, the values change in God's open revelation. The revelation is not ended. Jesus says, "Greater things than I have done, you shall do."

Jesus did not have this computer sitting on his desk; Jesus did not have the jet plane that could put him in New York in five hours from L.A.; Jesus did not have radio, television, a printing press—or stained-glass windows. We will change our values, when it is convenient for our prejudices; but when it's not convenient for our prejudices, we don't want the pain of change. So, the Bible is constantly to be interpreted, because the truth of the Bible, the chief value in the Bible, is not racism, sexism, or exclusivism. The chief value is love, and that will never change because the essence of love is acceptance. Paul says that the love of God is shown, the love of Christ is shown, in that while we were yet sinners he died for us. Acceptance—acceptance of you just as you are—invites you only to rise to the best that you can be.

You said that lesbians and gay men are on the point of the spear. I think lesbians and gay men are often looking for a comfortable place in the church, whereas it seems as though our role and gift may be to be uncomfortable and to go through the storm.

You've heard the cliché about "whether to afflict the comfortable or to comfort the afflicted." It is the challenge of the gay front to afflict the comforted and to comfort the afflicted. They are minorities now, so they can empathize and plead the cause of other oppressed minorities because they are in that ditch. On the other hand, those who are comfortable in their prejudices, they prick their consciences, they question their morality, they lead to a brighter day. We must not ever be afraid of conflict. We must never be afraid of crises. There's a classic joke about Black people: This mother is watching the soldiers marching by, "Oh look, here come the soldiers, and look, there's my son, and look, he's the only one in step." Martin Luther King says that the salvation of the world is in the hands of the maladjusted: the maladjusted to be out of step, to march to the rhythm of another drumbeat. That, of course, must take conviction, or else with the first dart everybody ducks and stays down; but if you have the conviction that you have the right to be here, you have the right to be who you are, then when the darts come, as the African proverb says, "It is not the name you call me, it's the name I answer to."

Do you think that you've learned much from lesbian and gay men? Have you had interactions with lesbians and gay men in which you've seen some aspect of faith or humanity that you hadn't quite seen that way before?

Well, you see I would have a problem with that question, because I could not see a gay person or lesbian person as different than a mainstream person. I would think that everybody's calling—you have no option—is to come to life as a student. You don't come to life as a finished product or as a teacher. You come to life as a student. Therefore, every life you encounter from your awakening till your final sleep, every life you encounter is a challenge or is a learning situation. This moment is the only moment, this is the existential moment, this is the moment. I must deal with integrity, I cannot afford distortion, and I must be open to his world as well as my world. So to say, "Gay person, can you teach me something?" Yes. "Brick mason, can you teach me something?" Yes. "Therapists, chemists, can you teach me something?" Yes. "Three-year-old, can you teach me something?" Yes. So, I would not isolate. If you ask if I've learned something about the gay movement, fine, because that would be a specialty, but to say do they bring something to the table other than a lifestyle? My goodness, yes, because every human being brings something to the table, and it all depends on whether we want an inclusive banquet or an exclusive banquet.

I know that First AME has grown in numbers, and it would seem from what you've just said that that growth has been because many different kinds of people feel that they do belong and they are taken seriously there.

I think that the banner that's lifted up carries the message. When the banner says, "Come unto Me, All Ye, Weary, Heavy Laden, Doesn't Matter, Just Who You Are, All Are Welcome Here," then in a period of time you grow, if you structure that programmatically. It isn't enough as a shibboleth. You've got to structure it so that, for example, ushers are receptive. You are doorkeepers, you are the entrance. Officers: Move over, make room. Don't structure people according to how long you've been here, but according to, "What can you do to help us now that you are here?" Choirs—multicultural, multiethnic, youth. You go to Skid Row. They must know that they are welcome. To the hospitals, children's hospital: they must know. To the police, to the fire people: they must know.

On the other hand, there are some specifics that go with the generalities. There's a zero tolerance for intolerance. If you seek intolerance, we will not be married. If you seek to point fingers, we will not be married. If you are a control freak, you will probably encounter some freaky behavior. And that's where the line is drawn. You are free to decide to cross it and to come along. We do not want sheep; we want shepherds, a conglomeration of shepherds, and then together we go out to help sheep.

You come into the church to go out of the church. The front door is the exit; and when we sing the benediction, worship begins. They must know that, and it's up to the leadership to set that kind of climate. If then, a pastor has been there five years, ten years, and the people are still excluding people, the shepherd must be held accountable. Do not make excuses; this is what you wanted. I don't care what you found, what did God give you as a vision? You must have a map to chart the course, and unfortunately too many of our pastors can't even find the North Star.

What's in their way?

Acceptance and safety, because who wants to be maligned? Who wants the budget falling, since history is pulled by an economic engine? You make some people mad, they're going to withhold the money. Then the budget fails. Then your peers will say, "You failed." So, the question is to be as smooth as a serpent's tooth, as harmless as a dove. We can't just be the doves; we've also got to have the wisdom to know how to bring along those who can empower the church financially. You don't have to run all your people away; some will leave, okay, but my goodness, you don't have to split your church on an issue that is not necessarily a splitting issue. If it means we have civil war where we must, we must, but we do everything short of that. Can't you meet the people, can't you get some significant others and dialogue with them, can't you try to sensitize them, can't you programmatically set aside this year to do step one and then step two and step three then step four? It will not be accomplished naturally. It has to be done supernaturally—which means "as led by God"— and you can't lose with the stuff God uses. Another cliché, but so very true when used, "If you really are sincere and if you know you've got God on your side, what in hell are you afraid of?" What's in hell? The devil. Get thee behind me, Satan. You believe it or you don't. If you don't, do what is safe; bless everything that you find and inherit. If you believe in God more than the devil, then do a new thing: Change.

Can you give examples of potentially divisive issues that have not been divisive because of approaching them in the way you just said?

I was trying to think of what isn't divisive (*laughs*). There is no change that is comfortable for church people because church people, religious people, by their very nature are orthodox people. And if you're going to be neoorthodox or even liberal or neoliberal, ultraliberal, you make some decision.

I'll give you a small example: I inherited a church of white symbols. There were some three hundred; they were Eurocentric. My first year as pastor: anthems, Eurocentric music. And there was also talk, "We don't want all those new people in here." And it was ludicrous, because these were nice Pullman porters and head janitors and such people saying that. These were not necessarily your bourgeoisie, which may be bad enough. But fine, we wanted to take down the symbols of the white Mary and the white Jesus, because Black people need to worship with their own symbols as does every other culture in the world other than Black America. We're the only culture that works in the symbols of a foreign culture. And if you do a little study of the Bible, you have more reason to believe that Jesus was Black than to believe that he was white; or more reason to believe the earliest Israelis were Black than that they were white; that Zipporah the Cushite who marries and teaches Moses many things and Jethro, his father-in-law, who introduces him to the sacred mountain, teaches him how to govern, and tells him about Yahweh, were Black.

So, we had this picture up front that came from Italy. This building was erected in 1969; and one person gave that mural to us and it hung over the choir, so it was central. In my second year, I brought on board into ministry a young woman who also had some artistic capabilities. We met at midnight. The scaffold person put up a little scaffold that she could stand on, and she kinked Jesus' hair and darkened his complexion and did the same to Mary and Joseph. The following Sunday the young people noticed, but the old people didn't. They were so used to the picture that they took no notice of it, but gradually it began to eat into them. Then we wanted to go to the stained-glass windows, because we had Black heroes in the windows but the Jesus figure was lily-white. We got a donor to help us and got the stained-glass company to come out on a Sunday afternoon at 5:00, because no one was there, and we changed that.

Now, we have a new mural that replaces it all, and it's 100 percent Afrocentric inclusive of whites, Latinos, Asians, and all. It tells the story of "out of Africa" to the present moment, and we call it "God and Us." And I think that type of inclusivism is what we're about, and now the congregation is totally Afrocentric but inclusive enough to have the anthems. Our covenant congregation is Jewish Temple Isaiah. They come to us, we go to them. Our educational exchange centers go to Skid Row. We do projects together. I don't think in ten to fifteen years have I heard anyone complaining about anything other than sometimes the instruments—music gets too loud, hip-hop—but they'll adjust to that, too. It's the subtlety of planning, of not being dumb. It is blasphemy to be dumb when we serve a God of wisdom. If we can't cope with the snake in the garden, how are we going to save the world outside the garden? And our destiny is not to be in the garden. Our destiny is to live east of Eden. If we can't handle that snake, how are we going to handle them folks east of Eden?

Looking to the future, why do you have hope that different kinds of people will be able to talk and work together? Why do you think we're going to be able to get there?

There are two hopes. One is that reason will prevail. The prophet says, "Come, let us reason together." A minority of people is reasonable and will exercise some degree of sanity in decision making. That minority is the constant hope of the world or of a community. That minority, when incensed, then can influence the majority. That is one hope: that the people of conscience will exercise conscience and become prophetic, rather than pathetic.

The second push is necessity. Reason will give a positive pull; necessity will give a negative push. Now that we have modern communication, transportation—and even with the Web—we are only scratching the surface of a oneness of communion. That oneness of communion must lead to a oneness of commonality. No more will people be brutalized when they see those sectors of the world where people are not brutalized. That's why institutions are crumbling. With religions, denominations are crumbling. People are crossing borders by the sheer necessity of that restlessness on the part of the have-nots; and the haves must share, or the haves will join the have-nots. We will have a commonality. Whether it will be a commonality of haves or a commonality of have-nots, the jury is still out.

So, the necessity plus the positive pull of reason are our hopes as we go into the millennium.

And how do you see the presence of lesbians and gay men in the church playing a part in that hope for our future?

I think perhaps we will reach a watershed in our understanding of each other when we can reach that watershed in our understanding of ourselves, and the sexuality issue is the bell calling us to the center of the ring for this ultimate battle with ourselves. The gay community may very well be the bell-ringer. Out of this struggle then, other struggles will have their own answers. This is not the ultimate struggle, but it is a climactic and dramatic struggle. So, it's important that the gay community take the high ground, because when the victory is won it must not be besmirched by negativism or violence or anything that would mitigate the principles. Ring the bell. Come out. Fight beyond the final round. Then stand victorious, because the ultimate question is, "Does a human being have the inherent right to be what that human being is as long as it does not impinge on the is-ness of another human being?" The answer must come back, "Yes, I know who I am; why do I give a damn about what you are?"

What would be a low-ground way that lesbians and gay men should avoid? What should we not do?

The low ground comes when you adopt the tactics of your enemies, your opponents. Slander. Viciousness. Finger-pointing. Eye-for-an-eye, tooth-for-a-tooth. That is an option, but it must not be the live or ultimate option. As in the struggle against racism, Blacks cannot, must not, isolate whites and drag them behind pickup trucks; cannot, must not, hang isolated whites and castrate them; cannot, must not, lump all whites together and say that all white people are vicious or satanic. You must not adopt the tactics of low opponents.

Maybe that's also a good reason for lesbians and gay men to remain within our churches of origin instead of moving out of them to found separate communities.

Well, if we are integrated people, we find integrated societies. You don't change patterns by walking away from them. You change patterns by persisting and insisting. And in the final analysis you will win, if you are in the right, of course.

What's on your own agenda for the immediate future?

We are working this coming year with education. Our Education Center goes now from pre-K through eighth grade. Secondly, economically, a $20 million venture capital fund that will allow us to enable startup businesses and enable small, at-risk businesses to persevere and grow—a business incubator that would lean toward the high-tech industries of Hollywood to prepare minority businesses to bridge with them, to get the skill, to have the equipment available. To that end, we have obtained a building and are doing $2 million worth of renovation so that it will become an "intelligent" building with modern tooling. We plan to enhance our housing industry from our current eight housing projects to twelve, including senior citizens housing and an AIDS hospice to house families afflicted with AIDS. And each of those, of course, would call for collateral ministries; thus, our Coalition of Health Professionals would work with the AIDS hospice, our Seniors' Coalition would work with the senior housing, the Men's Organization would patrol communities to keep the drugs out. So, we would move as a *gestalt* in those areas. Our forty task-force ministries cover and address just about every political and social issue, and each member of the congregation is encouraged to join at least one task-force ministry. The door is open. So, if God accepts somebody, we accept him or her. If God accepts us, we accept anybody. And that's the guiding principle.

You must be in your mid-sixties.

Seventy. I turned seventy two weeks ago.

And you're not planning to retire soon, right? (laughs)

Aw shucks, it's a question that my sensitivity will answer. When I am less than a firebrand, then I take me out of the people's face. I don't think you can accomplish anything—in life or in ministry—unless you are on fire. When I become cold, then I become history (*laughs*).

Chapter 7

Rev. Msgr. Raymond G. East

*S*ince 1997, Raymond East has been the senior pastor at the Church
of the Nativity of the Lord in Washington, D.C., where he has previously served several other parishes, including Saint Teresa of
Avila. The Archdiocese of Washington is the third largest Black
Roman Catholic congregation in the United States. Sixteen percent
of Catholics in the Archdiocese are Black; twenty-five of its 140
parishes are predominantly Black; and there are six Black pastors,
three of whom are monsignors.[1]

Before entering the priesthood, Father East was active in lay ministry with Vietnam veterans, farm workers, and prison inmates and
was business manager for the National Association of Minority
Contractors. Currently he is a member of the Archdiocesan Council
of Priests, the board of Food and Friends, the D.C. Catholic AIDS
Network, and the Church Association for Community Service. In
1989, he was elevated to Reverend Monsignor.

*Would you give some of the characteristics of the Church of the
Nativity?*

Nativity is a predominately Black Roman Catholic parish in the
upper northwest part of the District of Columbia. We're in a neighborhood of both apartments and many single-family homes. It's a
parish that's economically diverse, with some moderate and low-
income families mixed with lots of middle-income and some upper-
income as well. The parish has been here for ninety-eight years.

Was it originally founded as a Black parish?

It was a white congregation. In fact, as things developed in
Washington it was a whites-only congregation and integrated fairly

quickly in the '60s and then by the late '60s became almost all Black. But there have always been a handful of white parishioners from the old time who have remained in the parish.

Saint Teresa of Avila is in the Anacostia neighborhood in the southeast district of Washington. How is Nativity different from your previous parish?

The income level is the biggest difference. There's also a difference in level of education. Many of the parishioners here have postgraduate degrees. We have a judge, several lawyers, quite a few professionals, doctors, and so forth.

Does that make a difference in terms of the programs and outreach that you do?

It does a little bit. We had to have quite a few programs that served really basic personal and community needs when I was in Anacostia. And here that's not such a great problem. So, we tend to do the more traditional church ministries. What I call triage ministries aren't so necessary here.

What kind of programs do you have?

At Nativity we do SHARE, which is a food distribution program. The charity needs of the parish are taken care of by two organizations, the Catholic Daughters of America and Our Lady Sodality. A few people are interested in AIDS ministry, and we're trying to get that off the ground. We have several other ministries that are in formation, a young adult group and a bereavement group; and then there are the traditional worship-related ministries, like eucharistic ministers, choirs, ushers. We used to have a huge, very active teen club, but then all the kids grew up. The parishioners are older than at Saint Teresa's, and there is a senior citizen outreach ministry that meets every week.

Did you come to Nativity with any special expectations, or did parishioners have expectations of what they wanted you to do?

The way it works is that a meeting is called when there's a selection of a new pastor. At Nativity's meeting I think between sixty and one hundred people showed up. The whole parish is invited to attend; it's a listening session. They are able to voice their expectations of the new pastor. Neither the old pastor nor the incoming pastor attends that meeting, but the council and the parish leaders are all there. At Nativity they said they very much wanted a continuation of many of the good things that were going on in the past. They were very happy with their former pastor, who had been there nine years. They also expressed interest in expanding outreach to the young people. They wanted to continue to look to the future in terms of survival, and they had a couple of problems that they wanted to see any incoming pastor deal with. One of those was the presence of the Nigerian Catholic community, which has been headquartered here for four years. They felt that the presence of a separate community was problematic, and they would rather see that community absorbed into the regular parish.

You've been here a year and a half. Have you done what new pastors usually do, which is to just sit tight for a while, or have you tried to make some changes?

I've tried for the first year to make no changes at all. I think the biggest change I brought was a little difference in the liturgy in terms of a little more singing. We're trying to get more spirited singing and participation from the congregation. And I moved the choir. They were in a corner of the church, and I moved them into the sanctuary.

Is the style of the worship at all Afrocentric?

It had been by default. The music always had been Afrocentric, but the style of the liturgy was not. It was very formal, short (*laughs*), and very basic. Kind of like, "Come and worship and then we'll get out." I've changed that a little by making the worship a little more spirited and Afrocentric, but trying not too much of that.

Has that been well received?

From plain to mixed reviews. Many parishioners expressed a great reluctance to have it happen. They said, "We don't want you to bring any of that stuff from Saint Teresa's or Saint Augustine's. We just don't want it." And yet, many of the parishioners here had left to join other churches that had more spirit-filled worship. There are some parishioners who would like it "back the old way," and so we have two traditional Masses and two Masses with more spirited liturgies and a gospel choir, which they've had here for years.

It seems as if the parish is more formal and traditional than other parishes.

Very much so. It's been known for that. Many of the parishes in this part of the city have that reputation. Washington is very much a parochial town known by its neighborhoods, districts, and wards. The upper northwest has always been a place for the more educated, wealthy, traditional, conservative African American community.

Does conservative liturgy translate to conservative social justice positions?

That's an excellent question. It translates into maybe a more conservative approach, and a lot of that has to do with the age of the members. I didn't find the strong community outreach programs I expected. We are members of an ecumenical association called the Carter Barron Cluster of Churches, a very good group of about twelve churches very much like ours. Some of them are former white congregations that have turned mostly Black, others are traditional Black congregations, but most of them have older parishioners. Most of Nativity's social ministry was going on through this Cluster and not initiated by Nativity itself. It consists of a tutoring program on Saturdays, working with public school children who have material needs beyond tutoring, an outreach to help senior citizens with transportation, and financially supporting about fifteen to twenty families transitioning from homelessness to independence.

So, individual parishioners participate through your membership in the Cluster?

Yes. And I'd have to say the participation is very weak. The tutoring program involved the most people, and that's ten to twelve people. We're talking about a parish of almost one thousand families. So, the social ministries are pretty quiet, kind of dead. Lately, I asked the parish if they might consider joining WIN, the Washington Interfaith Network, which is a Saul Alinsky model of church-based community groups sponsored by the Industrial Areas Foundation of Chicago.[2] There are a dozen of these groups in New York, a big group in Baltimore, and we started a Washington group about four years ago. Nativity has been in the process of joining primarily to provide after-school programming for youth and to address the issue of immigration, because we now have a high amount of immigrants, mostly African and Caribbean. The other social-ministry need waiting out there is Hispanic outreach. We live in an area where there are a number of Hispanic families. There's probably as many Hispanic Catholic families in the area as there are Black families in our parish. That's the extent of social ministries. WIN has the most potential for organizing and reactivating social ministry in the parish.

Your own past is quite social justice oriented, right?

I would say so (*laughs*). Not always consciously so. It's been based on my own reflection on the Gospel and looking at the needs of the community, relating not only community needs but community gifts and strengths to the Gospel, to the scriptures, and seeing the need for that to translate into action, both my own individual action and that of the congregation.

You're recognized in the District for progressive thinking and action.[3]

Am I? (*laughs*) Let me put it this way. I come from California, and I have enjoyed participating in a lot of the social movements that have come along starting with the Civil Rights movement in the '60s. I'm forty-eight years old, so I was eighteen when Dr. King was assassinated. I've worked on civil rights in the construction industry and in the church, and I've been involved with antipoverty programs and the United Farm Workers struggle. I had that background in civil rights and interracial justice, so when I came out here I sought to continue that kind of work. I've really enjoyed being involved in the impetuses that have come up in Washington over the last twenty-three years. I guess it is involvement, and not necessarily out-front leadership, but I certainly try to be involved.

In the past twenty-three years, what are two involvements that stand out most for you?

The things that needed to be done in a most severe way and that caught my attention were, one, trying to organize churches around a comprehensive response to the drug problem—the crack epidemic and the drug and teen problem that really have just decimated Washington. And the other thing would be involvement in organizing and working with churches in an interfaith way to respond to the AIDS crisis. In both of those situations, D.C. statistically suffered very much. We've always been the fifth or sixth city in the country in terms of the incidences of HIV/AIDS and the number of deaths. And we've been number one in the homicide rate related to drug-related violence for many years. Over the last ten years the District has been heavily impacted by AIDS and by the drug wars, and that's where I've focused a lot of my work.

How did you get involved in AIDS work? Was there a pivotal event?

I've been involved since we started to feel the epidemic in the mid-'80s. Nineteen eighty-four–eighty-five was a pivotal year for me. I was the head of the Social Concerns Committee for the Council of Priests, and I had the opportunity to direct the energies of the Council towards some areas I thought needed attention. One was the drug situation, and another was AIDS ministry. It happened that Nativity and the pastor then, Ray Curlin, had also felt a need for the church to respond to the AIDS crisis. He and my committee organized the first diocesan AIDS conference for clergy and religious leaders. It was mostly Catholic with about four hundred clergy present. A young man stood up at the end of the meeting and said, "I'm Lou Tesconi and I've just been kicked out of the Franciscans and I have AIDS." His statement was the beginning of the Damian ministry, which is one of our local ministries in D.C., and we've been working on HIV/AIDS ever since. That was a watershed moment.

When you first started working on AIDS, introduced it into churches, and were working on it at Saint Teresa's, what were some of the programs you implemented?

We did peer training, which was an attempt to get lay people to become outreach workers by giving them some basic knowledge of AIDS and helping them work with families that have been affected by HIV. We did several trainings and participated with other churches that had taken a lead, like Rev. Albert Gallmon of Mount Carmel Baptist Church. We put on workshops and were part of a formation of the Catholic AIDS Network. We also had the parish really connected with other parishes, other churches interfaith-wise, and community-based AIDS service organizations; and it was the churches that were called on to help achieve acceptance in the Black community of the Max Robinson clinic, which arrived in Anacostia very late in the struggle and only after a long, long fight and a lot of community rejection. Now the Max Robinson Center is a branch of the Whitman Walker Clinic that serves the African American community. There was a pastoral advisory group that helped community leaders look at the problem right in Anacostia on Martin Luther King Avenue. The other AIDS service organization that we primarily worked with was Food and Friends, which provides hot meals and packaged food at no charge to people and families living with AIDS. So, we were able to get maybe twenty churches involved as sites and to get hundreds of volunteers from the African American community. The volunteer aspect of getting people involved was the important part of the work, and a subset in that work was the whole effort to help churches deal with homophobia. That effort is still ongoing.

It sounds as though there was resistance but also some real success. Can you explain what the resistance was and how you were able to implement the programs?

I think the resistance came from AIDS being perceived as a white gay disease, and there was a great stigma attached to that—both the whiteness and gayness. And yet AIDS had an immediate impact on the Black community, but the community went into denial. They said, "This doesn't affect us, we don't want to have anything to do with it. We want to keep any kind of AIDS outreach out of our churches, neighborhoods, and communities"; and then a lot of people started getting sick. I'm talking about neighborhoods in which on a third of the streets there would be at least one person, and on some streets—like P Street, S Street, T Street, and on Good Hope Road—there would be five, eight, ten people living with AIDS. It had the same impact as the death rate caused by the crack-cocaine wars, which also affected many, many people. We would do dozens of funerals, and lots and lots of people were sick. But there was a lot of resistance to any recognition of the fact that we had a problem we had to deal with, that we had sick people who needed love and compassion. When AIDS came home, when AIDS came to the church, when church members started being affected by HIV, then it was a real wake-up call.

And that was the reason for the turnaround, the breakdown of the resistance?

No, it would not have happened automatically without conscious and conscientious activity that came from the congregations. We were going against the tide, really fighting and struggling to raise awareness. The easiest thing would have been to do just what many congregations did: not to do anything, not to recognize that there were some great needs out there in the community.

So, there were certain parishes or congregations that saw the issue as needing attention and then provided leadership in the Black community?

Yes, and they saw the need even to struggle with it a long time before figuring out what to do. A couple of the Black Episcopal congregations were aided very much by having an outreach program that started around 1986–87 called ECRA, Episcopal Caring Response to AIDS. ECRA was well-organized, staffed and funded to a level so that it became the premier church-based, parish-based AIDS outreach in Washington. We also started a couple of initiatives. One of them was the Washington Religious Roundtable on HIV, of which Saint Teresa's was a charter member. I think the Roundtable helped a lot of clergy break through the wall of resistance in the congregations, because we had a chance to meet at least once a month, to address policy and education needs, and to support one another with AIDS fatigue. There were other groups, such as Associated Catholic Charities, that got involved and funded a position for working with HIV. Washington Interfaith Conference put out a statement and did some education around working with people with AIDS and the church's compassionate response. The religious leaders of different congregations—Cardinal Hickey, Bishop Haines, and other adjudicatory heads of the churches—also were helpful and supportive when they were called on and were challenged to do something.

Can you say something about what it's like to work on homophobia in either the parish setting or with your colleagues?

Homophobia was the stigma that kept churches from being involved. For example, to wear the red ribbon or to work with HIV, especially early on in the epidemic, meant that you were either gay or very gay-friendly, that you were tainted by the gay/lesbian/bi/transgendered community. That kept a lot of pastors from becoming involved in HIV ministry. It frightened so many people that the only way we were able to break through that was to get some real education by a couple of clergy activists like Pastor Rainey Cheeks, who founded the Inner Light Fellowship Church, a gay-friendly Black congregation.[4] Rainey was at everything that the Black and white pastors and Black community were trying to do in terms of the battle against AIDS. And there was also Elias Jones, a Black professor at Howard University and a very outspoken advocate.[5] Both of these men were either gay or bi, and openly so.

Elias had a strong connection with Saint Teresa. He was a frequent participant in the worship services there in the time of Father Stallings. Much of the AIDS outreach started when Father Stallings was there, and Elias was very supportive. The parish had a number of members who turned up HIV-positive and later died. So, I inherited a parish situation that already had a strong level of awareness, which made a great difference because some activists were very present, and Rainey and Elias were very good friends of mine, too. We developed this friendship by working together. I found them and others to be indispensable for keeping me involved in the struggle, for helping us very courageously to tackle homophobia. Helping churches to be really committed to serving their members and the community was a very important part of the struggle.

Can you say more about why you think working on homophobia is important?

I think it's important because AIDS was one of the first medical situations in America that I've been aware of during my lifetime that has a specific link to the gay community. It was first felt and experienced in the gay community. It was mistakenly called a gay disease or GRID, gay-related-immune-deficiency. Because the impact was first felt in the gay community here in the United States, it was the gay community that first responded by developing programs and processes. Whitman Walker Clinic here was a gay health outreach program and became the number-one funded organization helping people. The effort to find a cure for AIDS and to minister to people with AIDS started in the gay community, and that meant quite a bit of resistance in the Black community because of a certain cultural homophobia that comes from the Black community. It would just hit us in the face every time we tried to deal with the disease, so we said we've got to deal with this.

Would you describe this cultural homophobia?

The way that I experienced it in the Black community started at a very early age with an image—a false image—of what it is to be a man. It's a Black machismo that is very much related to images of athletes, entertainers, and rap artists. It's supposed to represent what it is to be a man in the Black community, and that is be anti-gay, physically very strong, and to demonstrate male sexual prowess. It's a cluster of myths regarding the Black male, and embedded in the heart of it is hatred of people who are specifically gay and lesbian. That was the model that was held up and that many people bought into. It was expressed in schools with a very big preoccupation on not being a "sissy" or a "fag" and with kids calling each other that name. The most pejorative names in the Black community come from the prison system, so you have boys calling each other "bitches" in a very dominant way or the using the pejorative term, "faggot."

Do you think there's also within the Black community an openness or sensitivity to the outsider or the oppressed that counters homophobia?

As much homophobia as I perceive in the Black community, there is also on the other side some very interesting things. There's always been a sense of hospitality and a countercultural acceptance of people. For example, the transgendered community has always been a little bit more visible, and there would be people who were transgendered, differently gendered in the Black community and "somewhat" accepted. It just goes along with being community. Another part of that would be the maternal acceptance of anybody's child. The church mothers will say, "Well, that's my child, and it doesn't matter to me whether she's lesbian or whether he's gay or whether he's a cross-dresser. I'm still going to love and accept him." So, there's that kind of community/maternal acceptance of people, and with that goes a little bit of hospitality.

But that's really counteracted by the other very strong image, the Black male myth. We see kids still struggling with it, and what it does is deny the fact that bisexuality is very much prevalent. There are many gay dads in the Black community, and there are many women who have partnered or been together and bonded together both for family and affection and as a means of survival. In my view and experience of the community, there was always a presence of gay people, but it's also very much denied; and the community would deal with it with anger and hostility, especially in the church. Pastors were and still are vociferous in preaching against homosexuality and any other alternative sexual expression and also in coming out with the same stock line, "God made Adam and Eve and not Adam and Steve." For example, when we had the Washington Religious Roundtable on AIDS, many preachers needed almost at every meeting to say the anti-gay creed just to let everyone know that they had not softened in terms of their religious or moral approach to homosexuality, and yet they still wanted to be engaged in the ministry to people with AIDS.

It sounds as though Saint Teresa's was a place in which gay people could be open.

I would say so, especially in the days of Father Stallings. In my understanding of that time, there was a much larger and visible presence of the gay community. But so many people left the church with him. About fourteen hundred families left, and I had a remaining congregation of four hundred families. Much of the gay community left with Father Stallings.[6] Not all, because the teaching, atmosphere, and preaching of acceptance of all members continued. In the Roman Catholic Church, we haven't specifically developed a program whereby parishes publicly declare themselves to welcome and affirm gay people, as the United Methodists, Unitarians, Lutherans, and some others have done.[7] The pastoral care of gay men and lesbians is to be done within diocesan-approved outreaches. For example, the Baltimore Diocese has a gay and lesbian outreach called AGLO. Several dioceses have adopted that pattern, and some parishes have such an active ministry here in Washington, but it would only be a handful. I would say that the Cathedral of Saint Matthew the Apostle, Saint Augustine's, and Holy Trinity in Georgetown have a diocesan-approved outreach to gay and lesbian members. Saint Augustine's has certainly been a parish that has been recognized as being very gay- and lesbian-friendly and has many gay members. By our preaching and teaching love and acceptance, people know whether a church is open or closed.

What do they know about Nativity?

Nativity is an interesting situation. It's a much older parish, and many of the young adults have gone down to Saint Augustine's. We have a handful of gay people who attend individually or as couples, but are not really recognizable. And yet, I don't give out the "God made Adam and Eve, not Adam and Steve" message. That's just not my pastoral approach to preaching. Instead, it's based on God's love and acceptance of all of us, of where we are, and on understanding our gifts and the giftedness of human sexuality, an approach that is consistent with the church's teachings but that would be friendly and warm and open to all people who would come through the door.

What is it in the Roman Catholic tradition that requires you or other Catholics to be open to lesbians and gay men?

I'd say, first, there is the insistence on the dignity of every person, that every person is entitled to human dignity and respect. That actually needs to be defended by the church institutionally and by individuals in the congregation who need to take an active role in defending and lifting up every person. That is and should be a hallmark of the Christian faith in general and the Catholic faith specifically. The other part is that since the Second Vatican Council, the church has struggled to find words to articulate a growing consciousness and awareness of gay, lesbian, bi, and transgendered people. It's struggled with looking at human sexuality and articulating a ministry of compassion. As the church in the United States has done that, as our bishops have worked with that, and as organizations like the now-banned Dignity,[8] New Ways Ministry, and others have tried to see the light at the end of the tunnel, I think a more balanced perspective has developed as indicated by the bishops' letter, *Always Our Children.*[9] That's the direction in which I think the church in the United States is going. When Rome seems to crack down on the church's ministry of compassion to gay people, there's always a group that has found a way to support that ministry and keep it in the forefront. I think a diocese like Los Angeles and the leadership of Cardinal Mahoney and other bishops around the country like Bishop Gumbleton in Detroit[10] have been very affirming of lesbian/gay people in the church and have helped people to integrate their sexuality with a realization of fulfillment and wholeness. And for me personally, I think that's a big part of the gospel message. Christ came and said, "I have come that they might have life and have it to the full."

I think Always Our Children *is quite a remarkable document.*

I think especially with the more conservative climate of our bishops and the fact that over the last ten or fifteen years we've appointed many more conservative bishops, especially explicitly conservative bishops, *Always Our Children* is a miracle, because it percolated through that more conservative climate of leadership. I think it represents a big step in the right direction. For many people in the church, the shutting down of or disassociation with Dignity was a very sad day for the church, because it marked a real separation and a closing-off of connection with and ministry to gay/lesbian Catholics; but I think immediately following that were a lot of responses that were positive with people trying to keep dialogue going. The work in AIDS ministry, I think, has been a bridge in that reconnection, because so many members of the church had been affected. Another big outreach here has been Mother Teresa's home for people with AIDS who had no resources and needed a place to die in dignity and respect. Mother Teresa personally came to Washington many times, and she never hammered on the issue of sexuality. She just talked about God's love and compassion and about living and working and the light. Her Sisters, too, have been very open. Probably the biggest spiritual light in my life at Saint Teresa's was to have Mother Teresa's sisters right there in the convent. They were very open to all people, and their ministry was very much a ministry of love. I think that's the direction that the church needs to keep going in.

Do you have any advice for Black lesbian, gay, bisexual, or transgendered Catholics who are seriously dealing with the issue of finding a place in the church and wanting to stay with the church but feeling really uncertain about doing so?

Sure. First, know that their place is in the church in the largest sense; and, then, know that explicitly through its preaching and pronouncements the church is open to all of its members and—that regardless of sexual orientation—the church sets pretty much without compromise a certain moral standard in terms of genital activity. It holds all its members to a certain standard of relationship and behavior. But in terms of its openness to all peoples and peoples of all colors, all backgrounds, and its ministry to all people regardless of faith or belief, the church has a very high tone of openness and welcome. At least that's what it's supposed to do. That's the goal. In terms of specifically Black gay and lesbian people in the church who are struggling, I've found that the parish is the place where acceptance is and should be felt. If your parish doesn't have a critical mass of visible gay people and lesbians—like at Saint Augustine's or Saint Matthew's where you can readily identify a lot of people or at least a warmth and a vibe of openness—but is a suburban parish or a more traditional and older parish like Nativity, still the parish is the place of welcome, hospitality, acceptance, and challenge, too. I think that while I would probably steer people who are looking for community to parishes like Saint Augustine's, I would never chase anybody away from Nativity. In fact, I'd encourage them to stay at Nativity and help God's garden of love and acceptance grow right here.

Chapter 8

Rev. Altagracia Perez

Since 1994, Altagracia Perez has been the rector of Saint Philip the Evangelist Church in South-Central Los Angeles. Established in 1907 because Blacks were not welcome in white parishes, Saint Philip's was one of the first Black Episcopal churches west of the Mississippi.[1] Recently, the church's mentoring, art, and AIDS prevention programs for Black and Latino youth have received national recognition.[2]

Before her appointment to this position, Rev. Perez was the coordinator of youth ministries for the Episcopal Diocese of Chicago and the Midwestern Province of the Episcopal Church and the associate director of a gang prevention program on the south side of Chicago. She also served on the Diocese's Commission to End Racism and its AIDS Task Force, on the advisory council of the Chicago Women's AIDS Project, and as president of the Hispanic AIDS Network, of which she was a founding member. She is included in *Who's Who among Black Americans*.[3]

She was appointed to serve on President Clinton's Advisory Council on HIV and AIDS and is the cochair of its Sub-Committee on Racial and Ethnic Populations. Involved in many community projects in the Los Angeles area, Rev. Perez was at the time of the interview organizing support for food-service workers and hospitality staff at the University of Southern California to win a written guarantee of job security.[4]

How did you get to the position at Saint Philip's?

The Suffragan Bishop of the Diocese of Chicago mentioned to the Suffragan Bishop of Los Angeles, Chester Talton, that he had a person who was looking for a job, was willing to relocate, and was a good priest. I must say it was kindness. Talton said he had a church that would be perfect for her. It was a church that was in conflict because it was a traditional Black church, the first Black church in California, and the community had changed from 80 percent Black/20 percent other to 80 percent Latino/15 percent Black/5 percent other. The church had started doing Hispanic ministry, got off to a bad start, and didn't know how to deal with the conflicts and challenges. I was the first rector in eight years who could give the same message to both congregations—in Spanish and English.

How did you get started, and what has worked well?

I think part of what was good was that I was a new priest. I had never served in a parish on any consistent basis. I had served on diocesan staff and went to parishes regularly, but to resource them. So I had a sense of how things are supposed to be done, but I was more of a manager working for nonprofits and writing grants, which this church thought it wanted to do. Before I figured out anything, I just said some basic things had to happen in different areas, things like redoing the finances and seeing clearly what they had here that wasn't going to work. I said, "I'm not going to go after grants unless our infrastructure is in good shape." Those things ended up being important, because if they manage to stick at all they will have transformed the institution from being controlled by small groups of people with a lot of power and a lot of mistrust to people learning how to work together, trust each other, pray together, and make decisions together.

Have you done any grant-seeking for Saint Philip's yet?

Very recently, yes. I gave in and I wrote a grant because I decided they had gone far enough and were doing much better. We received a grant from the Cathedral Corporation to start what's called the Saint Philip's Safe House Community Choir. It's a community choir of the young people who come to our after-school program and other young people who are being prepared to sing at nursing homes and community events. It's to supplement the lack of music programming in the public schools, and it allowed us to extend our after-school program from four to five days a week and to do something that makes the young people feel good about themselves.

How would you describe the neighborhood the church is in?

We're in the northeast corner of South-Central Los Angeles, one of the poorest neighborhoods in the city and an immigration point. It used to be the center of Black life in Los Angeles in the '30s, '40s, and '50s: the Black music scene, the Black Hollywood, the Black Downtown. With the onset of integration, the community dissipated and people moved elsewhere. Now Latino people are everywhere. My Latino parishioners reflect the community. They are all poor, whether they are working poor or on welfare or less. Some are in the process of being legalized under the Amnesty Act. We've also gotten several new English-speaking families who are bilingual. They're Black and identify with the Black community and do things in English, but they're like me, where they speak Spanish as well; so they become bridge families, because they are the ones that facilitate the work of the church to happen in two languages at the same time. Culturally, they can interpret behaviors, help smooth out misunderstandings, and literally communicate with all groups in the church.

Are most of the Black families from the original time of the church?

The majority are, but the new families that I talked about are a mixture of Belizean, Jamaican, Costa Rican, or other Caribbean islands. The American Black people used to live in this neighborhood, went to the neighborhood high school, and now live throughout the county. Yet, they have a commitment to this church because they remembered when they weren't allowed to go anywhere else. Once they could, they still wouldn't. So, it's the hard core that is left.

Do they still live in the neighborhood?

No. I now have one person who lives in the neighborhood, walked in about four months ago, and keeps coming. Ortherwise, not one of the Black members lives in the community, not even the new members. They come from as far as Long Beach and travel as much as an hour to come to church.

Did your being a Black Latina appeal to the church as someone to create better communication among the various groups?

Bishop Talton saw that for sure and then he sold me to the church. When the church interviewed me, they were sufficiently impressed that I was a regular person, that I wasn't a charity case (*laughs*), that I was a good candidate regardless of the fact that the bishop had submitted me. There were enough people in the leadership who felt that part of really dealing with ministry in our church had to be dealing with the Latino piece. Their voice was loud enough to override the people who began a petition to withdraw the offer to me because they felt they gave the search committee the power to get an African American priest. A Black Latino was not going to work for them.

The traditional Black families wanted an African American priest?

Right. What ended up happening was that only over time did they realize that I was very Black, that I could speak to the Black experience, that I considered myself a Black person. And then it eventually became an asset.

Can you give me an example of something that convinced them of that?

I don't know, maybe because I kept telling them that I am Black. They would ask me questions about why I would say that I am Black, and so I had to explain the African diaspora to them because they missed this. The last Black thing they did was integration. They think everyone should try to be integrated, so why would I make more distinctions about myself, especially when in their eyes I could take a position that was of more benefit to myself, because Latinos are seen as more white than Black? Why would I identify with them?

How do you explain the African diaspora?

There were Black people who were taken to be slaves, and they were dropped off in various locations. America is very self-centered about itself, so it thinks it's the only place that's lived with anything, but the structures of racism based on slavery happened in all the countries where slavery happened, which is a lot of places. So there are Black people of African descent in many places, and they have similar experiences in their countries of origin. What unites us is the fact that we were stolen from a country and had our identity taken away for the purposes of economic gain and exploitation. We share that history no matter what country we come from, because that's how we got there. Otherwise, we'd all be in Africa. There's a connection. We have more in common with each other than with people who actually live in Africa, because what we share is the history of the people who were sent everywhere.

And that made sense to people?

Eventually they got it. The Belizeans, the Jamaicans, the people who were from another country, basically got it right away. They were like, "I see what you mean. I consider myself Black, but I'm really from Jamaica; and you say you're Black, but your parents are from Puerto Rico and the Dominican Republic." Other people didn't get it until they saw me act, and then finally one guy who had a really hard time with it eventually came to me about two years later and said, "You know, I think I get it, because you really are more Black than any other Black clergy we've ever had." But it was because I would talk about racism and other issues in a way that made it clear that we shared a similar experience. I mean, after all, I was born in this country and l was raised in the ghetto. There are cultural differences, but the experience of racism is the same.

So you were addressing the issues that were their issues?

Right. And I didn't make any changes in the church for the first two years. Not a thing. I did every single thing the way that whoever was the last person to modernize things did them. There was another whole nightmare about the last person because he was gay. There were certain people in the church who wanted me to sign off on something that said that I would not preach that homosexuality was not a sin, and so I had to take this stand before I got hired. I went back to the senior warden and told her, "I cannot sign this because, one, I am not being hired to be your personal chaplain. I am a priest of the Episcopal Church, which has a certain doctrine that homosexuality is not a sin; the doctrine is that it is a sin to act on it. So, first of all I can't sign this document because it's against church doctrine and I'm a priest of the church. Two, not only do I think it's not a sin to be a lesbian or gay person, but I think that as long as you live within the standards of what we consider to be committed relationships—which we value, because we value covenants—then that's fine. I would offer all the sacraments, including marriage, to all people equally. Third, this has affected me personally and I have struggled in my own personal life with this issue and especially how it relates to the Bible. In the end, from all my experiences I ended up deciding that it was not a sin, and I come from a much more fundamentalist background than any of you did. So, four, I'm happy to talk about what I believe, and I don't need or want to convince everybody; we can study the Bible as long as we admit that there are people in our congregation who everybody knows are lesbian or gay and that we deal with it. As long as we start with the reality that these people are members and leaders in our church, then I can talk about anything you want." And I thought I wasn't going to get the job. But it apparently was the agenda of a very small group of people, the same ones that submitted the petition about my not being an African American. And I guess they got over it.

At one point, they pushed me on same-sex unions, and I said I would never do one to make a statement. I would use the same standard that I use for everybody else in terms of having a relationship to the church. And because it would be something that is not necessarily approved by the church, I would bring the vestry into a decision-making process. So, I would only do it for somebody who is a member of the church and knows their household. We did several Bible studies about homosexuality, which apparently they had not done according to the canons of the church. We were mandated to do those years ago as part of a study on homosexuality. It was supposed to happen throughout the denomination, and this church hadn't done it.

How did they go?

Very well. People who were not going to be convinced no matter what I said didn't show up. A couple of people who wanted to understand what the church taught, even if they disagreed with it, came. And then there were other people who were very sweet. They were the people who touched me the most. They were grateful for the Bible study because it allowed them just to say they were really concerned that this was an obsession of the church, that they thought that it really went against Christian charity, that it had been a real conflict for them, and that even if they didn't know what they exactly thought, it at least allowed them to *act* the way they felt was right.

One woman gave an example of her neighbors, a couple who have been together forever. She has had a real hard time with the fact that she tries to be a good Christian and follow scripture, but at the same time she knew that these people were the best neighbors she had. They were kind people. She knew that they were believing people. So she had had trouble making a reconciliation, and this discussion helped her. Even though she wasn't sure that she could make a decision about what she thought, at least she knew that we could be God-fearing people, that lesbian/gay people are a part of our community, and that there is a way we could talk about that.

And then there were a few people who already have lesbian/gay friends and other people who are more sophisticated around theological arguments and are not convinced that we should be marrying people in the church, but should do house blessings instead. Those sessions and discussions were good. The people know my stance. All lesbian/gay events and programs from the diocese get put in the Sunday bulletin and on the bulletin board. If we're going to do church, we're going to do the whole church. We are not a "congregational" church; we are a "catholic" church. And so you deal with the whole thing, when it works for you and when it works against you. That's what it means to be catholic.

Would you explain that difference?

A congregational denomination exists with each local church having their own mission and vision loosely connected toward the denomination within broad, defining boundaries. The local churches make decisions unto themselves that govern their congregations, whereas in our catholic tradition—though the process is democratic and hopefully includes input from every level with a balance of power—there is a hierarchy. Even though the way the decision gets made is democratic, once the decision is made it applies to everybody. Everybody gets to participate in the decision making, which is what general convention, diocesan conventions, and all these million of studies that the Episcopal Church mandates are about. When the solution is reached, you may dissent on personal conscience, but if somebody asks you what your church teaches, it's clear. It doesn't change from parish to parish. All Anglicans think certain things, and you can agree or disagree. I disagree with my church's policy on marriage for lesbian and gay people, but I'm still here. There are members of my local church who disagree with our bishop, who is very progressive and supports lesbian and gay unions and ordinations, but they are still here.

Where do you disagree with your denomination?

That the church makes a distinction between an orientation and a behavior. They want to say that an orientation is not a sin, but to have sex based on that orientation is a sin. I think that's not good logic. What's generated by that kind of law is that some people are first-class citizens and some people are second-class citizens. So, to get ordained it's okay for heterosexual priests not to be celibate, but homosexual priests have to be celibate. In the parish, heterosexuals can express their sexuality and relationships, others cannot—by church law.

What's the catholic part, the church's message on lesbian/gay issues that you feel obliged to give to your parishioners?

I make it real clear what the book says. I try to tell them exactly what the church says on the books, which is that homosexual orientation is not a sin, only homosexual behavior. And then I proceed to give my personal opinion and reasons for why that doesn't work and how this reflects a tension in the church, which is why at every general convention there's legislation proposed about lesbian/gay issues and the arguments about them are not pretty. It's the church at its ugliest in some ways.

Are the notices you put in the Sunday bulletin and on the bulletin board about things going on within the Episcopal Church or within the wider community?

Within the Episcopal Church—church things, diocesan events. We have a Diocesan Commission on Lesbian/Gay Ministries—just as we have a Commission on Hispanic Ministry and a commission on everything else—that does programs, retreats, conferences. Some local churches with a lot of lesbian/gay members and leaders do special series, like a Lenten series targeted to the lesbian/gay community.

Do you think that lesbians and gay men see Saint Philip's as a friendly place?

We are on paper. There is a process in the Episcopal Church, facilitated by the Bishop's Commission on Lesbian/Gay Ministries, where vestries can vote to sign on to a statement that their church welcomes lesbians and gay men. My church signed on before I was here, which is why I think the other document they wanted me to sign was kind of a backlash to what the vestry and bishop decided to do. I think the welcome is for real, but it has quivers, like the church knows it's the right thing to do but didn't always have the words to discuss the issues. I think it's helped that I'm very pro-gay and especially a Black person who's able to integrate gay issues into the life of the church in a way that doesn't cheapen any of them but challenges all of them.

What do you mean when you say it doesn't cheapen them but challenges them?

Sometimes Black people feel lesbians and gay men are too quick to compare the civil rights struggle with the lesbian/gay human rights struggle. I don't personally have a problem with it, but they experience it as something like, "I don't know enough about your gay community for you to be using what I know about my community to explain what's going on in your community," and mixed feelings about whether gayness is normal or not, good or not, contributes to the problem for them.

So you avoid the civil rights kind of comparisons?

No, I talk about it in a nuanced way, and I talk about the fact that the Civil Rights movement was not monolithic, that there were people who were forced into a tide of civil rights activities who had no intention of challenging the institutional system and were therefore conservative, whereas other people were progressive. Martin Luther King's position on the working class, labor unions, and wealth was way left of most people in the Black community. So I say it wasn't a monolithic movement, and they should stop pretending it was. It was not at all these God-fearing, conservative church folk who did that movement. It included radical people, people in the middle, and people in the right; and it was successful because it included everybody.[5] I challenge them around the fact that they want to make the Black experience unique to all other oppressive experiences in America. But they also hear me challenging the agendas of white liberals who claim to have dealt with racism because they had some dialogue with us but will never spend a day in the ghetto. So I challenge everybody equally.

I also use lesbian/gay struggles in my sermons because they are good examples of scripture about how we treat the stranger and the outcast, whom we are ministering to, who makes up the kingdom of God. The outsider is central to a lot of theological themes, so they get put in there regularly because for my church Black people are not the outsiders. It's these other people: Latino people, gay people, Asian people, people who are other than them and who they feel threaten them. Whenever the stories of the Samaritans come up, I deal with women and gay issues, because it was such a given that the Samaritans were less than human. They weren't "as good as us," and I think that's how women and gay and lesbian people are perceived now.

Do you have lesbian/gay friends and colleagues in the Los Angeles area?

Yes. When I came here I went to the gay/lesbian center, to the gay bars and dance clubs. I got the magazines and newspapers. I hooked up to what was going on, and since I've been serving on the President's Advisory Council on HIV and AIDS, I've made both straight and gay friends who are also on it and live in the area. So, yes, and also because I do a lot of community work across different issues.

Did Saint Philip's see your earlier AIDS work as an attractive quality?

I guess because the interim person had connected them with Minority AIDS Project, they thought it was cool. There was a family in the church who had already lost someone who had died of HIV, and there was a woman who was currently dealing with a daughter who was HIV-positive. So I think they liked that part of my background. I don't know if it was a great plus. I think it made who I am and what I do clearer. I told everybody, "On most issues that you think of in terms of left and right, I'm left-falling-off-the-street; but I don't have a drum to beat. If I can challenge you to grow, since I think it's about growing, fine. And if you also remind me of stuff that I don't know about, then we are really doing church."

Are you pleased to be on the President's HIV/AIDS Council and with the work it's doing?

I think that we've done a lot of good things and that we have an incredibly responsible group of people. I value the friendships I've made. But I'm most interested and involved in prevention education, which is of course the most critical piece for communities of color who don't have access to medical care, and we've gotten nowhere on this. I'm the cochair for the Sub-Committee on Racial and Ethnic Populations, and honestly it's been real frustrating. Now it's better because the Council made a radical move in adopting and making its primary objective for the rest of its tenure through the president's term the issues of racial and ethnic populations. So, that area got better, but prevention is still a real problem.

So the Council's focus has been on treatment and research?

Right. Everybody loves treatment and research. "Give them more money for the Ryan White CARE Act, let's create a research institute, let's push human studies." We're doing that level of sophisticated stuff, preparing vaccinations to be used. All of that and we still can't say "condom" in public high schools.

Will you talk about the AIDS prevention work you're doing at your church?

We got a grant to be a subcontractor for a national pilot project to use Teatro, which is a traditional sort of political theater that Latinos, especially Mexican Americans, have used a lot to educate and promote community programs in the past. We applied Teatro to the HIV/AIDS education process in Latin American communities, especially because Latinas are one of the largest groups at risk. They often miss education because they don't always go to college. The sixteen-to-twenty-five age group was the hardest to get to. We did the Teatro project, and I was responsible for creating the theater. I was the producer. I hired a director. We recruited the kids, did the training around HIV/AIDS awareness, and they learned about theater and drama. It was a mixed group—some of Saint Philip's people and some people from the broader community. We had a script that was developed nationally, which we adapted for what's going on in the Latino community in Los Angeles.

The story is about a young Latina woman who finds out she is HIV-positive, the changes she goes through in her feverish recollection of what got her to that point. It talks about the complexity of her life—issues of racism, having a boyfriend who was not good to her and pressured her to have sex, her mom loving the boyfriend because he was white. It connected the complex issues of her life—economic, racial, lesbian/gay—through different characters.

It was very well received, and some of the people have gone forward to try to get more funding for it, because the goal was to interest both public and private funders—community-based agencies—to create this kind of project in various locations. It's taken off. Some of the schools are doing them.

The diocese is also doing TAP, Teens for AIDS Prevention, the Episcopal program for AIDS prevention. I'm sure that because I'm involved in AIDS work, the kids here decided to do this program. It targets teens to be leaders to do AIDS education and awareness in their communities, and the kids have committed to it. Actually, when I was in Chicago I helped create the TAP guidelines for use in churches. It's good because it pays attention to racial and ethnic issues and to biblical issues.

What's your message to Black lesbian, gay, bisexual, and transgendered people who want to remain in the church?

I think we should believe that there are no rules, that however we can live with integrity within this institution is okay given where we are, that it's not fair to expect everybody to be out or to be pure. None of that works. We have to see our real goal, to really see our agenda, especially as people of color who are also more varied in our sexual orientation, as bringing together pieces. We can explain pieces about power and justice to other communities. We can serve as a bridge—not that everybody wants to be a bridge, but at least the way we live shows that there are issues that Black people and lesbian and gay people have in common.

And then there are also all kinds of ways in which justice struggles are simply justice struggles—whether it's the workers at USC or whether it's the couple who called me yesterday and asked if I would do a same-sex union, and I told them, "Yes." There are others who, because they're really damn good Christians but are outed by mistake, will challenge the whole system of the church by virtue of the fact that nobody knew and thought they were wonderful. We play different roles depending on who we are and what we live. What we show people is that justice and love and mercy are the centerpiece of the Christian gospel and that we live that out; and sometimes there is a remnant, there's a group that gets dumped on more than anybody else. That's okay as long as we're getting hurt for doing good and not for doing evil, and God says we're blessed. That gets to be our role, and our kids won't have to have that role.

My daughter doesn't know that it's not okay for women to be together. She thinks that's how lots of people are, that they find somebody and they're together. She can't figure out why there are no Disney movies that reflect this, however. She's four years old and she realizes that some girls have girlfriends and some boys have boyfriends, even though that's not on TV. It's got to mean something that no matter where we are, if we act with integrity and are ourselves in the best way, our kids won't deal with that kind of obstacle. No matter what they're dealing with, they won't have to deal with that. And that means a lot.

We're pioneers in the sense that no one wants to talk about it, but we've been there all along. It's like discovering America: it wasn't that it was really lost, it's just certain people hadn't discovered it yet. But it does make us pioneers, and that means that our kids will be better for it—all of our kids, whether they're really ours or all the lesbian/gay kids who are going to come out in the next ten years. In my church, kids know that we don't talk negatively about certain things, and they have friends who are lesbian and gay. I have a girl in my youth group who is working on Madison Shockley's campaign for city council because she has a gay teacher who lives in that district and she wants him to have rights; and Madison Shockley builds coalitions with lesbians, gays, and straights.[6] And she thought that was important. You know, our kids are 50 million years ahead of every little thing we do. They go to the right place because they don't have to be warped by homophobia and racism and classism. At least not as bad as we were.

Chapter 9

Rev. Dr. Arnold I. Thomas

*I*n 1998, Arnold I. Thomas was appointed conference minister of the Vermont Conference of the United Church of Christ (UCC). As a national denomination, the UCC is divided into thirty-nine regions or conferences. Within each region, a conference minister counsels local pastors, coordinates the work among local congregations, and administers programs, meetings, clinics, and workshops for their benefit.

Before his current position, Rev. Dr. Thomas was for eight years the pastor of First Congregational Church in Williamstown, Massachusetts. Previously, he was the Protestant chaplain at Wesleyan University in Middletown, Connecticut, and pastor of First Congregational Church in Little Rock, Arkansas. He received his Doctor of Ministry degree from Hartford Seminary in Connecticut.

Active on various denominational and civic committees, he has served on the UCC's National Open and Affirming Structural Committee. The Open and Affirming (ONA) program encourages and helps local congregations publicly declare that they welcome lesbian/bisexual/gay/transgendered people.

I know that First Congregational Church in Williamstown voted to become Open and Affirming when you were its pastor. Did you initiate and guide the church through the process to become ONA?

I guided them, but I didn't initiate it. It was on the burner before I arrived. The discussion about Open and Affirming had been initiated by the members of the church, and the interim minister before me got the message and organized a committee to look into it. They had planned a series of discussions to present to the congregation but decided to get my feeling and approval as the new minister coming in. After looking at the schedule of discussions, I felt it needed a biblical perspective on this issue and it also needed to invite people who were gay and lesbian members of the church either in a pastoral or lay capacity to speak. They agreed and asked me to present the biblical perspective.

So this is a congregation that was ready to discuss the topic. Would you say that readiness comes from a history of being open to difficult issues?

Yes. A few years before I arrived, it addressed the topic of sanctuary for Central American refugees. But it's not what I would consider a liberal congregation. I would consider it more moderate, because the issue of providing sanctuary lost by about six votes and divided the congregation for a period of time. Even those who won on that issue felt upset because of the way they were being perceived by other members of the congregation. It took a while for the congregation to heal and for members to feel comfortable with each other again. As soon as that matter was somewhat resolved, we addressed the issue of Open and Affirming.

We went into this issue being very careful and caring of the different points of view present in the congregation and trying to make sure that they were heard as respectfully as possible. And I think they were. After the vote to become an Open and Affirming church, I called one of the dissenting members to see where he was in relation to the congregation. He said that his membership remained firm. He recognized that his point of view was not one of the majority, but he also felt that his point of view was heard, respected, and considered very seriously. He appreciated the way we handled this matter.

What do you think the congregation saw in you as a prospective minister that qualified you to handle this discussion in a constructive, nondivisive way?

I presented myself as a person who grew up in a religiously conservative household, who was very appreciative of that conservative experience, but who was no longer a conservative. I also told them I grew up in a very mixed community—racially mixed, religiously mixed—and that atmosphere provided a means of challenging me, my religious perspectives, and a lot of other things that I had to deal with in life. So I came into this church with that kind of history. I had friends who were Jews, Christians, Muslims, atheists, gays, lesbians, as well as heterosexuals.

I'm sure they appreciated what I brought to this discussion from that experience.

Can you say more about your religious background?

I was raised in Ohio. My father was a Baptist minister and very fundamentalist. He felt that homosexuality was a sin. What he did not realize until very late was that my brother Leroy—we referred to him as Lee—was gay. That really challenged his perspective. Unfortunately, when Lee made it known to my folks that he was gay, he also told them that he had AIDS, so it was a double blow for them. But Dad always said that regardless of who we were, what we believed, and where we went in life, we would never cease being his children. He asked Lee to come home, so he and Mom could take care of him. But Lee had developed a very strong community of support in New York City as a member of the First Presbyterian Church there, which was a More Light congregation with a sizable number of gay and lesbian members.[1] That's where he died on Good Friday morning of 1984.

As I said, it shook Dad's religious perspective to his foundations, but he was convinced that Lee was good and with God. Lee also shook me from my conservatism. Those individuals whom my father and my conservatism had warned me against were now sitting next to me in the person of my brother, whom I loved very much. My love for him and also the fact that I looked up to him caused me to take a fresh look at what Scripture was saying and to see the different points of views in it, to realize the Bible does not speak with one voice and often is a dialogue of different religious perspectives about how God relates to the people of Israel, to the church, and to us today. It became important to me in light of that diversity of religious perspectives to try to formulate in my own mind what I consider a God principle—a principle of what I think and believe my life is about—and that was a principle of unconditional love by which I reentered the study of scripture and tried to discern from it where God was speaking.

Was 1984 a turning point on gay issues for you as well as for your father?

The turning point for me happened well before that, during my college years when close friends came out to me and informed me they were gay. That prepared me for Lee informing me that he was gay, which he did while I was in seminary and well before he contracted AIDS. My college years were a time of turning for me in which I was no longer under the conservative religious environment of my father, a time in which I was exploring and discovering new outlooks on life.

That's really where I experienced an atmosphere in which my religious questions were appreciated. In my father's church and in the conservative religious environment in which I grew up, questions were seen as doubt, and doubt was seen as sinful. It was in the educational environment of Hiram College that my questions were appreciated; and it was under, you might say, the tutelage of a UCC minister who was a professor at the college that I was able not necessarily to find answers but provided with the religious and sacred means to explore my questions. That exploration eventually led me to membership within the United Church of Christ.

When for you did the issues of homosexuality and lesbians and gay men become so important that you knew they were going to make a difference in how you thought and in what kind of a minister you were going to be?

I think it really became an important issue when my brother informed me that he was gay. My brother felt he had a calling to ministry long before I felt the call to ministry. But Lee realized that he would probably never be accepted as a minister, certainly not within the Baptist Church in which we grew up and possibly not within any other church. So, he went in a different direction and he made that clear to me when he informed me he was gay. I was a bit saddened but more upset that the church would do that. That's when my ministry took on another dimension to try and provide, as best as I possibly could, a place where all people could find their space and their voice within the church. I felt that the United Church of Christ could do that. I felt it was a church that was attempting to do that—struggling but attempting.

I was also inspired by some passages of scripture that Lee alluded to in his revelation to me. One was the passage in Acts where Peter confronts Cornelius in his house. It was a place where Jews were not allowed to be among Gentiles, but Peter's proclamation was that God is not partial and will certainly seek anyone who seeks the love of God. Peter realized that he could not hold back the spirit of God from this household, and the entire family of Cornelius was baptized.

There are various passages of scripture that influenced me, but the one that really challenges me and speaks to my heart is the First Epistle of John, chapter 4, where it says there is no fear in love, but perfect love casts out fear. I think the church is a place where members are attempting to love without fear, but that's a very difficult task. We have so many ingrained traditional norms that prevent us from loving without fear. Our racism, our sexism, our homophobia—just to name a few—have been sanctioned by the church in many ways. And it becomes very difficult for us to see these norms as antithetical to the way of God, because we have been so used to seeing them as normative. The great challenge for the church is to try and overcome these barriers, to provide a place for those whom we have for a long time feared and considered evil, to recognize that God's spirit is with them, too. And if God favors them, we must favor them as well.

So that is the challenge, and Lee helped me realize it. After he informed me that he was gay, it was no longer just a matter of my friendships with gay people, because Lee was a part of my family. He was the brother whom I wanted to grow old with. He was that close to me. So his revelation of who he was, but also who he was in relation to God, was very important to me. One thing he said that I will never forget was that for a long time he prayed that these feelings would go away and they did not. Then he prayed that God would allow him to accept them and accept who he was. And then he said that God answers prayer. So, Lee really provided the turning point for me.

Do you think that people who come out of conservative traditions are often more genuine than liberals when they do address this issue?

Yes, I do. I think that when a conservative—or a person who grew up in a conservative background—is supportive of gays and lesbians being affirmed and assuming positions of leadership in the church, it marks and testifies to a radical shift that such individuals had to go through. Moving from conservatism to a more liberal posture theologically is an upsetting and sometimes wrenching experience for an individual. It certainly was for me, because I moved from a place in which I was trained and indoctrinated to think that I and other people like me were the exclusive favorites of God and anything unlike the community in which I grew up was anathema to God. So it took a strong, supportive, theological environment to help me move from that position with some peace of mind about myself. To move then from there to the position of being supportive of gays and lesbians took another step that distanced me even further from my conservative upbringing, and those steps could only be taken after much soul searching and much personal experience that really shook my foundations in such a way that I could be convinced that this was the right and godly thing to be doing. That's the way it was for me. It was not an easy move, but when it was made and when I made it with the assurance that this was where I should be in relationship to God and the rest of world, it became a testimony.

And that's where the conservatism remains true. People who grew up in a conservative background such as mine, when we find ourselves in liberal communities we're somewhat—and I need to speak for myself—concerned about the quietness of people who have religious experiences and are afraid to share them for fear of offending other people. I think we can share our religious perspectives without offending others, but we do need to share them because they are so meaningful and important for us. The notion of testifying about what you have experienced is an attribute of my conservative religious upbringing that I don't want to be rid of, to be ashamed of, or to shy away from. The experience that I and others like me have gone through needs to be revealed. People need to know about it, and it needs to be shared in a way that is not disrespectful of other points of view, but as a perspective in which individuals are certain that these are events in which God was very much present.

What do you think it is that liberal Christians don't quite get about conservative Christians who do go through this process and end up with a different viewpoint?

I think a lot of liberal Christians have given up on conservatives. I think that they feel that they're so strongly rooted, and many of us are, in our upbringing and traditions that there is just no shaking our foundations. But when we do make this change, the reaction of liberals is almost as if "so what else is new." They've been there, done that. But they haven't gone through the struggles as much and don't appreciate the sense of confused identity that one had to go through to get to that point.

Do you think as someone who's gone through that process there's something fundamental about your conservative theology that is intact and you're glad it is?

Yes. I personally think that conservatives are better able to speak to other conservatives. People who have grown up in a conservative atmosphere, who now think differently, are better able to speak to other conservatives who are homophobic. I appreciate the strength of my upbringing as far as the importance of knowing scripture, so that I am able to speak to other conservatives who also hold a high regard for what the Bible says in what they do. It's still important for them to refer to scripture and know what the Bible has to say before they do just about anything. I'm not of that frame of mind now, but having grown up in it, I do hold a high regard for what scripture says. I do believe that the Bible speaks to us in our present day, but unlike many conservatives I don't think it speaks in one voice. However, to challenge conservatives I need to know from which I speak, and therefore I need to know the Bible to the extent that I can challenge their points of view from a biblical perspective. I think that many liberals in the pews and also in the pulpit do not appreciate how conservatives regard scripture, and as a result they have difficulty speaking to conservatives.

How do you engage conservatives in this discussion?

The discussion usually takes the form of asking conservatives what is their foundation for their belief regarding gays, lesbians, and homosexuality in general. And they will cite passages of scripture—Genesis 19,[2] Romans 1:18–32,[3] Leviticus 18:22, 20:13—to back their points of view. I will respond by citing those very passages and giving a different perspective on them. This perspective would inform them of the contexts in which these statements were made and the kind of impressions biblical writers had of homosexuality, which today would be considered narrow-minded and uninformed, as narrow-minded and uninformed as assuming that all heterosexuals are rapists, pimps, or child molesters. It is, for instance, also interesting to note that if we regarded the rest of the Levitical Code as seriously as we regarded the mandate condemning a man who "lies with a man as with a woman," I doubt if any of us would escape the condemnation of death.

I will also challenge them by saying that if they believe that God spoke in this way to the people of Israel and also to the church, do they believe other statements in the Bible presented as clearly and forcefully as words of God, but that contradict or challenge each other's point of view? These differing points of view result from the people of Israel and the church becoming exposed to new communities, people, nations, and experiences, which opened their eyes to the awareness that what they had thought was the word of God was more the word of their social and tribal perspective, and it no longer applied to their current experience and thinking. However, in that evolution of change, God did remain present and they acknowledged God's presence.

But to be able to talk with conservatives, you need to show them chapter and verse where the Bible does not speak in one voice. For instance, Deuteronomy 23 and 24 make it very clear who is of the house of God, who is invited into the community of God and who is not. Ammonites and Moabites, because of their hostility towards Israelites when they came out of Egypt, were said not to be part of God's chosen community. Disabled people and eunuchs were not allowed in God's communities. But this passage of scripture is openly refuted by Isaiah 56, which says that even eunuchs who seek to follow the way of God will be included in the house of God and that God's house will be a house of prayer for all peoples. So, in Old Testament scripture you find clear examples where the voice of God, as conveyed to prophets and leaders of Israel, does not speak in one voice. All you have to do to refute Deuteronomy is read the Book of Ruth. Ruth was a Moabite who was an important link in the prophetic line that leads to King David and also to the Christ. And certainly in the New Testament, Philip's baptizing of the Ethiopian eunuch refuted Deuteronomy. What I seek to do is to challenge the conservative who feels that the Bible speaks with one infallible voice and to present the Bible as a composition of many and varied theological impressions conditioned by the cultural, ethnic, sociological, and sexual biases in which they were written. This is not to say that God's word is not present in scripture, but it has to be discerned from the context in which it is presented.

I acknowledge that there seems to be at least two conflicting voices, two conflicting schools of divine interpretation, in scripture. One school is a strong legal tradition: God says it, and therefore we do it and don't question it. So, when God tells Saul to destroy the Ammonites and Saul does not do it, Saul is condemned by God. The other school is the spirit of the law, and it's a tradition I encourage. The spirit of the law is a message that is very inclusive and that desires all people to follow God's way. It's apparent in the Book of Isaiah and in the way of Jesus in the New Testament. But in both the New Testament and Old Testament, you find the tension between the legalistic, literal interpretation of the law and the spirit of the law. You find them intertwined with each other—sometimes in opposition and sometimes collaborating—but there has to be for me a principle by which you can discern one from the other.

That's what I refer to as a God principle, which for me is partly found in First Corinthians 13, where the greatest of faith, hope, and love is love. Another part, as I said earlier, is found in First John, which says there is no fear in love, for love casts out all fear. The main part, though, is really found in the ministry of Jesus, who challenged the notion of what was considered pure and clean by being with communities and individuals who upset the status quo in ancient Israel. I think the role of the church is to be with and to include individuals and communities who upset the status quo in our present-day world. That principle openly provides a radical alternative of living and of community so that those who see us will say, "This clearly is a different way." And I hope conservatives would eventually say this clearly is a way of God.

Is there a particular part of the discussion when you see people changing?

Yes, when I can prove to conservatives that what they cite in one passage of scripture is refuted in another, because conservatives in many ways are like many of us. We only read what we have been directed to read in scripture, and we don't look at the complicated nature of scripture. When we are allowed and free to probe and explore, we will discover that there are a lot of challenging aspects of scripture that we need to accept and that the Bible is not as easily controlled by our traditions as we would like it to be. When I open the level of doubt in their minds about the harmonious nature of scripture, I've made an important step. And that does happen. All you have to do is direct them to those passages and to the context in which they were given. And when that happens I feel another important step in their faith journey has been accomplished, because I see myself in them. To challenge them is a service in the same way I felt that individuals who challenged me from my conservatism into a different way proved to be a service for which I am thankful. Initially, when you find yourself being challenged, you certainly are not thankful for it. You're upset. Everything you held dear becomes challenged, and you really struggle to try to make sense of it. I am very much aware that challenging a person's spiritual beliefs can have both positive and negative results. And I'm very fearful of that, but I also realize the greater damage that could happen if those beliefs are not challenged. People's lives are affected and destroyed when others continue to believe in a narrow-minded way. So, I realize we're talking life-and-death kinds of issues either way—by challenging or by not challenging. It's important for me to be mindful of that, but nonetheless to pursue a direction I hope will bring people out of a more narrowly focused perspective of scripture into one that allows them to realize that there is something more at work here than what we have been led to believe.

Is there an anecdote from the Open and Affirming process at Williamstown that sticks out for you or captures what that experience was about?

Yes, even in the environment at Williamstown that appreciates different points of view, I learned after the process was over that we had not been speaking to the already-converted. I was wrong even about those people whom I assumed were very open-minded and in favor of the church becoming Open and Affirming. They had their own stereotypes and biased perspectives to overcome. So, I've learned to assume nothing when it comes to this issue. As with trying to address racism, people came into the Open and Affirming discussion assuming their minds were open and they were accepting of others, only to realize as we explored this issue that they were not. There were challenges they had to overcome, such as what happens if their own children come out to them, how they feel toward covenanted relationships between gays and between lesbians and whether they should be sanctioned by the church and occur within the sanctuary of the church. People discovered that as this issue entered the realm of their sacred beliefs, sacred traditions, sacred ground, and sacred norms, they were most challenged; and they discovered their liberality was not as open as they thought it was. By bringing this issue into the realm of the church, you upset and challenge a lot of positions and feelings held sacred even by liberals. That's why I really appreciate the church addressing this issue, because we are confronting people of different stripes regarding homophobia, and to bring a sacred dimension to this homophobia is probably the most upsetting task.

Can you say a little more about what you mean by the "sacred dimension"?

The sacred dimension is where we're redefining what is sacred by including people into the community of God whom we have excluded in the past. Accepting that Blacks and people of color are part of the community of God means that the traditions we bring to the Christian community influence and affect this community. And that means if the church is going to be a truly multiracial, multiethnic community—not just in its wider dimensions but in its local dimensions—some of the traditions we consider to be sacred, our way of singing and worshiping and what we view as sacramental may have to change. That applies also when we affirm the place and leadership of gays and lesbians in the church. Even though marriage in itself in some traditions is not viewed as a sacrament,

I do personally view it as a sacrament, because—especially when marriage takes place in the church—it is a calling of God's presence into the lives of these individuals and it is saying that the marriage relationship should be as mutually affirming as the relationship that God has with the church. So, we're using religious images and examples to bear in the relationship of a marriage between a man and a woman. The same understanding of mutually affirming, God-inspired relationships should apply in covenanted relationships between lesbians and between gay men, and that challenges and expands what we understand as sacred and sacramental in the life of the church. When you cross those borders of tradition and challenge members of the church to expand their understanding of what is sacred and what is understood as God's presence in the lives of individuals and in the lives of the church, that's upsetting.

Where do you see this going in the future? What's your vision for change?

My vision of the acceptance of gays, lesbians, and bisexuals within the church is part of an overall understanding of the transformation of the church as it becomes a more multidimensional and inclusive kind of church. I see the Open and Affirming issue of accepting gays, lesbians, and bisexuals as part of a larger transformation that the church is making to become a more diverse community. And I think there's going to be a lot of tension and fighting to preserve the old ways, just as our nation is experiencing a resurgence of racism as it comes to grips with the fact that in the next couple of decades it will no longer be a predominately white nation. So, I expect much struggle within the future before the inevitable occurs concerning the full inclusion of gay, lesbian, and bisexual Christians within the church.

The challenge for the leaders of the church will be to try to present this struggle as a creative tension that has to take place if the church is going to survive, that will ultimately be good for the church even though people cannot see it presently. The church is dying partly because we don't have the zeal and the conviction—or we're not perceived as having the conviction—that the church had in its early years when Christ was with them and God was a part of them. In fact, in many ways, the church today is very reminiscent of the church in the first century. We don't control the issues anymore. We're not a church of Constantine anymore. We're not a church that influences and shapes the direction of government anymore. We're starting all over again.

I think we can start all over again with a sense of being reborn to a new creation. And God is definitely with us in our attempts to discover that renewed quality. In fact, we should be most suspicious when the world tends to acquiesce or feel comfortable around us. When we embody a level of tension and an alternative that is not the status quo and is clearly inclusive and unconditional in its love, that's a very radical posture. If we can continue to embody that in spite of what the world desires and compels us to be, we'll do fine. We may have to suffer decreasing numbers before the message kicks in that this is ultimately a way of God that people need to take seriously.

If people ask, "Where is your hope for making this inclusive church actually happen?" what do you say?

The hope is knowing there is a divine spirit in every one of us. And the hope is knowing that ultimately as the message becomes clear and as our embodiment of that message becomes clear, God's presence in each human being will acknowledge that this is where they should be going. I think that should be our Christian message. I'm a person who tends to favor a very interfaith approach, but I also believe that we can say this is what we do because this is what we believe as Christians, this is what we do because Christ is the centering force in our lives, and this is how we interpret his force and ministry. So, I think we can do this work from an interfaith perspective, but also from a very Christian perspective. We claim Christ as the example by which we move. I am hopeful that the message will be embodied in the work of the church. Being very convinced that that will ultimately occur allows me to look at the tension we're now in and realize that it will lead to greater things. I'm very hopeful of that. I also firmly believe that those people who have affected my life, Lee being one of them, are still very much a part of my life, and that everything I do is being watched and observed by these spiritual influences. It's almost as if they have become a part of the spiritual community going back to Christ that is observing, guiding, influencing, and informing my actions, and that I cannot do otherwise. I have to act in accordance with how those individuals have shaped my life. I have to be faithful to my relationship with them. These are the reasons that make me very hopeful.

Do you have advice for lesbians and gay men about their life in the church and what we may need to do more of or to do differently?

Yes, I would give this advice only from my own experience as a Black person in a predominantly white church: That your presence in the church is upsetting for most people. I realize when I come into a predominantly white room, in some ways I am upsetting what is going on in that place. All eyes become focused either directly or indirectly on me. The same is happening with gays and lesbians in the church. You are upsetting what's going on in that church, and all eyes are directly or indirectly focused upon you once they know you are gay, lesbian, bisexual, or transgendered. The upset that people are feeling and experiencing is good. They may not acknowledge it as good, but they will also not acknowledge it as guilt. It's good that they realize that they're feeling upset, and that feeling will hopefully allow them to say to themselves, "Why am I feeling this way and how can I move from this?" That's where I think gays and lesbians can be a great help: by helping congregations to know that as individuals and as a church they are good people, but none of us is where God wants us to be. We need to be challenged and we need to be open to the various ways God affects our lives and is more present in our lives. That means accepting the challenges among us. My advice to gay and lesbian Christians is to be patient but persistent with those who are upset around you, by acknowledging that they can be changed, that you're not alone, that God is with you, God is in you, and God is in them. God can do some wonderful things within all of us, in transforming us from where God wants us to be. So, for words of advice: Be patient and persistent, and also hopeful and faithful.

Chapter 10

Rev. Dr. Jacquelyn Grant

*J*acquelyn Grant is the founder and director of the Office of Black Women in Church and Society and the Fuller E. Callaway Professor of Systematic Theology at the Interdenominational Theological Center (ITC) in Atlanta. She is the first African American woman to earn a doctoral degree in systematic theology, which she received from Union Theological Seminary in 1985. The author of many books and articles, including the groundbreaking *White Women's Christ and Black Women's Jesus: Feminist Christology and Womanist Response,*[1] Dr. Grant is generally credited as pioneering the recognition of women's contributions to the Black church.[2] One of her current research projects examines Black people's understanding of the divine through Black theology and Black art.

Rev. Dr. Grant is also an ordained itinerant elder in the African Methodist Episcopal (AME) Church and serves as associate minister at Victory AME Church in Atlanta. An active participant and leader in the Ecumenical Association of Third World Theologians (EATWOT) and a former participant in the World Council of Churches and National Council of Churches, she lectures widely in the United States and abroad in colleges, universities, hospitals, prisons, and churches. She is included in *Who's Who among Black Americans.*[3]

When did you first realize that you or your denomination needed to take seriously the concerns of lesbians and gay men?

Probably early on in my academic work, as a seminarian and Ph.D. student at Union Seminary in New York. The gay/lesbian caucus was just being organized during the time that I was there. The issues were dealt with in the Union context rather than in the wider church. At that time in that context I also became aware of the fact that these issues were also critical to some African Americans who were beginning in some ways to become vocal, still not freely or openly so, but I guess the term "relatively so" might be a way of describing what was beginning to happen in those days. Increasingly, as I began to realize that these were issues that impacted not only the white church community but also the Black community, they became more and more important to me.

What were people beginning to struggle with?

To become open or not to become open, to come out of the closet or not to come out of the closet, a typical issue for lesbian and gay persons. The interesting thing is that it is still an issue today more than twenty years later. That still seems to be a challenge and struggle for many people who are lesbian or gay.

Did you see any people in those earlier years make the decision to be open, and what happened when they did?

Yes, I'm sure I did, just recalling the context, but Carter Heyward is the one person who sticks out in my mind as having been open and an advocate of lesbian and gay rights.[4]

Did you see the issues and problems for lesbians and gay men in the Black church as different from those who were trying to come out in the white church?

There are some levels at which the issues are the same. At other levels, they are much more complicated. Yes, people talk, stare, quote Scriptures when confronted. So, intracommunally they may be the same, but intercommunally Black gay/lesbians are faced with the added dimension of racial discrimination. Put another way, intracommunally you get the same kinds of rhetoric in the Black church and the white church: "Hate the sin and love the sinner." You get the same kind of question in the Black church as you do in the white church—"How do you convert gay men and lesbians from a life of sin to embracing Jesus?"—which means transforming oneself, one's being in terms of sexuality. Intercommunally the additional question is, "How do we affirm the humanity of those who are Black and gay/lesbian?"

Some African Americans say that not being able to be who they are in their church is like being cut off from their people, whereas white lesbians and gay men usually don't quite speak of that same kind of connection with the church community. Does that kind of response make sense to you?

Well, it makes sense if your religiosity or your spirituality as manifested in a religious context, within a church context, has been critically important to you. I guess it really depends on how one is raised, how the church functions, has functioned, or had functioned in the life of the person. It is true that the church as an institution has been involved in or a part of the life of the Black community perhaps in ways that the white church has historically not been a part of the life of white people in the white community. I don't know. I can't make that judgment. But it's not uncommon to hear expositions on the role of the church in the life of Black people historically, and I think a big part of that is true. It's not to say that all Black folks are members of churches or that the church has been important in the life of all the Black people, but I think it is true that the church has played a significant role in the life of Black people in the context of these United States historically. Just given that reality, it means that the church has been a part of the lives of a good percentage of Black people in general, and it's not unreasonable to think that the church played a significant role in the rearing of Black gays and lesbians, which therefore means that their life in the church would take on more significance. But my point is that it really depends on the role that the church plays in the particular and individual lives of gays and lesbians.

Do you think that places like ITC and other seminaries are doing much or anything to prepare pastors to deal with the issues of lesbian/gay people in their parishes?

I think some preparation is going on. I know that there are some professors who deal with gay and lesbian issues in the context of the classroom. I do, and there are others who do. That's not to suggest that we're solving the problem of heterosexism or homophobia, but it does speak to the fact that we are attempting to raise up a new generation of seminarians who will go forth and minister to and with the entire community in constructive and creative ways. We are successful in some ways, and we're not successful in many ways.

So, you see yourself as not alone but as having colleagues who are also tending to gay issues. I understand that at ITC Randy Bailey is doing Old Testament analysis in a way that is not anti-gay.[5] Do you feel that while there may not be a movement of such people, there are recognizable individuals who are open to these issues?

Sure. I don't participate in a movement, but I deal with the issues. And there are others here.

Are there lesbians and gay men, either churched or unchurched, whose writings you use or that have helped you?

I use Renee Hill's essay, "Who Are We for Each Other? Sexism, Sexuality, and Womanist Theology," and Toinette Eugene's essay, "How Can We Forget? An Ethic of Care for AIDS, the African American Family, and the Black Catholic Church." And also a piece by Anita Hill and Leo Treadway, "Rituals of Healing: Ministry with and on Behalf of Gay and Lesbian People," in Thistlethwaite and Engel's anthology, *Lift Every Voice: Constructing Christian Theologies from the Underside.*[6]

What do you do in class to introduce the issue?

A section of my systematic theology class every year is on liberation theology, and I treat gay liberation theology in that course.[7] As I talk about liberation theology in general and liberation theologies in particular, I address issues of homophobia and the ways in which we have, consistent with other expressions and forms of oppression, developed similar kinds of oppressive models with regard to gays and lesbians. I see the issues, like other liberation theological issues, as issues of justice, as issues of basic humanity. I think it's not accidental that those of us who do liberation theology are constantly involved with reconstructing and constructing different understandings of what it means to be human. It's no accident that gays and lesbians are challenged at that point just as other oppressed groups are: Basic humanity is generally denied.

So, in doing constructive theology, we are doing a lot in terms of conceptualizing and talking about what it means to be human and challenging the ways that our humanity has been rejected and denied historically. I think that's a big part of the struggle of gays and lesbians whose lives are defined for them by sexual activities. I mean, they're not even defined by sexuality, but by specific sexual activities. That kind of narrow definition makes us unable to recognize that we are all sexual beings and that sexuality is not only relevant when we talk about issues of homosexuality. The rhetoric is usually framed in such a way that it's almost as though when we talk about gays and lesbians we're talking about sexual activity and only sexual activity. But when we talk about other people—nongay people—then we can talk about other things that impact people's lives, like justice, love, righteousness, and all that other stuff that preachers like to talk about (*laughs*).

So, issues with regard to gays and lesbians specifically get relegated to the physical body; and I try to get students to see how that's just as inappropriate as women being relegated merely or only to things of the body, or as African Americans being Black and relegated only to things of the body, or other groups of people being relegated only to things of the body. I never argue that all the issues are the same. What I argue is that if you do some comparative analysis what you'll find is that the victimization of people by virtue of their sexual orientation is sometimes similar to the kinds of victimization that other oppressed peoples experience. They are not the same, but there are similar kinds of attitudes that develop, and similar kinds of projections are made about their basic humanity.

How do you show that the oppression of lesbians and gay men is different from and similar to other forms of oppression?

African Americans, for example, are victimized by virtue of who they are by the color of their skin, which really means then that gays and lesbians do not always have an identifiable characteristic. To be female, one has an identifiable characteristic, which historically has become the object of blame, shame, and oppression. To be Black is to have an identifiable characteristic that determines that you do not warrant the advantages of what it means to be human. That's not true for gays and lesbians, and one of the critiques that I have always had and continue to have of the gay/lesbian movement is that I'm not sure that they are as persistent in dealing with other issues, such as racism in particular—and perhaps sexism, too, I don't know—that impact other people and even some of those who participate in their own community.

For example, to get back to when I first encountered these issues at Union Seminary on an intellectual as well as on a personal level—that is, by way of knowing people who are gay and lesbian—I remember there were some gays and lesbians who were trying to identify themselves and to clear up who they were as African American and gay. I remember one of the things that I heard was—now, this was in the later part of the

'70s—that "the race issue is irrelevant at this point; we've dealt with the race problem already; we need to deal with issues of homosexuality now," which for me kind of created a problem.

If one could say that the gay/lesbian community was actually free of racism, then one could agree with that statement and then begin to understand where these folks were coming from; but since we know that that is not true, the question becomes how then are Blacks who are gay/lesbians able to creatively and constructively wrestle with the issues of their sexual identity and still not lose sight of the struggle that they face even within the gay/lesbian movement itself. So, it's quite clear to me that the issues cannot be the same. They can be related, they are similar, there are ways in which they function in similar ways; but as long as gay folks are still racist, then there still needs to be creative ways of wrestling with racism apart from the gay community and within the gay community itself.

It seems that one of the places that African American lesbians and gay men should be able to turn to in the hope of wrestling with both their racial and sexual identities would be the church. Do you know churches in which lesbians and gay men feel comfortable to do that?

Well, there is the gay Metropolitan Community Church,[8] but when you speak of these issues in the Black church context, it really depends on what you mean by "feeling comfortable." There are many lesbians and gays who are connected to Black church communities and who worship, live, and work in Black church communities and do so comfortably. Now, that does not mean that these communities are embracing of them as gay/lesbian people. What it means is that the community is embracing of them as human beings and as a part of that community. What that means essentially is that the issues are still not being dealt with above the table. It means that it's almost (*laughs*) Bill Clinton's "don't ask, don't tell" kind of approach to the "problem." You can find a lot of situations like that. There are so many. There are churches that function in a way that everybody knows that so-and-so is gay, but he's a darn good musician, or everybody knows that so-and-so is lesbian, but she's active in the community. You find a lot of that going on in most churches, but these churches having gay/lesbian caucuses? No, you wouldn't find that. Or these churches sponsoring lectures on gay/lesbian issues? No, you're not likely to find that. Now, you would find churches inviting a gay/lesbian person to preach or to teach or to sing, but to address directly and concretely issues of homosexuality? That's not likely. That's another story, as they say.

In your work, you write about how Black women have been the backbone of the church but remained in the background. Do you think there's a similar pattern with gays in that they are very much a part of the church, but they haven't yet found a way how to be in the foreground with their own identities?

Yes, I think that is the reality.

Do you think they themselves are going to have to push toward more open recognition, or does that need to come from the pastors and clergy? If there is going to be a change, how would it happen?

I think it's going to happen. What I tell my students is that even on the women's issue you are not always going to be able to confront the issues directly; it may be that you may just need to model. Sometimes in my presentations in churches, as I broaden my analysis and talk about Black women's need to be minimally tridimensional in terms of our analysis and ultimately multidimensional, I name the contradictions to which I'm referring. I talk about racism, sexism, classism, and many times I add heterosexism and homophobia. You throw it in there with the others; sometimes they are accustomed to dealing with the others, sometimes not. Many times when you add homophobia, it does generate discussion. Many times when you add it, then you get this response: "Oh, she's going to hell!" You get those kinds of responses, but the more you begin to talk about it, the more people are able to think about it and ask, "How do I participate in destructive ways when I relate to people who are 'different from me'?" Sometimes you can address these issues directly, sometimes you cannot.

There are other ways you can talk about these issues without confronting people all of the time. You can model the issues by addressing situations when they present themselves or by responding to comments that come up in your classes that clearly manifest homophobic attitudes. The way a professor responds to a question or a comment that comes from a student who thinks that homosexuals are going to hell says a lot about how the other students may begin to think about their own attitudes and beliefs about homosexuals. That can be done in many different ways. Sometimes I identify them specifically and sometimes I don't. When I do

my chart on the board in terms of different perspectives on liberation theology, I identify gay/lesbian issues as one of those perspectives. I do it
sometimes in the church even. You can probably lose a good part of your
audience when you do that, but at some point you're going to have to
begin to wrestle critically with these issues.

*When you're working with your students and the issue comes up, what is
usually the stumbling block for them?*

I think it's socialization, really. We are socialized into a heterosexual
culture, and we're not given to be tolerant of those who do not accept that
normative "culture." You don't generally get into that kind of a discussion
in class, not on a seminary campus. My impression is that folks are generally responding to a history of having been socialized to see same-sex
relationships as inherently evil.

*What is it that helps people cross over and begin to talk about and take
seriously lesbian and gay issues? What's the connection that somehow
makes sense to them?*

It's hard to answer, because I think it's different things for different
people. For some people it's knowing someone who is openly gay or
knowing someone whom they love and respect and whom they suspect
may not be heterosexual. I don't think there is any one answer to that. I
think there are any number of things that bring people over.

*You mentioned before that you work out of liberation theology, and that's
usually when you can identify lesbian/gay issues. Do you think there is
anything else out of your theological tradition that either requires or
encourages an openness to lesbian/gay/bisexual people?*

Well, just the basic affirmation of Black humanity, really. Even those
who do not subscribe to liberation theology—and there are many Black
folks who don't—that's the reality. Those who do not subscribe to liberation perspectives and who would not use liberation language to define
their theological or political stance can still speak out of a basic acceptance and ability to affirm Black humanity. And most often I think that
comes when you know "somebody who is"—a kind of "I have a family
member who is" reality in which people are able to see that "this person
is human, just as I am human." I'm sure there are other possible reasons

for people's ability to affirm the humanity of gays and lesbians, but then there are still many people who do not.

What do you think is the contradictory theological tradition that some people may hold to that doesn't let them?

Well, I don't know. I would say that all situations of prejudice, such as prejudice against gay/lesbian people, come out of a basic need for some reason to differentiate. There is a variation of that will to power. There's a sense in which people sometimes have the need to be the norm, which I think is a variation of the will to power, so that it becomes necessary to make a distinction between "me and them." And for many, a convenient "them," a convenient "other," is the lesbian/gay community. I don't know what explains it other than a basic arrogance that many people are taught: "My way is the best way, if not in fact the only way, and you will either be like me or you will be wrong." For me that's just a basic proclivity towards sin. So, I don't know what drives it other than just our sinful tendency.

What kind of advice do you have for African American lesbians and gay men who are trying to find a church or who are thinking about leaving the church?

I usually recommend that they spend more time—which can be liberational, but not necessarily so—searching for a church where they can feel comfortable. One of my former students graduated and went to a church in which she was openly lesbian and welcomed the lesbian community. Of course, she got into trouble with the church for that and has ended up moving on. I think now she's doing a new church development in another denomination. She's just starting, and it is an intentional community that will be focusing on gay/lesbian people and issues. I think there are those kinds of churches that are being established. I don't think that gays and lesbians always have to leave traditional churches to find comfort, but I suppose that more and more of them are becoming increasingly frustrated with the traditional context. But I suspect my advice to gays and lesbians would be the same as my advice to women who become overly frustrated and then struggle with whether or not to leave their churches and denominations. My advice most times is, "Well, if you leave the church, who's going to be there to fight; who's going to be there to struggle; who's going to be there to change things?" That sometimes helps some of them to make a decision to stay or to stay longer. Others simply declare that they're tired of the fight. That's legitimate, and I recognize that as a respectful way as well. But merely to move to churches that are overwhelmingly gay and lesbian does not, I think, necessarily solve the problem. Unfortunately, we don't have a whole lot of churches like Cecil Williams's church in San Francisco, where you have a public, open stance on the issues.[9] But I think it's less likely that we will develop more of those churches when gays and lesbians continue to move on, turn their backs, or find new territory. I say that not as a criticism. I say that as a reality, because I do affirm those who decide that they must move on. I affirm their right to do that. But I simply say that is not their only option.

I see your willingness to deal with homophobia and to accept lesbian/gay people as compatible with—and perhaps a logical extension of—your work with Black women who have not been recognized within the Black church and your multi-issue instead of single-issue approach.

Yes. Because African American women have been victimized several times over, I think we bring the capacity for a level of compassion that enables us to be able to see the victimization of others. But that's not always the case. There's just as much homophobia in the African American women's community as perhaps in some other communities. But I do, in terms of my own consciousness, attribute my ability to see those various levels and my having experienced those various levels of victimization and oppression as a way of enabling me to see that there are other groups, such as gays and lesbians, who experience similar kinds of discrimination. Frankly, after saying that though, I do recognize that homophobia is a part of my community, too. It is an issue that is not being addressed in any significant way in my community, but as people grow, develop, and feel more empowered—and I'm sure that as we get more and more folks like Renee Hill and this young woman I mentioned who is just starting another church—we're going to be able to get more advocacy on this issue in the Black community as well.

Have you seen Kelly Brown Douglas's new book, Sexuality and the Black Church?

No. I'm aware of it, but I haven't looked at it yet. Why do you ask?

Because she begins her introduction with the same claim about Renee Hill. I have it here. She writes, "My journey began with a trenchant critique by Renee Hill, one of my friends and theological colleagues. She stridently and rightly observed that her womanist theological colleagues had imprudently ignored issues of sexuality."[10] And she quotes Hill as saying:

Christian womanists have failed to recognize heterosexism and homophobia as points of oppression that need to be resisted if all Black women (straight, lesbian, and bisexual) are to have liberation and a sense of their own power. Some women have avoided the issue of sexuality and sexual orientation by being selective in appropriating parts of [Alice] Walker's definition of womanism. This tendency to be selective implies that it is possible to be selective about who deserves liberation and visibility.

So obviously, Hill's an important person in this whole discussion.

Yes, she is one of the few Black persons in the Black community who is dealing directly with these issues.[11]

PART III

Making the Connections

Chapter 11

Rev. Edwin C. Sanders II

*E*dwin Sanders is the founding pastor of Metropolitan Inter-denominational Church, which is located in a working-class neighborhood of small houses in Nashville, Tennessee. Lesbian/bisexual/gay/transgendered people are welcome and encouraged to participate in the life of the church. I attended a packed Sunday morning service in June 1998 and interviewed Rev. Sanders in the afternoon.[1]

How did the church get started?

I had been the dean of the chapel at Fisk University. I left in 1980 in a moment of controversy. A new president had come, and we weren't able to mesh. I left and had nowhere to go. I didn't have a plan. And instantly there were folks who had been part of the chapel experience at Fisk who wanted to organize a new church. I felt no spiritual interest in organizing a new church, but seven months later I felt like I clearly heard the voice saying, "This is something to do." I'm glad it worked out that way, because I think if I had done it directly after Fisk it would have been born out of a reaction and we probably wouldn't have developed the kind of identity, sense of mission, and direction the way we did. Twelve people came together and said they wanted to do this.

One of my good friends, Bill Turner, is a sociologist, and we were at Fisk together. Bill had a theory that institutions—and he built his theory around Black institutions—could not break out of the mold from which they were born. There was something about the way an institution is framed in its beginning, and no matter what you do you don't escape it. I thought that was absurd, but in time I came to think that he had something. The congregation was a mix of white and Black men and women from all kinds of denominational backgrounds, and that mix turned out to be significant, because from the beginning people identified us as being inclusive at least in racial terms and definitely inclusive and equal in gender terms. The first Sunday, one of the reporters from the local newspaper covered the service. We went to a lot of effort to have a well-structured, sophisticated worship experience, but he chose to focus on the fact that women who wore pants served communion, which probably began to say something about who we were going to be. In traditional African American churches women don't wear pants, and the service is male-dominated.

In that original group we had also a young man—one of my very dear friends—who was gay. Another one of my dearest friends went through a major mental breakdown at the time we were starting the church. I felt it very important not to abandon him and to include him. So we had a guy going through major psychological problems, somebody who was gay, and we had the racial mix. We did not have the class mix at the beginning. Most of the folks were associated in some way with the academic community. Nothing like we have now. Today we have an unbelievable mix of people. There are people who are doctors, lawyers, dentists, and businesspeople, and we also have a lot of folks who are right off the street, blue-collar workers, in treatment for drugs and alcohol, going through a lot of transition. And that mix has evolved. Although we said in the beginning that's what we wanted to be, the current mix goes beyond that of the original twelve members.

The presence of Don, the one gay Black male in the original congregation, had a lot to do with our current mix of people, and it had a lot to do with how we got so involved with HIV/AIDS ministry. The church began in '81, and he died in '84. It's almost hilarious when I think about it, because I'm so involved in HIV/AIDS work now, but when he died, we didn't know what was going on, and they told us he died of toxicosis. I remember saying, "What in the world is that?" I researched it and found out it had to do with cat and bird droppings, but Don didn't have cats. It was AIDS. You'd hear people talking about this strange disease, because then it was 1984, but what that meant for us was that we got involved before it became a publicly recognized and discussed issue. Don's presence and death pushed us in ministering and responding to folks with AIDS and in dealing with the issue of homosexuality.

I think the Lord's hand was in this in a way that I don't completely understand. It's bigger than me and the people, because it's amazing to me some of the things that were a part of us from our beginning. For example, there's a poem that we have used since the very first Sunday we began. We could never have imagined that it would end up being so much of what we do. It's called "The City" and was written by an Episcopal priest up in Jersey City in the 1970s. It talks about knowing God's face in the ways in which God is present to us in the city and talks about the God who drinks cheap wine and experiences the sting of a needle. It's interesting we'd end up now seventeen years later—and until recently the only religious organization in the United States—to have a needle exchange program. Little did we know that what we were saying in those words would become so much a part of our reality. But it has over the years.

The other thing I was going to tell you about, which is kind of funny, is the name. I will never forget when I told one of my friends we were going to name the church Metropolitan Interdenominational. He asked, "Are you sure you want to do that?" I said, "What do you mean?" I was pretty naïve. He said, "All the gay churches across the country are called Metropolitan churches." I said, "That's where I feel the Lord leads me; I feel Metropolitan." Nashville happens to have been the first metropolitan government in the United States, the first place where the county and city combined. My image of Metropolitan was a church of all of the city, all-inclusive. But my friend said to me that everybody is going to instantly say you're the gay church. I said, "So be it," and we went on with it. Like I said, there was a hand bigger than mine at work.

Where do you do the needle exchange and HIV/AIDS program?

We do part of it here at the church, and we do a lot of it as street outreach. We do most of our needle exchange out of vans. We go to where people are, to some of the heavy drug areas. We're blessed in that we've been able to work out some fine relationships with the various powers that be. The health department here in the city actually is a partner with us in doing this. The police department has been cooperative in that they've been willing to acknowledge the identification cards we give to folk who exchange needles. The cards simply say the person is part of a program designed to curb the spread of HIV/AIDS and please understand that is why he or she has paraphernalia with them. The district attorney has been very cooperative with us. He's been willing not to prosecute us. Nobody will give us that in writing, of course. They're unwritten agreements, but they've worked out real well for us.

What was the turnaround point for the class mix? How and when did it happen?

Early on we got involved in prison ministry. Going in and out of the prisons we started to develop relationships that translated to folks coming out of prison and getting involved in the church. After I had done the prison ministry for a while it became crystal clear to me that 80 percent of the people I was dealing with in prison were there for alcohol-and-drug related issues. I started reassessing this whole issue of drugs and alcohol and decided that's an area we had to begin to focus our ministries. So I got involved, did the training, and became certified as a counselor. I would venture to say that 25 percent of the people in this church are folks whom I first met in treatment. Thirty to 35-plus percent of this congregation are folks who are in treatment from alcohol and drug use. This is a place where a lot of folks know they can come. We've got all these names and labels, you know, the drug church, the AIDS church. But it's alright, because that's what we do. We hit those themes a lot.

I've learned some things over the years that I pretty much hold to, and this is one of them: We say we don't celebrate anything in this church other than our relationship to Christ, that's the vehicle for liberation in our lives. We don't say we are a Black church, we don't say that we are a gay church or a straight church, we don't say that we are anything other than a church that celebrates our oneness in Christ. I'm convinced that has turned out to be the real key to being able to hold this diverse group of folks together. I must admit I'm a person who has a negative thing about the word "diversities." I don't use it much. We don't celebrate our differences; we celebrate our oneness. That ends up being an avenue for a lot of folks being attracted and feeling comfortable here. New folks say, "I got here and I just felt like no one was looking at me strange, no one was treating me different. I was just able to be here."

There are a number of folks who come who are cross-dressers and folks who are in the midst of sex changes. People know they are here but just don't pay any attention to it. Folks get to where they say anyone can come here and it's not something that people pay much attention to because those various differences tend not to be a focus.

We probably struggle with not celebrating difference more on racial terms than on any other level. We would not have a racial mix at all if we were not very intentional about it. Our substance-abuse initiatives have helped us to maintain a racial mix more than anything, because my clients come across racial lines. We've discovered that for many folks, other than African Americans to some degree, this is a point of reentry, of coming back to discover a spiritual foundation for their lives. I'm thoroughly convinced that churches are as segregated as they are because they are so culturally distinct and completely one-dimensional. It's one of those things you always need to be resisting. Folks tend not to be open to cultural experiences other than their own. It's a heavy thing. We did some strange things to avoid it for a long time. For instance, we went twelve years without a choir. I was very intentional about it because I know that choirs do end up taking on a lifestyle of their own and getting locked into an identity. I knew for us it would end up being the contemporary gospel sound. But sometimes I buckle down and fight people's tendency to celebrate cultural difference and sometimes I give in. With the choir I eventually gave in, but insisted that they do spirituals and anthems as well as the gospel sound.

I was impressed by the informality of the service today. People seem to relax and fit in. The choir is less focused on performing than on interacting with the congregation. Your own manner is informal and lets people in. You don't just say all people are welcomed, but actually do something to let them feel at home.

Yes, we do have the sense of informality. People are arriving from the time we welcome the guests at the beginning until just after the sermon when there's maximum presence in the audience. People come in slow, and we give folks an opportunity to leave early. We even say it in the bulletin, "If you need to leave, just leave quietly." And we know folks do. There's a lot of folks who want to hear the choir or the sermon, but they don't want all the rest of it. One of the real hooks for just about everyone is the fellowship circle at the end. We actually have a few Jews and a couple of Muslims who worship here regularly. The Muslim family does a very interesting thing, which helped me to appreciate the significance of the fellowship circle at the end. We offer communion—the Eucharist, the Lord's Supper—every Sunday, and they stay until we get to that part of the service. Then they go outside or into the vestibule, but they come back in. I remember when Omar first started attending, I said to him it's interesting to me that you don't leave at that point. He said, "No, no, no, I wouldn't miss the fellowship circle." And it made me realize that the communion of the fellowship circle is more important than the bread and the wine. Probably the real communion is what we do when we stand there at the end and sing "We've Come Too Far to Turn Back Now."[2] We do that every week. It's our theme. That's a very significant moment. I've heard people tell me when they have to be late that they rush to get here just to catch the end of it. One woman said to me it was enough if she just got here for the fellowship circle.

A lot of the informality is very intentional. For instance, the only thing at Metropolitan that's elevated is the altar. Nothing else is above ground level. None of the seating is differentiated. In most churches the ministers have different, higher, bigger chairs than everyone else. We don't do that. We sit in the same seats the other folks do. My choir director is always telling me we'd get better sound if we could elevate the back rows. I say no, everybody's got to be on the same level and got to sit in the same seats. We do a lot of symbolic things like that.

Do other clergy give you much flack for working with needle exchange, welcoming gay folks, and working on issues that they may see as too progressive?

They do. But let me tell you, I have been able to have a level of involvement with ministers in this community that probably has brought credibility to what we do. I would like to think that we have maintained our sense of integrity, especially as it relates to our consistency in ministry. Folks tend to respect that, so even when they disagree, they also look more seriously and harder at what it is they're questioning. They've come to know over time that we've been a group of folks who try not just to be politically correct but to think and act about where the teachings of Christ will lead us.

We just had James Earl Ray's funeral here. He, as you know, was the convicted assassin of Martin Luther King Jr. Some people, including members of King's family, do not believe he was guilty. Doing his funeral here was one of the more controversial things we've ever done. The one thing that we say all the time about ourselves—it's almost a cliché—is that we are inclusive, we are reconciling, and we are engaged. Those are our three words. We are inclusive of all, constantly involved in issues of reconciliation, and engaged in the issues. One pastor who was a leader of the local Civil Rights movement and a friend of King's seemed symbolically right to do the funeral, but his church said no way. And then another congregation here that's very active and in the heart of the African American community said no. So, Metropolitan was the only place that was open to it. To me that's living out who we say we are. We simply say we acknowledge all folks as being children of God and of course the situation with James Earl Ray made it easy, because even though there were all kinds of contradictions in his life, the fact is he was a baptized believer. We have to believe that he had the promise and the guarantee the same way we have it. Obviously, folks here were challenged. We had a lot of positive support, but we've also had folks asking, "What are you doing?" And I responded that we say we are a "whosoever" church, and James Earl Ray was one of those whosoevers.

"Whosoever" is from John 3:16–17: "For God so loved the world, that he gave his only begotten Son, that whosoever believeth in him should not perish, but have everlasting life" (KJV). Has it been an expressed theme from the beginning?

It's been our theme for the last seven or eight years. The theme from the very beginning was Citizens of the World. We've always had a visual focal piece. First it was the Citizens of the World banner. And then for a long time it was the cross that's on the wall in the corner that looks like it's made of *kente* cloth from Africa, but it's actually cloth made in Guatemala. It's a kind of cloth that people all around the equator make—in Asia, the Americas, Africa. That symbolism is important to us. The circle, the cross in the middle of the circle, the cross of cloth made by people circling the world. That was our focal piece for a long time. When we were ready to make a change, I had a vision for one thing that will work. David, a young artist who does our children's church, did the new theme piece that has the "whosoever" on it.

We're growing in this inclusivity all the time. The language issue was big for us. We try to use inclusive language.[3] If somebody comes into the church who is not into that, it sticks out like a sore thumb. Does our inclusivity also mean that there is a real tolerance for folks who are perhaps not where we think folks should be in terms of inclusive language, sexuality, gay and lesbian issues? I think the answer is yes, you have to make room for those folks, too. That's a real struggle. Another one of our little clichés, and we don't have a lot of them, is we say we try to be inclusive of all and alienating to none. It's amazing how easy you can alienate folks without realizing it. Hopefully, if someone comes and does not use the language as we use it or is not where we might be in terms of some issues, that doesn't end up being a basis upon which we exclude them. We try to feel for that person and their response. One of my favorite Howard Thurman quotes is the one where he says I'm not only responsible for what I do to you, but I'm also responsible for how I respond to what you do to me.[4] I think there is a way in which we try to get folks to wrestle with that, because even though someone might say something that is out of sync and not where our thinking is, we have a responsibility to respond in a way that isn't alienating to the person and doesn't create a breach.

You need to get beyond difference and engage the person in a way that is transforming for them.

If new people have trouble with cross-dressing, transgendered, lesbian, or gay people, how do you get them to stay and deal with it rather than leave?

We tracked that issue a couple of times. Let me tell you what's happened. Most folk are here for a while before some of it settles in, before they start to notice everything. It's amazing to me how people get caught up in Metropolitan. They'll join, get involved, go through membership class, and that's usually when it starts to hit them, that they say to themselves, "Uh-oh, I'm seeing some stuff that I'm not sure about here." But what we've discovered is that what seems to help us more than anything else is that folks end up remembering what their initial experience had been when they first came here. We even have one couple—this is my favorite story to tell—who has talked about coming here on one of those Sundays when we were hitting the theme of inclusion hard. They left saying, "What kind of church is that?" But then a couple of weeks later they said, "Let's go back over there again." They came back and then didn't come again for about two or three months. They were visiting other churches. They said when they got down to thinking about all the churches, they had felt warmth and connection here. They said, "You know, that church really did kind of work," and they ended up coming back. When folks are here there's a warmth and connection they feel, a comfort zone in which they'll eventually deal with the issues that might be their point of difference. We've seen folks move in their thinking, and there are some folks who have not been able to. I've got one young man—I really do think he just loves being here—who says, "I just can't fathom this gay thing. Why do you insist on it?" I said, "You know, you're the one who's lifting this up."

As I said, we try to make sure that when any issue is brought up, it's in the course of things. It's not like we stop and have gay liberation day, just like we don't celebrate Black History month. We don't focus on or celebrate these identities or differences, but yet if you're around here you can't help but pick up on the church's support for these issues and differences. Today, for instance, we sang "Lift Up Your Voice and Sing," which is known as the Black national anthem. But we call it "Our Song of Liberation," and I've tried to help people to understand that. One of the greatest things about that song, which is a little-known point, is that it was written by James Weldon Johnson for the competition to establish a national hymn. It was chosen for first place, and then the committee found out that a Black person had written it and chose the second-place song to win. That's when Black people started calling it the Negro national anthem. One of the most telling references in the song is "to our native land." Johnson wasn't talking about Africa. He was talking about America. It's such a great song of liberation for all Americans. When you think about the song, you can always make it specific to your own experience. It's a song that was written as an American piece and not as a Black piece.

I have a lot of divinity students who serve as my pastoral assistants, and most of them are women. This place has become a refuge for Black women in the ministry. There are not a lot of clergy opportunities for them, so I've tried to figure out how to incorporate them into the life and ministry of the church. They actually run a lot of our ministries. Most of them are extremely well-prepared academically—more prepared than I am to do the work—and they do it well. When they started coming, we suddenly became a magnet; a rush of folks out of divinity school wanted to come and be a part of our ministry. I probably seem like I'm extremely freewheeling and loose, but I'm probably a lot more intentional about how things are going than folks realize, especially as they relate to the focus of ministry here at the church. One of my concerns was not having the time to orient the young ministers, to bring them into a full awareness of what makes this place click; but I discovered that if I get the inclusive piece established in the beginning with them, I don't have to worry about the rest of it as much, about keeping my eye on them all the time.

Can you name people who prepared and inspired you to do this kind of ministry?

Yes, I can. My parents were most influential. My dad laid the foundation for nonviolence in my life. He had been a man who was a fairly ruthless and aggressive businessman in his early life and went through moments of transformation to become a minister. He turned his life around. Because he'd been a person where guns and violence were a part of his world, he never would allow me to have toy guns. He died when I was eleven, but he was a tremendous influence.

Of people outside my family, one is James Morris Lawson. He's now the pastor of Holman United Methodist Church in Los Angeles. Martin Luther King referred to him as the leading strategist of the nonviolent movement. Jim Lawson was my minister in Memphis. I worked with him when I was fifteen years old, running errands for the folks who were doing the important work. He was a student of Gandhi, truly an apostle of nonviolence. I think the first time I ever heard the word "reconciliation," I heard it from Jim Lawson. So, the theme of reconciliation came into my life through him.

The other person is Vincent Harding, who I first heard speak at Wesleyan University when I was an undergraduate there. That was a life-transforming moment for me. Vincent preached about the gift of Blackness and took as his text First Corinthians 13 that speaks of love as the greatest spiritual gift. He was the first person I heard speak to the truth of the pain of Blackness, not compromising in any way the horror of the experience, yet being able still to have a word of hope and compassion. The gift of Blackness is about how God uses experiences like that of adversity, which translates into great gifts to the world, like the blues and jazz and gospel music and poetry and all that has been a part of the humanizing factor in the world. So much of what he said in that message became a part of the reality of our day. It is very significant to me that it was "We Shall Overcome" that Lech Walesa was singing in Poland, that they were singing in Tianenman Square, that they sing in South Africa; and it's what he was talking about then. He was saying what we do has to be driven by our love.[5]

A third person was Phil Hallie, my professor at Wesleyan, a Jewish philosopher. Phil was the person for me who always posed the challenge of, "Can this idea work?" He challenged me about ideas that were unfolding in my head. For Phil the important thing was the practical. It was hands-on, up-close, very personal. I miss him a lot. When I was preparing for the James Earl Ray funeral last week, I found myself picking up *Lest Innocent Blood Be Shed*[6] and realizing that the truly uncompromising, unconditional love he saw in the lives of the people of Le Chambon who hid Jews from the Nazis was the kind of love that I knew had to be at the center of what we were doing with James Earl Ray's funeral. The only frame of reference for the villagers of Le Chambon was to live in the way Jesus had described. I would like to think that's the kind of community that we can develop around here. It's not something that anybody figures out, it's just what you do if you're alive and doing what you understand to be right. That shapes how we deal with the presence of folks who have any kind of alternative or different lifestyle. The first point is, "Here is another human being." Everyone who is a human being who is breathing and alive in this world is the handiwork of God. No matter how obscure, how deeply it might seem to be out of place, the evidence of God's presence is there. And we have to look until we can see and deal with folks. I've had a lot of experiences in life that have helped me to know that it is always there. Working with death-row inmates helped me so much in that regard. Folks who had committed some of the most heinous crimes you could imagine, but you deal with them. You find that point where you know this is another child of God. There might have been all kinds of circumstances in life that led them to a moment of doing something that was outrageous in every sense of the word, but at the same time this is still a person who has within them that spark of the presence of God that ultimately is about something that is good and right and positive. I'm always willing to look for it.

You know that the example here of accepting and welcoming lesbians and gay men is an anomaly in the church. Most gay people feel alienated from their churches, but I've found that African American more often than white gay people emphasize the importance of religion in their family, community, and history and say that most of the pain and sadness in their lives centers around the church. They claim that being rejected by the Black church is especially devastating because this institution has been, and continues to be, the only place where they can take real refuge from the racism they experience in the society.[7] Clearly, that's not happening at Metropolitan.

We realized when we started doing our HIV/AIDS ministry there are organizations established by gay white men who had done a good job of developing services, but we kept seeing there was something that was not happening for gay and lesbian African Americans. And we realized it was community. No matter how much they tried to get that in other communities, there is the whole thing of cultural comfort. They were looking for the context where there were people who looked like them, who were extensions of their family supporting them. It became clear to me that what we needed to do was to establish a place where people could literally come and have a sense of community. Consequently, what we call the Wellness Center here is more than anything else just a place where you can come and feel at home. It has sofas and tables and chairs. Folks sit around. It's a place where there is a community that is an insulating, supporting place to come to. And although we provide some direct services for those folks, more than anything else I think the greatest service we provide is a safe place, a comfort zone, a community, a way to be connected to community. I know real clearly what you're talking about, and I've heard it spoken, too. It's one of the real issues for African Americans who are gay and lesbian. Our simple response has been to try to create a space where folks will have a certain level of comfort.

The problem I often run into, which speaks to what you were asking about, is that I think the greatest trouble we have sometimes is folks in the gay and lesbian community want to celebrate their sense of life and lifestyle more than Metropolitan lends itself to. In the same way, I have folks who don't understand why we don't do more things that are clearly more defined as being Afrocentric. There's a strong Afrocentric movement now within religious circles, and I end up dealing with them the same way I do with the folks who want to have ways in which they celebrate being gay and lesbian. I say the only thing we lift up is the basis of our oneness. I think the church has been a place where folks have not been able to find community, where they have been rejected. The African American church is a pretty conservative entity, always has been. It's probably been even better at holding up the conventions of American Christianity than other institutions. Folks can draw some pretty hard lines, and that's what we've been dealing with at Metropolitan. But the other side of the Black church is that it is known as being an institution of compassion. So, at the same time you have folks giving voice to some conservative ideas and practices, you can also appeal to a tradition and practice of compassion. That's why in our HIV/AIDS ministry we've been able to bring other churches into the loop. We're trying to get thirty churches to be involved in doing education and intervention on HIV/AIDS. We've been able to engage them on the level of compassion. Once we get them involved at that level, then we see folks open their eyes to other issues. African American churches have been very effective in compassion ministry for years around issues of sickness, death, and dying. What we're trying to do is get folks to put as much emphasis on living and not just ministering to sickness and dying.[8]

Another thing is the contradictions in the church, the unspoken message that says, "It's all right for you to be here, just don't say anything, just play your little role. You can be in the choir, you can sit on the piano bench, but don't say you're gay." We had an experience here in Nashville which I'm sure could be evidenced in other places in the world. You know how a few years ago in the community of male figure skaters there was a series of deaths related to HIV/AIDS. The same thing happened a few years ago with musicians in the Black churches. At one point here in Nashville there were six musicians who died of AIDS. In every instance it was treated with a hush. Nobody wanted to deal with the fact that all of these men were gay Black men, and yet they'd been there leading the music for them. It's that contradiction where folks say, "Yeah, you're here, but don't say anything about who you really are, don't be honest and open about yourself." I believe that the way in which you get the church to respond is to continue to force the issue in terms of the teachings of Christ, to be forthright in seeing how the issue is understood in relationship to Jesus Christ. One thing I've learned about dealing with inner-city African Americans is that you have to bring it home for them in a way that has some biblical basis. I'm always challenged by this, but I'm always challenging them to find a place where Jesus ever rejected anyone. I don't think anyone can find it. I don't think there's anybody whom Jesus did not embrace.

Chapter 12

Rev. Marjorie Bowens-Wheatley

At the time of this interview, Marjorie Bowens-Wheatley was the associate minister at The Community Church of New York. Founded in 1825, the church is affiliated with the Unitarian Universalist Association (UUA) and has historically been known for its "social activism and prophetic pulpit." It describes itself as "one of a handful of Unitarian Universalist congregations across the continent with significant racial, economic and cultural diversity. With nearly 400 adult members and over 50 children and teens in our Sunday school, we cherish the sense of community we find—the caring and friendship of diverse, kindred spirits. In 1997 we affirmed our inclusiveness of gay, lesbian, and bisexual persons by voting to become a Welcoming Congregation, a program sponsored by the UUA. In 1998 we adopted a new Mission Statement: 'to create a caring, anti-racist, diverse, spiritual community.'"

The church's social justice work is spearheaded by several groups, including its Black History and Culture Committee, Racial Justice Committee, Diversity Committee, and a local chapter of Interweave. Interweave is a denominational network of groups "dedicated to the spiritual, political, and social well-being of Unitarian Universalists who are confronting oppression as lesbians, gay men, bisexuals, transgender persons."

Rev. Bowens-Wheatley has held several positions on the denominational level and is currently the director of adult programs at the UUA national office in Boston.[1]

Can you tell me a little bit about how you got to the UUA?

I was raised Apostolic and for a variety of reasons did not find it a tradition I could continue in, partly the relationship of authority structures, partly theological and my need for greater freedom of thought. Mine was an independent church, not affiliated with a denominational structure, and therefore did not have the checks and balances that authority structures offer. Now, this is interesting, because if Unitarian Universalists have an issue with authority, it's the other way around, meaning they don't like or want authority. That's true with me to some extent. But on reflection, I never thought of the church in which I grew up as not having enough authority, but as not having checks and balances. The minister had so much authority—he was really the bishop with no one to check on him—that he became corrupt. I became aware that churches need systems of authority that are broad-based. So, one of the things that attracted me about Unitarian Universalism is congregational polity, where the whole congregation has something to say. There's a structure in which to say it and an attempt at democracy—something that I would have wanted in the church of my origin.

In any case, I left that church when I was sixteen; it was the church of my birth and of my family for three generations. It's hard leaving when you have that kind of connection, but on the other hand, I felt I needed to. I actually lost faith in God, because I wasn't able at that time to separate the church from theology. It took a lot of work to be able to do that, but in the interim when I was not going to church, I didn't feel the need for church, but yet I felt the need for spirituality. I was always a deeply spiritual person, a religious person, but I had no place to express this when I lost my faith. I probably really didn't lose my faith, but I lost my anchor.

I did become United Methodist for awhile because of my husband at the time. When I got divorced, I left and was kind of turned off by institutional religion for a variety of reasons, mostly theological. Certain things didn't make sense to me. What I wanted was a place in which I could question. It was the same thing that I couldn't have in my parents' church. When I asked questions about theological precepts that didn't make sense to me, I got the message that it's something you're just supposed to have faith about. I guess I was wandering for awhile and looking for a place that made sense and would allow me to question.

I came into Unitarian Universalism in two ways. One, I was doing my own religious search, independent reading, but in a fairly structured way. I did this for about four years. I would explore literature of various religions, and they weren't necessarily Christian. That's what originally broadened out my perspectives theologically. I ran across the works of Ralph Waldo Emerson and Henry David Thoreau and got interested in them primarily from a perspective of nature and the relationship between ecology, theology, and spirituality.

At the same time, my daughter, who was in middle school, wanted to go to church because her friends were going. They invited her to an evangelical church, one very much like the kind of church that I grew up in. I did not want her to be exposed to that as her first religious experience at that age. So I said, "Well, let's think about this. What other church could we go to?" She said, "Why don't we go to a Unitarian church?" which surprised me. I said, "How do you know about Unitarians?" and she said, "We've been reading Ralph Waldo Emerson in school." So I said, "Okay, great, I know a Unitarian church." It was really for her, even though Emerson had interested me, too.

We were living in Washington, D.C., at the time, and All Souls Unitarian Church was in our neighborhood. I knew the church—not theologically, because I had never been to services there—but I had been going in and out of that church for about five years because several of the community organizations that I was involved in as a social activist met in that church, and I knew the minister. He used to ask me, "Why don't you come to church sometime?" and I would say, "I don't do church." I was shocked when we *did* go, because I knew about fifteen people there, most of whom were active in some of the organizations I was already in, or they were students or faculty at Howard University where I was working. I looked around and thought to myself, "How come all of you knew about this and I didn't? You didn't tell me anything about it. I never knew that Unitarian Universalism was this kind of faith." It was almost exactly what I had been looking for all those years. So, we were enamored, kept going, and joined within a couple of months. My daughter and I had had no real religious or spiritual community, and we found it there.

After becoming Unitarian-Universalist, you went to seminary. Where?

Wesley Theological Seminary. I first became familiar with Wesley when I was a graduate student at American University. Even though I wasn't going to church at that time, when I had spiritual issues that I needed to deal with, I went to the chaplaincy program at Wesley. But I chose Wesley for two other reasons. One, I realized that the Christianity I was raised with as an Apostolic was not necessarily representative of mainstream Christianity; and I really wanted to know what mainstream Christians believed. And two, I wanted a seminary where there were people of color both in the faculty and the student body.

So, you were ordained in 1994, and The Community Church of New York was your first placement?

Yes, I came here as a temporary minister. I intended to go into a doctoral program after seminary, though not directly. When I finished seminary, I said very casually to some friends that I was looking for a place to hang out for a year before going back to do my doctorate. The associate minister here at the time heard that, so she called and asked me if I would be interested in being a part-time minister and creating something else on the side that spoke to my understanding of my ministry. For me, that was antioppression and antiracism work. For the first three years, I was on staff between one-third and one-half time at the church, and the rest of the time I did ministry in the UUA's Metro New York district, working with other congregations doing antioppression work. Then the associate minister left and the church called me to replace her. But I still only do this position two-thirds time—by my choice—so that I can continue to do the antioppression work. I'm a field consultant for the UUA's "Journey Toward Wholeness" Anti-Racism Program.

It sounds as though you were doing antioppression work before coming back to church.

I started doing that work when I was a United Methodist. Shortly after I got married in 1969, the neighborhood that I moved into—this was in Philadelphia—was a racially transitioning neighborhood. It was moving from working-class white to middle-class Black. The Realtors were blockbusting, but because of the class situation, a lot of the white people there weren't able to sell their houses. They weren't in a financial situation to move. It made for very interesting racial dynamics and actually some racial problems, such as when some of the white teenagers started harassing some of the Black people who were moving in. I was a housewife at the time with nothing better to do, so I started intervening and almost mediating, not even knowing that I was mediating, with some of the neighbors. Others saw what I was doing and called in the local United Methodist pastor to mediate, too, and we started working together. I became the block captain, and that led me to all kinds of work as an activist. I got involved in writing proposals for day-care centers and moved on to housing and women's issues. By the time I moved to D.C., I became involved in the antiapartheid movement, the Central American movement, and lots of community-based projects.

When did gay issues start to kick in?

I can tell you precisely. It started through the women's movement. I was one of the organizers for the National Conference for Women and the Law in 1977 in Washington, D.C., at Georgetown University. The women of color met separately, because we had separate issues to plan for the conference. In that meeting there were lesbian women of color, and they told the straight women that we had a problem. They thought we were homophobic as a group. So they asked for a separate meeting with us. We agreed to meet and see what the problem was. The meeting was around the corner from my house, and I had asked my then-husband to meet me there after the meeting. He and I had another meeting to go to together afterwards. Well, the meeting went fine. There were some issues of heterosexism, and we worked them out. My husband didn't know what kind of meeting it was, and I hadn't told him because I didn't think it was particularly important. It just didn't occur to me that this could be an issue. But when he came to this house to meet me and saw lesbian and straight women—the lesbians were very out—he accused me of being a lesbian. If I was at this meeting with lesbians then I must be one; he jumped to that conclusion. So, all of a sudden, not only was my consciousness raised about how heterosexism happens, but I had to figure out where I was on this issue. And basically I had to say he was wrong, not for calling me a lesbian—I didn't care about that—but I was concerned about his stereotyping lesbians and saying negative things about them. When I stood up to him, then I knew I could stand up to anybody. So, that's really when it started.

But that's not even really true, now that I'm thinking about it, because it started in my parents' church in terms of consciousness. The pastor was gay, and my choir director was gay. And everybody knew this. It was never discussed, but there were no put-downs either. There was never a sermon against gays and lesbians. There was an acceptance of them from the beginning. It just was. And it wasn't just of those two, because there was a small, informal caucus of gay Black men in the church of my birth and everybody knew it. So, I'd have to say it started there. But it wasn't out; it was silent. They weren't hiding anything, but no one talked about it. This was the early 1960s. The man who became bishop was born in this church, and from the time he was a teenager everybody knew he was gay. He was a friend of my parents. It never became an issue, but it was always a part of my life in that sense. He was always affirmed for who he was to the point where he became bishop. The fact is, though, silence prevailed;

nobody ever talked about it. These men had power, but their gayness was not acknowledged, so that dimension of their lives was oppressed. That's the tricky part about oppressions. They're rarely simple and obvious.

As you no doubt know, the UUA is the most pro-gay religious body. When did its progressive positions start to affect your work and play a part in your life?

I don't remember any one specific time. But, for an example, I can go back to 1987. One of our "new start" churches in Tulsa, Oklahoma, asked me to speak at their Charter Day, the starting of their congregation. I wasn't a minister then, but very active in the UUA. The name of the church was the Church of the Restoration. Restoration is a biblical image from the Old Testament Book of Isaiah, so I thought that I would go to that text to capture and evoke images of restoration. A part of the sermon that I did ended up getting excerpted in a meditation manual called *Been in the Storm So Long*, put out by the African American Unitarian Universalist Ministry (AAUUM) in 1991.[2] I had no experience at preaching and I didn't realize that a part of what I was saying in the sermon was a litany, but somebody else there who is a minister asked if it could be included as a litany. I gave permission and that piece was published there first, and then it ended up in our hymnal in 1993. When that came out, I started getting requests from other people to use it. When a group—I'm pretty sure it was the Gay Men's Chorus—here in New York asked for permission to use it in a performance they were doing, I thought, "Wow" (*laughs*). To me, originally it was just something natural for me to say. It's just who I am, and I didn't realize I had said anything that profound. It had to do with my theology and my vision of ministry and church as breaking down the barriers that divide us from each other. That's why I'm in ministry. Even before I made the decision to go into ministry, that's who I was and that's still who I am. So that "litany" includes everybody. It includes gays and lesbians, and it means getting past those differences. I was simply writing what I felt in 1987, but after I wrote it people started responding, and that's when things started for me as a public advocate and supporter of gay people.

Do any of your friends and colleagues ever say, "Come on, Marjorie, what's all this gay stuff about? Why don't you pay attention to more important things?"

No, I have held up this issue as an aspect of our faith, because I believe it is. So I've called people on being faithful to who we say we are. Our very first principle as Unitarian Universalists is to honor and affirm the inherent worth and dignity of every person. That has to include gay people, and if it doesn't, then there's something wrong with the way we express our faith. If that's not what we mean by it, then I'm not a Unitarian Universalist and I don't want any part of it.

So the response you usually get is positive?

Yes, but at the same time I'm not going to say that there hasn't been any resistance, but it's not widespread. There are people, including people at this church, who don't want to focus on and recognize our differences, but prefer a more universal claim, "We're all human." My response is, ". . . and we have particularities that we need to pay attention to; the way to the universal is through the particular." That's been a hard message to communicate to the point where people really get it. They are beginning to get it now, and we've had some real progress. Some of the people who were our most ardent detractors, when we were passing the "Welcoming Congregation" resolution, are now coming to films and programs that Interweave offers.

Why do you think you've been successful? As you've come into this situation and seen what needs to be done, how have you been able to do things that have worked, been new and helpful for this congregation? Are there problems here that are different, that you have had to adjust to?

Well, let me say that this congregation took ten years to become a Welcoming Congregation. When my predecessor was called, she was the search committee's second choice. The committee's first recommendation for that position was a lesbian couple whom this congregation turned down by one vote. So, there's history here. To get from that time up to now was a ten-year period. And it was a lot of work, and I wasn't here most of that ten years. When the resolution was passed, I had been here for four years. A lot of work was done to get people ready for greater acceptance. There's a chronology, and Interweave shepherded the process. Lay people took the leadership, and I as a minister have been supportive. That's the way that our UU congregational polity works. I don't mean that I haven't taken some leadership. I took the initiative to do a sermon on gay issues, which I think was significant, and Interweave felt supported by it; but the way that things change in UU congregations is more through the laity than by the ministers—on any issue.

Someone on the outside looking in on this congregation may say, "Why would a congregation that's open to all have trouble with the gay issue?"

That's a good question. The answer lies in our thinking we're unique, but we're not. I mean, yes, we're liberal, and yes, we have a liberal history, but we're also like other people out there with our prejudices and with our limited understanding, limited history, and limited exposure. There's a phrase—it's kind of a joke, but there is some truth in it, and the joke is that Unitarian Universalists are going to die from "terminal uniqueness," because we're not unique, in some ways. This came to light and became a larger discussion at our General Assembly this past year. Robert Bellah, the sociologist of religion, was one of the keynote speakers, and he basically told us how un-unique we are in relation to mainstream denominations.[3] I think that liberals often get off the hook by saying how different we are. And we're not that different from the mainstream in some ways, and this is one way in which we are not. We're part of society; we're influenced by the same things other folks are influenced by.

At the same time, though, to me it is because of our faith, our religious tradition, our purposes and principles that we can do some things differently and may have moved into places where others have not. There is no one Unitarian Universalist theology, but what holds us together is our principles and purposes, our various approaches to religion, and the way we want to run our congregations democratically. There is a greater foundation on which to build. When you start with principles that say "respect the inherent worth and dignity of every person," how can you then exclude some group of people, if that's what you say you affirm? To me there is a theological premise here, or a foundation on which to build, to call people to account when they discriminate or when they leave somebody out, or say, "Aren't we all human?" without wanting to discern and affirm our particularities and differences.

What do you think is the big gay issue for Unitarian Universalists now? And what are your own recommendations for it?

Gay marriage. The president of our denomination gave a good witness to same-sex marriage at our General Assembly in 1997. As a testament to and support for gay marriage, he asked gay and lesbian people who were there and who were partnered to come up on stage. That's an example of leadership from the top and something that the whole General Assembly, which was more than three thousand people that year, could see. Previously, the 1996 General Assembly passed a resolution in "Support of the Right to Marry for Same-Sex Couples."[4] But the other supportive actions are by local ministers doing ceremonies openly and with pride. I did a ceremony here last year, and I was so happy to see that the sanctuary was as full as on any Sunday morning. It was a wonderful ceremony. When doing those ceremonies becomes normative, the more we continue to do them, we're making a statement and more people will come to see them as just life. To me, doing these ceremonies is even more important than a resolution passed by the General Assembly because a resolution is a statement of conscience on paper. But you have to do it, witness it, let it become part of the normal life that people come to expect.

African American lesbians and gay men often say the Black church is an anchor for them in a world that is otherwise hostile and alienating. So, to be cut off from the church, if their church is being homophobic, is "to be cut off from our people."[5]

That's true.

Do you also see this as an issue for African American gay men and lesbians within the UUA?

It's a curious kind of question because it has to do with what attracts people to Unitarian Universalism in the first place. What I think attracts people is: (a) a level of comfort with ambiguity, (b) a level of comfort with difference, and (c) having the ability to make up one's own mind rather than following the pack. So, when you ask that question, what first comes to my mind is that there are some people who chose this faith to get away from some of the traditions of "the Black church," specifically because they need liberty and freedom just in terms of thinking instead of having a set of theological rules or a set of church hierarchies that say they should find that freedom in the Black church. They have made some intentional decisions about the African American community, which may be less important for them than some of these other concerns about thinking freely and questioning. At least, that's my take on it. That's not to say that that applies to all people or any one person completely, because I miss the culture and music of "the Black church" and the sense of cama-raderie and community that you just don't find in many UU churches. The answer is both yes and no. There are people who were uncomfortable with "the Black church" for a variety of reasons—a lot having to do with authority—and have become Unitarian Universalists partly because of that. The decision of some may have nothing to do with gay and lesbian issues, but simply with feeling more comfortable. There are other people for whom the Black church tradition was and still is very important.

But there's another issue here, and that is that everybody Black wasn't raised in "the Black church." That's important to say, because within the Black community there is great diversity theologically, culturally, and in terms of church history. What one feels comfortable with culturally to some extent is related to the church. One of my best friends, a Black woman in seminary, and I are very much alike on almost everything except what kind of music we prefer in the church. And I relate it right back to the fact that she was raised Roman Catholic and I was raised Apostolic. So, I don't want to make the assumption that African Americans who are Unitarian Universalists were necessarily raised in "the Black church." That's not always true. When I was a United Methodist, it was in a Black community and the church was a Black church, but the United Methodist Church is not a historically Black denomination. It would be interesting to see some figures on the distribu-tion of Black people raised in historically Black churches versus in main-stream denominations. There are lots of Black people who are Catholics, Methodists, Lutherans, or Nazarene.

There seems to be a popular perception that I've heard from white and Black people that the Black church seems to be more homophobic than the white church.[6] In my previous research I found it went both ways— Black pastors and congregations could be anti-gay or pro-gay[7]—but that was true of white pastors and congregations, too. So I decided to go out and look for particular examples of Black pastors and churches who do welcome and affirm lesbians and gay men.

I can give you two examples. The first is anecdotal, but not strictly anecdotal because there was an article written by James Tinney who observed that there is a preponderance, a higher proportion of gay men in Pentecostal churches.[8] I have definitely seen that to be true, especially in the ministry of music. If you go into any of the Black churches, Church of God in Christ as well as some of the Baptist and Pentecostal churches,

it's all over the place. It is so out there. I don't know if anyone has documented this, but it's evident. It's very strong, and anybody who knows
these churches will admit that. So that's why I spoke earlier about the way
I was raised in the church, because I frankly never really saw any homophobia there at all. I never did, except for the fact that it was never
affirmed, because they weren't out. That has something to do with the
times. So, it's a very curious thing when you hear that Black churches are
more homophobic.[9]

My second example is current, creative, and more specific: Rev. Alma
Faith Crawford and Rev. Karen Hutt in Chicago. They're both African
Americans and started a church called Church of the Open Door about
two or three years ago with specific outreach to the Black gay and lesbian
community, and it's still working. Two denominations are involved, the
United Church of Christ (UCC) and UUA. Alma has clergy standing in
both denominations. Karen is Unitarian Universalist. They're partners
and recently had a service of union. I've been to that church, and it's a
remarkable place. It's a new congregation and a really fantastic one.
There was an article about them and their church in our denomination's
magazine, *The World*.[10] Even though they started the church to serve a
particular community, it attracts more than that. It attracts friends and
allies, as well as families and their children. They're meeting a need that
goes beyond, I think, the gay and lesbian community.

*I know that's also true in other gay-identified new churches in the UCC.
Eventually they attract all sorts of people who simply like to come to them
because they find community there.*

Well, to be frank with you, when I was visiting Chicago, I attended out
of curiosity and because they're friends of mine. I wanted to support them
in their ministry. But because of the racial imbalance in the UUA, I also
found something there that I don't find in most UUA churches. Because
I was raised Apostolic, I need a sense of connection culturally with the
Black church—some other folks need it, too—and finding ways to get it
is a creative act, much in the way that Karen and Alma have done. So, if
I lived in Chicago, I would probably choose to attend it as my local
church for that reason, because there was a sense of spirituality there that
I don't often find in UUA churches.

Chapter 13

Rev. Dr. James A. Forbes Jr.

*J*ames A. Forbes Jr. is the first African American to serve as senior minister at The Riverside Church in New York City. Founded in 1927 by John D. Rockefeller, the church is affiliated with the American Baptist Churches in the U.S.A. and the United Church of Christ and describes itself as "an interdenominational, interracial, and international congregation" whose twenty-four hundred members "come from more than 40 different denominational, national, ethnic, and cultural backgrounds." In its mission statement, the church "commits itself to welcoming all persons, celebrating the diversity found in a congregation broadly inclusive of persons from different backgrounds of race, economic class, religion, culture, ethnicity, gender, age, and sexual orientation." Maranatha, one of its social-justice ministries, "brings the concerns of the lesbian, gay, and bisexual community to the church in the form of education and action, while providing fellowship and spiritual community for gays, lesbians, and bisexuals."[1]

Rev. Dr. Forbes is ordained in two denominations, the American Baptist Churches in the U.S.A. and the Original United Holy Church of America. He received his Doctor of Ministry from Colgate-Rochester Divinity School and is the author of *The Holy Spirit and Preaching*. *Newsweek* magazine named him one of the twelve most effective preachers in the English-speaking world. Before his installation at Riverside in 1989, Rev. Forbes taught for thirteen years at Union Theological Seminary, where he continues to hold a chair as the Harry Emerson Fosdick Adjunct Professor of Preaching. Since 1992, he has cochaired A Partnership of Faith, an interfaith organization of New York City's Protestant, Catholic, Jewish, and Muslim clergy. In 1998, he gave the keynote address at President Clinton's Initiative on Race meeting in New Orleans.[2]

When did you begin to deal with the issues of lesbians and gay men and to make them a part of your ministry?

I grew up in a Black Pentecostal church. My denomination was totally opposed to the inclusion of gay and lesbian people, but still there was an "understood" inclusion—that is, everybody knew there were lesbians and gay men in the church, but preachers often preached against the lifestyle. So, as a kid growing up I came to the position where I generally agreed with my tradition that gay was not the way. Then I came to Union Theological Seminary where I experienced the lesbian and gay community raising this issue in a serious way. During that time I worked my way from a position of opposition to one of inclusion and affirmation of the whole family of God.

I often like to confess that in that process I was asked to co-celebrate communion with Karen Ziegler, a student and ordained minister in the gay Metropolitan Community Church. I refused, because I was in the middle of trying to work my way through the issue and did not like the political pressure to say yes. Political correctness was urging me to "have to," and I was feeling, "No, I can't do it right now." Often, the transition to inclusion involves hedging when being pushed to full political solidarity. I wanted to grow slowly in the Spirit into what I hoped to be a more mature position, so I wasn't ready yet. By the time I left Union for my position at Riverside, I was very much aware that homophobia was a sinful dynamic and one form of immaturity in the faith, and that I should rise above my own conviction to become a champion of inclusion.

Interestingly, though, when Riverside was wrestling through its inclusiveness statement and I was still at Union, Lee Hancock, who was the chaplain at Union, and I were invited over to Riverside to talk about biblical and spiritual resources for their reconsideration of homosexuality. One of my students had written a paper reexegeting the Sodom and Gomorrah text, and I had pretty much affirmed the interpretation she put forth that the text was about the condemnation of inhospitality rather than of homosexuality. But most of my growth was along the lines of the Pentecostal hermeneutic based on the Gospel of John passage that says, "There are many things I have to say to you, but you cannot bear them now; however, when the Spirit of truth has come, I will lead you into the further truth." So, I started thinking and talking about the issue of "more light" from the Spirit and believing that, as human sciences illuminate the nature of the development of sexuality, it was necessary to grow with the Spirit into the understanding that if you have a false premise—mainly the old concept that people basically choose what they want to be—you come to understand that there is in some significant degree a givenness to your sexual orientation, but also that the best of Christian faith affirms the capacity to make choices even within the framework of givenness. Then all of a sudden you have to revise what you've been saying. So, some of us began to be proactive in terms of Riverside's inclusiveness statement.

I guess the biggest "card burning" occasion for me and the more difficult was during my first year here at Riverside when I marched with Maranatha in New York City's Gay Pride Parade. It was not a joyous occasion for me. It was a conflicting occasion, because as I was walking down Fifth Avenue and saw the television cameras, I realized that for me this event was a coming out in terms of my theological perspective, and I was thinking (*laughs*) that all over the nation people who had raised me in my Pentecostal tradition were watching and saying, "My God, Jim Forbes is out there! Has he gone crazy?" Of course, it's a very liberated moment to be able to say to yourself, "You have come to a theological change. Are you prepared to experience the break with your tradition in a public advocacy area? It's one thing to have a different theological position, but are you willing to let the bridge be dismantled between you and those who are intensively homophobic? Are you prepared to say that in this matter I take a break from the tradition that has nourished me?" Not an easy thing to do if you have had a seriously intensive formative experience in a very strong conservative environment that has made you think that if you are not with that tradition, you've actually forfeited your right to enter into the gates of heaven.

So, for me the first go-around was a very serious bearing-the-cross kind of advocacy and not a joyous one. However, the rationale was very clear. While I was not basically conjoined by my card-burning experience, I was able to see how if your childhood had been restricted and you were gay and had not had a chance to celebrate that, the parade would serve to relive and release the childhood, adolescent, young adult, and also some of the more mature adult dimensions of that restriction. And as one who was willing to confess to being a part of the oppressive arrangement, I should be grateful there is an opportunity to celebrate the release from oppression. If I could celebrate the release of Nelson Mandela from prison, I should be prepared to celebrate the release of my brothers and sisters from hiding and silence into open celebration in the public parade. But still, I'm not fundamentally a parade-type creature, although I did get arrested yesterday in the demonstrations for the Amadou Diallo case here in New York,[3] but I'm not a professional Act-Up kind of demonstrator.

Nevertheless, to learn to let your values override initial stylistic discomforts is a part, I think, of learning from the gay development how to be more inclusive.

Did you get any reaction from people who saw that you had marched?

No, that is not the point at which I got the greatest reaction to my advocacy for gay folks. I don't think anybody even said anything to me about the parade (*laughs*). Chances are people already know where your perspective is heading. The more difficult piece was two years ago when I was the Luce Lecturer at Harvard and the music album, *Bold,* came out by the Winans sisters with the song, "It's Not Natural."[4] I was asked to speak on Tavis Smiley's show *BET Tonight.*[5] Oh, my goodness! I took them on on the basis of "Your song is a beautiful song. That's its problem. Your voices are beautiful. The rhythm is contagious. But carried with it is the encouragement of the legitimization of the elimination of people. Because if it is not natural and an abomination in the sight of God, then the logic is that you, who would never act upon it, would give license to persons who think that in the name of God this unnatural reality should be actually expunged from the face of the earth. And there is someone somewhere who out of your beautiful sound will do a dastardly deed. And you therefore will have some responsibility for that. That's my position."

There were Pentecostals, Evangelicals, and other types who were also on the show. One said, "Now, Rev. Forbes, I know you to be a man of the Spirit, a man who believes in the Bible. How can you possibly overlook the biblical basis for the condemnation of homosexuality? I mean, I've always respected you, but. . . ." Oh, boy, did I get riled up! I'm usually committed to rising above the more combative kind of public debate, but I got so riled up I didn't even let anyone else speak. And the host of the show tried to interrupt me, "Rev. Forbes, Rev. Forbes . . ." But I said, "No, no, I'm not going to let this bigotry continue. . . ." And he said, "Rev. Forbes, Rev. Forbes, please, we want to hear. . . ."

My son said to me after, "Daddy, you're always on TV and most of the time people come up to me and say, 'James, we heard your daddy on TV and he was really good,' but after this program they came up to me and said, 'James, I saw your daddy on TV'—period," as if it was an abomination in the sight of God. A lot of people mentioned they saw me on *BET,* but commented even more on the intensity with which I attempted to be an advocate for a more open position. So, more than the Gay Pride Parade, that TV show was probably the greatest public exposure of my perspective in a context that was conflictual. My sense is that it was a more public debate between visible evangelicals and a liberal like myself than had happened before.

I saw the show and was amazed. My reaction was, "He's really going to bat for us! No other non-gay clergy stands up to anti-gay bigotry so forcefully." I felt excited and encouraged. I knew it wasn't your typical style, but it seemed one of those rare moments that deserved a different approach, and the one you used was appropriate.

I thought that if my intensity lacks discretion, it would be more indiscreet not to be indiscreet. This is not a minor issue in which cool heads should find a way to ignore it. I felt it was combat with a spirit, so let's acknowledge the nature of the exchange.

In the life of the church, what role do you think this issue has? It's an issue on its own, but it also seems to have a connection to other issues. Is that your sense or not?

Out of my Black liberationist struggle,[6] I have come to wonder how to frame this issue so that it becomes a part of a broader liberation of struggle. And I think it has. On Monday I was arrested with Liz Alexander, who is on my staff, is Presbyterian, is working on handgun control, is a gay woman who had a bonding ceremony here, and is in charge of the Department of Children and Family Services in the church. If she is working with me in regards to getting arrested for Amadou Diallo's death, isn't it natural that I and others, who are not gay but are struggling with myriad social-justice issues, should respond when a gay person is killed or attacked, as seems to happen almost weekly? So, a liberationist aggregation is beginning to function here. And I think that within the church that is generally understood. If you're going to be for liberation, you really want to be for liberation in general, not just for some folks whose liberation prolongs liberty for themselves but has no sensitivity to the liberty that others also pray for, work for, and sometimes demonstrate for. I think it's happening.

However, you should know from a pastoral perspective I am not really keeping up. Obviously, I know the new words to be added to gay and lesbian are bisexual and transgendered. But the truth of the matter is I don't have any theology on transgender issues. The movement is taking its place alongside other liberationist causes, but there are elements and dynamics of the movement that are still evolving, and many of us have not worked through our basic solidarity with it to a more sophisticated theological understanding. It is much more ideological solidarity. I can tell you what the basic issues are that led to the expansion of terms for Black folks from Colored, to Negro, Black, Afro American, and African American, but not for gay issues. I can and do speak about the generalized acceptance of persons for who they are and who they claim to be, but I cannot tell you what transgendered is, what is on the cusp of that term and issue. Nor can I really tell you about the ethical implications of the inclusion of bisexuals. Is it serial monogamy or is it "try one for a while and then another after that"? I don't know the answer to that. I don't even know what the questions are. I do not know the debate that led to the adding of these names, but they're a part of the family, and I'm for the family whatever the family is.

But I also know that I can't just lump this issue in with every other issue. I need to recognize that there is a continuing curriculum. There is, so to speak, a "second semester to this course" and I've only done the first semester, which is about moving from homophobia to inclusion. Surely, I've not taken the second semester that would address the growing dimensions with respect to marital bonding and unions, what gift has come from the gay movement that should enrich the perspectives of heterosexuals on these issues, what is the latest wisdom about our critique of marriage in general that has led to some improvements in the way bonding is envisioned. So, I'm aware that my solidarity needs deepening in terms of the continuing debate with the issue itself before it is simply folded in with an "also ran" quality.

A lot of us gay people in the church are used to battling the people who are against us, but there are those who aren't against us and who are looking for something from us other than to fight with us. So, for the "second semester," what is it that gay people could do to help people who want to move along?

I have always said from my Black experience that there seems to be a trajectory of release from oppression. You state the case, you battle resistance, you win some concessions and make some gains, you celebrate a fundamental inclusion as family members without need to apologize. Fine and good. But all you've been through must have given you a perspective such that now you are officially viewed as a family member without having to make the case that you are. You could not have gone through all that struggle and suffering without having been given some unique wisdom that belongs to the larger family. So, what should the next chapter or second semester involve? I think one important issue is how do we together determine the moral and ethical principles which will sustain the social fabric with the least amount of tear and prospect of violation. That is to say, what about the training of children for inclusion? We need to have that conversation. We now have a common pool of kids from different backgrounds in the church. How do we train them so that those who are or will be gay will not discover that this world is not congenial to their development? And for people who are heterosexual, how does the training of people to include and celebrate gay kids also help develop and celebrate their own heterosexuality?

Usually, the new kid on the block has all the energy. So, gay people may be feeling more strongly right now than others about their identity and development. But how do we frame "be who you are" in such a way that it does not create the impression that it is better to be one or the other and can be used instead for the inclusion of all people? How do we create the environment in which that can happen? I'll use the example of the struggle to see Black music as having the same basis of excellence as white music. In the early stages of that fight you had white people feeling that "They're saying that our music isn't worth anything. I mean we've got Gregorian chants, but these Black people are coming in here and acting like if it isn't a spiritual and hoop-dee-do it isn't anything." So, the new group that's making a case for their inclusion often gets the reaction that they're saying theirs is really better. How do we work to stay together and project to children that they can discover and not be told who they are and that they do not have to feel defensive?

What is the ethic that informs people who can go either way? A number of macho folks in the Black community who see somebody leaning towards being a lesbian would consider it as a mark of their virility if they could talk her into being straight. Is it right to do that in that case or in general? No. If somebody is on the borderline, is it okay? Is the new ethic that in a community people should test out their affectional proclivities and, as in heterosexual situations, this woman simply may not be interested in you and you just let it go? What are the boundaries that would determine where there is a violation of pressure to deny another the unfolding of the uniqueness of whatever they are doing? We don't know the answer to that.

How should we have all-church parties? During the church's sixtieth anniversary, I told Dick Butler, "I don't care what they say, I'm going to dance with you, brother; we're going to be together as a family." And I was dancing with Dick—and with dancing now, you know, you don't have to hold each other—but the women who are likely to be my strongest supporters and want to protect me from the brunt of anybody's critique joined in, and all of a sudden it's a heterosexual dance. When we have couples clubs, should gay couples meet separately from straight couples? When we have social dances, should they be mixed? In safe-sex seminars, is what's safe for gays different from what's safe for straights? Can these programs begin to be done together?

What about the public manifestation of gayness and the public manifestation of heterosexual affection? Are there things that ought not to be done in public, and I'm not talking about touching and kissing? What is the public face of the gay movement? It relates to how Black folks sometimes say to each other, "If you all don't want to hurt the cause, don't do this." Are there things that you can say to gay folks along those lines? Are we prepared to say these things together? With respect to marriage, bonding, and people who are not going to be married, how do we talk together about helping sexual expression in the context of not legally committed relationships? How does the Bible work on this, and how do we interpret the Ten Commandments from a gay liberationist perspective on adultery?

I've often thought that what the church ought to do is to organize TLC clubs, Tender Loving Care clubs for children, in which there would be opportunities to do sex education with a real level of sophistication. Is the goal that people should have premarital chastity? What is that? I haven't married anybody in years who had it. Why should some people not have had sexual experiences on the basis of trying to live up to those standards? So, maybe we should teach them differently. What would a really first-rate orientation to sexuality for emerging adolescents and young adults look like? Would we have touchy-feelies, would we be naked, would we look at and be shown what we have to look forward to?

I've thought it would be fascinating for the church to say, "We want to develop a people for whom sexuality is a normal and beautiful part of their lives, and we want to take away the fear dynamic that comes from not knowing and that probably stimulates our libidinal energy to override our hesitation and fears as well as our acting as responsibly as we should." Is the church ready to do that? Is it in this church that the children will see each other, see male genitals, see female genitals, understand how they work, and be told the reasons for why you can do this or that, or instead will they be told they have to work on their own libidinal energies and know how to be responsible for themselves without the support and help of a caring community?

I've thought it would be really fascinating for the church to be proactive instead of saying, "Don't do it." But I don't think that heterosexuals can do that by themselves. So, what would an inclusive curriculum for the preparation of sex education look like? What are the principles that would apply? I think that never again can heterosexuals list what the basic principles of mature sexual relatedness look like. You know, we list principles of mutual vulnerability, consent, noninjury to body, and on and on. But what about gay or straight sadomasochism and domination: how do you get your head around that? We're talking "second semester," and "second semester" classes cannot be with straight people alone. Equal numbers of gay and straight are required for such a class. The class together would have to determine the issues, because one half of that class does not know the issues as they are viewed by the other half.

What I hear you saying is that the first semester was about getting people to struggle with the church so that gay people could fit into it. Now it's not just about gay people fitting into the church but about shaking and shaping the church.

Yes, that's the issue. And to shake it together with those who come from different perspectives or orientations. And that's what I look forward to. Also, what would be the social agenda beyond gayness in which gays would be joined with others? Everything in the first semester would have been done to help continue the struggle. I know gay people are interested in other people besides themselves and in other things than sex. How do you mature to a liberation struggle whose agenda diminishes with respect to any particularity and a longing simply for solidarity and now enlarges with respect to actual interactive experience among different people?

You mentioned Liz Alexander. Are there other gay people shaping a larger social agenda with other kinds of people at Riverside?

At our church, we have gay people who are as active in the Stewardship Committee and other commissions as they are in Maranatha. Some who used to be the most militant advocates in Maranatha have mellowed into raising funds for a variety of programs. All of us mellow as we go along. We can't fight that long after a certain age anyway (*laughs*).

There are others—I don't know if they are gay, but I sense they might be—who are simply working in general areas, including the AIDS ministry, which is not gay-specific. They're doing good work in helping the church to get on with many issues. There are gay pastors who don't preach gayness but teach the gospel, but in the gay form in which they find themselves the message is there anyway. The gay community here is, I think, approaching the maturity that I'm talking about.

You travel and speak a lot outside of Riverside. What usually is the stumbling block for people when they deal with the issues of gay men and lesbians?

First, I think the absence of a basic consciousness about sexuality in general continues to be the condition in which homophobia grows. It isn't about homophobia, but about sex in general, especially regionally. The South continues to be, I would say, pre-K in regards to candid, open conversation about sexuality. Second, again mostly in the South, there are those biblical verses that override any other considerations, in spite of all the good work that biblical scholars are doing to reconsider them. And third is the attachment to a very simplistic "natural" theology in which it is a given that when you see a penis it seems natural that it would be seeking a vagina. People just think in terms of the natural theology of heterosexism and the birth process, a theology that can't begin to understand how two women even do it. They assume that lesbians have to use a dildo because they don't have the "natural" equipment to do it. The "natural" conditioning of our understanding of sexuality is reinforced by the Bible verses that are learned by heart, and an invitation to a freedom and glorious liberty of sexual expression is nil. The absence of a deeper and liberationist theology from childhood up makes it hard for some folks to make the transition and get on.

Public display of affection is still a hard problem for some folks who are almost willing to let homosexuality go if it's done in the closet, but not if you hold hands in public. There are still some folks who link gays with AIDS. Many cannot yet see how it can be normal for two men to raise a child. Their questions are, "Can they raise a boy, can they raise a girl, is pedophilia involved in this?" Pornography, which is peeked at even by Evangelicals sometimes, feels to them as though it blurs the lines. In anything X-rated, the chances are there's going to be some gay sex in it with respect to women. Men are intimidated by the tenderness with which women seem to be able to make love to each other without the benefit of their masculine presence. It's frightening for somebody who has less than the strongest sense of their own identity. So, those are some of the concerns I run into when I talk to groups.[7]

When people do break through some of that, what is it that let's them do?

A child being born in the family who is clearly gay. A person defending them who's clearly gay. The unfairness to gay people seen as just not right. They can say, "I know gay isn't right, but it's not right what they did to them." So, the sympathies can shift on the basis of the brutality experienced by gay people. Less frequently, well-reasoned arguments help, but mostly for people who already have inclinations and impulses towards a new perspective.

What about their pastors? If their pastor takes a position, does that make a difference to them?

If they love the pastor whom they want now to reject because they think he's gone off the deep end, they may use the tension between the rejection of his theology and the love they feel for him as a person to help them adjust, to get used to things. I think there are people in my church who love me enough to say, "Rev. Forbes, we'll go along with you on that," and after awhile the new way of thinking doesn't seem so unnatural or unusual anymore.

Do you think that Black clergy have more moral credibility when they speak against homophobia and are listened to more seriously?

Black pastors are really more respected and have a little more authority than white pastors in general, I think. And so I would assume that if a pastor says, "Leave these people alone, because they're God's children just like everybody else," that would go a long way towards at least first repressing homophobic expression and perhaps over time getting people around to moving toward a more inclusive place.

Have you in your pastoral experience dealt with Black lesbians and gay men who feel alienated from the predominantly white gay movement?

Yes, but it's usually economic—that white gays get more of the money. So, GMHC, the Gay Men's Health Crises Inc.,[8] here in New York is thought to be more skillful in lobbying for the money for HIV/AIDS and not to have been sensitive enough to Black concerns. Namely, racism doesn't disappear just because you're gay. Black folks assume, "Okay, the misery index gives us a predisposition to solidarity; but as white folks work through their particular misery, they go on back to being white folks, messing over Black folks." That's the theory or typical way of understanding that.

If gay people are feeling discouraged about organized religion and the Christian church, what is your word of hope for us? Many of us want to give up and run.

Right. One of my colleagues at Union had a T-shirt that said, "I may not be perfect, but parts of me are excellent." Isn't that great? (*laughs*) The church may not be great, but parts of it are excellent. You could take a kind of elitist attitude to say that those of us who are Christians and have heard the grace of God applied to our lives are very secure and don't need the church to reinforce it too much. So, maybe in gratitude for God's grace you could stay and help minister grace to this church that needs the wider truth. So, that becomes a kind of heroic message that your church needs some people who might let it off the hook for its narrowness.

The other way is from a Black perspective where you say it goes in cycles. You get in on a good cycle and ride it as best you can, and the chances are that each round will go higher and higher, but be fully aware that it could circle back around instead of going higher. So, here we are today approaching Easter Sunday, which is the anniversary of the death of Dr. King, and it's also the time we're looking at Abner Louima,[9] Amadou Diallo, and racial profiling.[10] It seems like "déjà vu all over again," but we know that we've made some progress and that the trouble now is on a different level than in Dr. King's time. So, you say that you stay and do it for unborn generations. You don't let the church off the hook. Your presence will continue to impact the shape of the church in ways that will make it better for somebody else who's coming along.

For example, in my early years here at Riverside, by just walking through the door I knew folks were asking, "Why did we ever accept a Black man to be our pastor, plus he's Southern, and sometimes he even splits his verbs, and he leaves off consonants at the end, and he's not quoting the best-sellers?"[11] But now it doesn't look so strange to see me walk through the door. Oh, there may still be a little when I get to carrying on as my old Southern Pentecostal self (*laughs*). So, I would suggest that you've got to be in it for the long haul and do it for the sake of God and for others who will follow. All things being considered, it's probably not a bad institution.

Anything we haven't covered that you would like to talk about?

I anticipate preaching a sermon about heaven, and I wonder if the eschatological perspective—a perspective from "the final days"—might offer wisdom to the gay movement. Recently, I preached a sermon in Chicago about sex. I said, "Yeah, you all worry about sex, but genital sex is not that big of a thing. If you want to feel the full orgiastic life, it happens when you're flying through the streets of heaven and all you do is rub wings. That's the big O; just rub wings." Reinhold Niebuhr said that sexuality is the elevating of one of the vitalities of life to a level of ultimacy. I think that ought to speak to us. You see, I'm sixty-three. I'm not as sexually active as I was. I can make it on much less sex than I used to. Sex is not nearly as sensual. It has a way of not being, you know, the be-all and end-all. How can younger people who are in the height of sexual energy see it from an eschatological perspective and not as a singular ultimacy, so they can bring a little more balance in terms of physical, emotional, and spiritual love?

So, I would wish to see a good discussion about when the sexual energies wane, will we have developed other dimensions of human relatedness that are fulfilling and binding, since we all know it's not about the big O anyway, not really? It's about the fact of human relatedness in its metaphysical dimensions. I think that in a super sexually stimulated society, putting sex in perspective is going to be a gift that gays and straights can offer society when they look at things with different perspectives. Eschatological theology may offer such a perspective, so I use a theme entitled "at the end of the day." At the end of the day, will God be called "Mother" or "Father"; at the end of the day will there be any basic difference between male and female; at the end of the day will the difference between gay, straight, lesbian, bisexual, transgender really matter? We go through all these distinctions now, but where is life tending toward and what does that broader perspective do to relativize any of our typically intensive antipathies or obsessions?

Chapter 14

Rev. Msgr. Russell L. Dillard

*P*opularly known as the "Mother Church of Black Catholics," Saint Augustine Roman Catholic Church was formed in 1858 through the efforts of emancipated slaves. With two thousand registered members and three thousand calling it their home church, Saint Augustine's is now one of the largest parishes in Washington, D.C. In 1990, Father Russell L. Dillard was installed as the first African American pastor in Saint Augustine's history, and in 1991, he was elevated to Reverend Monsignor. In an invitation to the public, he says: "It makes no difference who you are, where you are from, or what you look like. As long as you come to praise the Lord, then you are welcomed."[1]

Do you think that Saint Augustine's is seen by lesbians and gay men as a place in which they are welcome?

I guess the ultimate answer is yes, just based on the fact that we have lesbians and gay men in our congregation and there seems to be a sense that they are certainly a part of our family.

What do you think your parish is doing that makes lesbians and gay men feel welcome?

I think they are accepted as people. I think Saint Augustine's has always been known for its being a welcoming place. I was just part of a symposium on HIV and AIDS, and one of the things that I tried to emphasize was that the church has to be welcoming to people who are living with the virus. That means not only what the pastor does, even though that gives some direction. It's much more what the people themselves do and how they receive other people. I think that's what people find when they come here. They feel that they are welcomed for who they are, and that's always been the way it is here. That preceded me.

So, Saint Augustine's has a tradition and reputation for being that kind of a community?

Exactly.

Why do you think that is? I mean, how far back does that tradition go?

Because Saint Augustine's was formed by emancipated slaves who felt that the church at the time was not as welcoming as it should have been, the tradition of being people who would not put other people in that circumstance has grown from 1858.

Are there parishioners who have trouble welcoming lesbians and gay men?

If there are, certainly nobody has come to me to express it. And nobody has come to me to say they have seen that from others. I think the thing is that people who are lesbian or gay don't wear signs. They become a part of the community. They're not separated from or on the outskirts of, but a part of the community. It's not like people ask what your sexual preference is. If it comes up in conversation, it comes up in conversation, but it's not something that is solicited or put on a form. You come to worship the Lord in the spirit of this Afrocentric liturgical expression, and you're welcomed as a part of this community.

Can you say something about the Afrocentric worship style?

That is probably Saint Augustine's signature. The gospel music and Afro American spirituals touch the roots of the gospel and speak to having been bonded, enslaved, and separated and to wanting to come together as a people. The services, even the ones that are more traditional, are for the most part lively and engaging so that people are called to it and feel a sense of participation. The idea is that if you come into our church, you've come to praise the Lord. You're not coming as a spectator or as somebody sitting on the sidelines; you're coming as somebody who is called to praise the Lord and to offer your gifts and talents at the table so that others may benefit from what you bring.

Is your parish more or less Afrocentric than others?

Probably no more than others; probably more than some. Certainly Saint Teresa's, Holy Comforter/Saint Cyprian, and Saint Augustine's are all on a par. But I think Saint Augustine's is known for it because it was a church that people were sent to if you were Black. In other words, you could go to a "white church" or the church that might be in your parish boundary, and people were very clear that you didn't belong there. For instance, our location now, the present Saint Augustine's was the former Saint Paul's. In Saint Paul's there were five pews out in the back of the church allocated to Black people. The rest of the church, which seated six hundred, was for white people. So, when Saint Augustine's built its own church, the current building, it did so with the idea that they were going to worship in a style that was comfortable to the people who were building it. From the very beginning to this day, there has been a diverse congregation. Back in the days when it was first built, for instance, Justice White used to come and had a pew. Congresspeople did and still do come because of Saint Augustine's very well-known music ministry. The choir was always a point of magnetism for people. People come for what does not separate them but brings them together, and that is the love and praise of the Lord.

Could you say something more about the diversity you talked about?

Sure. Saint Augustine's now is probably 85 percent people of African origin. However, on any given Sunday at the Mass that is the most popular you'll find many non–African Americans, including many visitors from Europe. We are part of bus tours, and people are pointed to Saint Augustine's if they are Catholic and want a place to worship. People come who have seen videos of Saint Augustine's or heard the choir's tapes, especially from France, Italy, Portugal, and Germany. Everybody's welcome; however, people who come realize that this is a church that celebrates and worships in a way that is most comfortable to people of African origin.

Does your music ministry rely heavily on gay people in the way that Black Protestant churches do?

Not really. There are gay people in the music ministry, but the predominance of the ministry is not by gay people.

Are there lesbians and gay people at Saint Augustine's in leadership positions?

Yes.

You were born and raised in D.C. Which parish did you attend when you were young?

Saint Anthony's. At that time it was a paragon of diversity. We didn't know racial differences. It's unfortunate that it wasn't documented more as to how Saint Anthony's was such a melting pot, but it truly was. I guess from there I got a sense of how that was how church was supposed to be.

Do you think that you are more open to welcoming lesbians and gay men than some of your colleagues?

That's hard to say, but certainly the priests that I have worked with throughout my priesthood—and I can only speak from that vantage point—have been open to and welcoming of all people. I think that what I'm not finding is gay people themselves making the distinction and pulling themselves apart. So, if you're gay or lesbian, then that's not the thing that is most known about you. You come as a person who wants to praise the Lord or wants to involve himself or herself in the ministry, who wants to serve God. But there are times; for instance, there was one young man who was taken into the church about four or five years ago, and one of the things he said about Saint Augustine's was he came here as a gay man, was accepted as a gay man, and has been accepted as a gay man. Now, I'm not certain that everyone in the church knew he was gay, but his feeling from other church members is that he's a part of this community, part of the family. And he said it as a witness statement either at the Easter Vigil or Easter Sunday, one of those two big events.

When did you first realize that welcoming lesbians and gay men was important for the church to be doing?

Well, again, because I'm African American, I know that to be left out, to be put aside and left there, is no good for anybody. So, as far as I'm concerned, people are who they are. If they are coming to be a part of this community, they are going to be embraced as a part of this community. Whether you are lesbian, gay, or heterosexual, if you are living the spirit and the light of this community in ways that are appropriate to church life, then nobody is going to take you aside and say "Let's talk." But if, for instance, you are a heterosexual who is acting inappropriately, whatever that means, some of the elders of the church are going to take you aside and say something to you. And in the same vein, if you are gay or lesbian and doing similar kinds of things, somebody is going to say something to you. They won't do it as a means of chastising but as a means of fraternal or sororal affection—"You're a part of us; and we don't want to see you as not a part of us. In order to do that, let's talk about this."

Do you think that the Black Catholic movement may be more progressive than other parts of the Catholic Church on lesbian/gay issues?

That's real hard to say. Black Catholics probably as a group, like Black Americans as a group, are relatively conservative on many issues. In terms of welcoming lesbian and gay people, the question becomes, oftentimes, what your background is. I know some denominations are obviously much less tolerant, if that's the word, of people who are lesbian or gay than other denominations are. Certainly within those individual denominations, there are local churches that are more accepting. So, I think that what I'm finding in the Roman Catholic Church is that probably is true across the board. However, I do feel—and this is only a feeling, not something scientific—that the Black Catholic Church is much more accepting of people, because there's something about the importance of church as a place for people who are sinners, and that's all of us. That has always pervaded the Black church. We know we're not coming here because we're better than anybody; we know we're coming here because we are full of fault and need to have ourselves graced by the love of God. So, if you are one of us, meaning an in-flesh individual who is a sinner, then you belong here; and that's everybody. So, if you come to the doors you are saying you're coming to seek the salvation and the grace of the Lord to try to do the best that you can with the life that you have been given. I think that mind-set is pervasive and allows for more acceptance. We don't see ourselves as better Christians or better people.

What other ways has that acceptance been shown within Black Catholic churches?

Certainly for people living with HIV and AIDS and people who are addicted to drugs and alcohol. We've always had outreaches to people with addictions. Many of our churches, if not most of our churches, have some kind of outreach programs to people, like twelve-step programs. We're not about being overly, fancily dressed, not that there are not people who come dressed very, very high, if you will; but if you don't have anything, that's okay, come in the door. It's not about how you look, how fine your clothes are, or how nice your car is that makes you a part of who we are; it's the fact that you want to be a part of who we are.

Do you think you have class diversity?

Oh yes, very much so.

Can you say something about the HIV/AIDS symposium you just did?

It was the first one sponsored by the Archdiocese under Msgr. Ralph Kuehner, who's the director of the Community Organizations and Issue-Based Coalitions part of the Office of Social Development. It brought together two priests—myself and Msgr. Ray East—to make presentations about what our parishes are doing or have done with and for people living with the virus. There were about two dozen priests there and about half as many lay leaders from other churches who came, most of whom did not have HIV ministries in their parishes. They came to learn how they could establish ministry and what our ministry entailed.

And can you say briefly what your ministry does entail?

We're big on education and also Food and Friends, which provides free meals and prepared food to people with AIDS. Continuously keeping peoples' consciousness raised, in addition to providing direct care, is extremely important because people are too willing to think that the battle is over, the cure is at hand, and people aren't becoming infected or being affected by the HIV/AIDS epidemic, when in fact in our African American community we are overly represented in HIV/AIDS infection. For us, it's to keep our people's heads in the game, so they know there are people all around them, sitting in front of them, next to them, across the table from them at home who could very well be infected. And they have an obligation to reach out as brothers and sisters to our brothers and sisters who are walking this journey.

Is that message communicated in the worship services or educational programs or both?

All of the above.

And you address social issues like HIV/AIDS in your homilies?

Absolutely.

For you, what is it about the Roman Catholic tradition and theology that creates the opportunity to be open to lesbians and gay men?

I think the foundational piece is obviously what Jesus kept talking about, how he lived his life, the importance of the individual person—that because we are all children of the same heavenly Father, then we have an obligation to be in relationship with our brothers and sisters no matter who they are, where they are from, what they smell like, what they talk like. It doesn't make any difference. We have an obligation to do that. And I think that in order for us to be true to the Lord, then that kind of belief has to be fundamental in all that we are; and it has to be spoken, affirmed, and lived. So, that's the foundational piece: Everybody is a child of God. And, again, remember we're talking about people whose experiences or whose ancestors' experiences have been of exclusion. So, obviously it's not wise for us who have been excluded to now exclude others. It's not who we should be; and it's why, I think, we find that it's important not to let people think they cannot be a part of this community.

Is that point—the one about Black people having been oppressed, therefore not going on to oppress others—one of the lessons you often find yourself making?

Oh, yes. I think that in this day and time we can be very self-righteous, in that "I've made it, I've got mine, now you get yours." I think in this area of Washington, D.C., where a lot of African American people are successful, where there are a lot of middle- and upper-middle-class African American people, you have to remind people from whence they came or from whence their mothers, fathers, and grandparents came—not in a finger-wagging way, but in a way that just says, "Let's not forget our roots and let's realize that there are still brothers and sisters who are nowhere near where we are now." It's continuous, because we always have to say—and we always get a lot of "Amen" behind this—that none of us got where we are by ourselves. Somebody sacrificed something along the line so that we could be in these pews, houses, or jobs.

When you're working with your parishioners and, let's say, someone has problems with lesbians and gay men, what do you find is most often the stumbling block to acceptance and what's most helpful for getting them over it?

The stumbling block probably would be behavior.

Sexual behavior?

Right. What I've experienced is that it's the same stumbling block they would have with heterosexual behavior. If you are, for instance, not married, then you should not be involved sexually with somebody else. If it is known that you—either as a gay or lesbian or heterosexual person—are involved sexually with someone who is not your partner or spouse, then that becomes a bone of contention. Now interestingly enough, here at Saint Augustine's I have had people talk to me about a heterosexual who might be in a relationship that is inappropriate many more times than I've had someone mention anything to me about a person who is lesbian or gay in a relationship that is inappropriate. I don't know why that is. Maybe lesbians and gay people are much more discreet with their relationships, for their own reasons.

How do you get people over that stumbling block?

First of all, if it's an individual, we talk about it together. We talk about the fact that people know what our church teaches about sexuality in the context of marriage, because it is preached from the pulpit. When I'm speaking from the pulpit about behavior, I'm talking about behavior in the fullest sense. It's all people, be you lesbian, gay, or heterosexual. So, when I talk to individuals I remind them of that which is spoken about here. And I also let them know that if they really have difficulty with what another person is doing, I will certainly speak to the individual. But I also say we have to respect the choices that people have made. We might not agree with them, we might not even in the context of our doctrine believe that those choices are right, but we're not going to throw someone out because somebody is doing something that we believe to be inappropriate. Is it my job to say something to somebody who is being very indiscreet? Absolutely, but that's happened to me with people who are heterosexual, not with people who are homosexual. The few times when people who are homosexual were acting inappropriately, it was their friends in the choir or in the ministry who have taken them aside to talk to them about it. And again, what is that but a family member dealing with a family member?

What is your message about relationships, whether they are heterosexual or homosexual? What is it that makes a relationship good?

For me, I'm not a radical in this Roman Catholic Church. I do believe in the sacrament of marriage. I do believe that the proper context, and I say this to all our kids as well, is the sanctity of marriage. And I say, however, that that should not and never should hinder one from good relationships with other people that are healthy and loyal and in which you can tell the innermost secrets of your life. So, for me it's important to affirm the church's doctrine on sexuality while at the same time affirming the beauty of relationship. What I find myself called to is affirming responsible friendships, loyal friendships, friendships that people can count on. And in terms of sexual relations, those relations should be within the context of sacramental marriage.

But you know that for gay men and lesbians, that context isn't available, right?

I know. For me it's a struggle, because I know that people are in very, very good, long-term relationships. As a Roman Catholic priest I certainly can't bring those relationships to the altar for the sacrament of marriage. But I certainly can speak to those relationships as being loyal, as being truly friendships, but I also have to say that in the context of my belief they cannot be sexual. Now, if that is unfair, it could very well be. I'm not wise enough, I guess, to be able to know differently.

Have gay people ever challenged you on that or presented it as a problem?

Let me think. There have certainly often been discussions, and certainly people have been not happy with the church's position or with my position. But on the other hand, they want to be a part of the church and so they listen and try to understand what the church is saying. They don't always agree, and they say that is something that we are going to have to make some decisions about.

It seems that while you maintain the church's position, you also don't put yourself in a place of judging their relationships.

No, I'm not going to beat people over the head with it, because there is a pastoral side that always has to be kept in mind. Our people are more than just responders to words on a page; they are people, they are my brothers and sisters. They carry with them the disappointment that the church places on them for being who they are and also the joy the church offers them as truly being accepted as God's people, just as my African American ancestors were told by the people of the church, "Don't come here, you're not really Catholic." But they themselves saw in the Catholic Church something that they truly wanted to be a part of. It's something that as a young Roman Catholic I had to hear from my non-Catholic friends, "How can you be a part of a church that allowed slavery, that allowed priests to have slaves, that white men rule?" and on and on. That's something that I had to think through a lot because it was true to a point. As I say, when you're two thousand years old you are going to have made some mistakes. But I came to grips with realizing that African American people still are part of this church, and I wanted to minister to my people who are part of this church. I think it's similar with lesbians and gay men in that not everything the church puts out for gay men and lesbians is what they want to hear, does not seem sensitive to their needs; but the voice of the church that they hear most frequently is the voice of the people in the pews and the clergy at the altar who call them to be "a part of" and not "apart from."

What do you think of the bishops' document, Always Our Children?[22] *Is it useful as a pastoral resource or tool?*

A couple of interesting things about it: One, it's a reiteration of what the church has been saying in fragmented terms in a lot of different places; and, two, it speaks to parents and is such an important pastoral tool because so many parents were pushing their children away. What I think this document says more than anything else is that that is wrong, that is something that we as Christians and Catholic Christians cannot condone. These are your children first. They are also the church's children, but they are your children first. And you have to accept them as God has presented them to you or as, in many instances, they have interpreted God having presented them to you. So, it's to be able to say to parents, "Please, don't look at the church as that which gives you sanction to say no to your kids. Look to the church as one who says your child is important to us, and we call you as parents to embrace and affirm those children as who they are and to accept those children as they feel they are called to be." So, that document has been a very helpful and strengthening tool for me to be able to say to parents with all sincerity, "Do not— the Lord does not call you to—separate yourselves from your children."

When you were talking about the symposium you did, I got the impression that one of your roles is not only to pastor your own parish but to be a teacher for other priests in the area. Is that a role you ever expected seeing yourself in?

Actually, no. It's funny. My first assignment as a priest turned out to be my home parish, which is unusual. I was like the kid priest. And then I went to Howard University and was serving the Catholics on campus and anybody else for that matter, and I was happy with that—you know, serving these kids and trying to bring the Lord to them. And then I became a pastor of a small church while I was still chaplain at Howard. I was pretty much unknown, because the church was small, inner-city, had some problems in the area with drugs, shootings, and things like that. That was my first eleven years of priesthood. It was the next nine years that thrust me into this other, more public position, which is both a burden and a joy, because I feel very unworthy to go before a priest group and talk about whatever it is I talk about, be it HIV/AIDS or. . . . I remember talking to a priest group about acceptance of people, the new immigrants, because most priests in this diocese are white. They are the children of the early immigrants: Italians, Poles, Irish. I said it is time for us to be the ones to open up our arms to the new immigrants. And I found myself doing more of that kind of thing. I do a lot of work in high schools,[3] I am a chaplain at a couple of places, I always like to challenge the young people about the beauty of the diversity they find around them, that they should relish and take that open mind-set they have been given in these schools to the colleges where they're going, because most will be going to colleges where that won't be the rule, be it the historically Black colleges or predominantly white major colleges. People won't run to one another and say, "I want to mix with Black kids," or "I want to mix with white kids," or "I want to mix with the Asian kids." They'll say, "There are some white kids, I'm white, let me hang with them; there are some Blacks, I'm Black, let me hang with them; there are some gay kids, I'm gay, let me hang with them; there are some straight kids, let me hang with them." And we have to understand, as the bishops' document says, we are all God's children. That has to be gotten across, and I find myself overwhelmed by the thought that I'm in a position to do that.

There seems to be a nice irony in that Saint Augustine's was founded as a place that people had to go so that they could worship. Now as their priest, you're the one other parishes are looking to for leadership.

Absolutely.

What advice do you have for African American lesbians and gay men who want to stay in the church but are having difficulty doing so?

I use an analogy when I'm talking to kids or even adults about the sacrament of reconciliation. I say, you know, the one thing that we have made clear since the Second Vatican Council is that the priest is there to offer you the forgiveness of the Lord. It's the Lord who forgives, but we are the agents to say those words. And if you go to a priest when you confess your sins, which I know it takes a heck of a lot of nerve to do, and he beats you up, then let me say this to you, "Find another priest." Don't go back to him and don't let him be the church for you, because he's not. There will be other people who will hear your confession, who will offer you the reconciliation and the love of Christ and the forgiveness of the Lord and who will walk the journey with you, who will not cut your legs off on the journey. And I say this also to lesbians and gay men: There are churches that are more open than others. People come to Saint Augustine's from as far away as Richmond and as far north as Columbia on a regular basis, because African Americans and people who like and need a different kind of worship experience are not finding it at their local places.

As I see that phenomenon, I say to lesbians and gay men that you might have to pass a few that are closer to you to get to the one that says, "Welcome, my brother; welcome, my sister," but you will find one. So, don't give up on confession because the confessor is not good; don't give up on your local church because they're not accepting of African Americans or lesbians and gay men. Find a place where you can feel that the Lord calls you to this home church. The good thing about our Cardinal

Archbishop is he does not say that you have to go to church within your own boundaries. All he says is if you go to church outside of your boundaries, register there. So, we have a whole bunch of people from northern Virginia, Baltimore, and other places coming here because they like the welcoming. And I tell lesbians and gay men there are churches like Saint Augustine's in Washington, in the archdiocese, in other dioceses. Please, don't give up on "the church" because you've had a bad experience with "a church." Within this wonderful thing called the church, find a church that can be your church.

Chapter 15

Rev. Dr. Renee L. Hill

*R*enee L. Hill is the senior associate minister for peace and justice at All Saints Episcopal Church in Pasadena, California.
Founded in 1882, it is now the largest Episcopal congregation in
the Western United States. The church declares that "the vision
which unites us is our commitment to be a progressive church of
God's inclusive love, rejoicing in our diversity, ministering to one
another's needs, challenging injustice and oppression, animated
by the heart, mind, and ministry of Christ."[1] Its Peace and Justice
Ministries includes programs for abused women, elementary and
high school tutoring, the environment, HIV/AIDS, children-at-
risk, lesbian/gay/bisexual/transgendered people, hunger and homelessness, substance abuse, intercultural and international relations,
and combating racism.

Rev. Dr. Hill received her Ph.D. from Union Theological
Seminary. She has served as assistant priest at Saint Mary's
Episcopal Church in Harlem, as assistant for youth and outreach
ministries at Saint Ann's Episcopal Church in the South Bronx, as
associate priest at the Cathedral of Saint John the Divine in
Manhattan, and as assistant professor of theology and director of
studies in feminist liberation theologies at Episcopal Divinity
School in Cambridge, Massachusetts. In 1995, she was one of two
women from the United States to participate in the "Beijing Young
Women Leaders Program" at the United Nations Fourth World
Conference on Women. Her writing has been anthologized in several collections, and her essay, "Who Are We for Each Other? Sex,
Sexuality, and Womanist Theology," is generally regarded as having
broken the ground for discussing the issues of lesbians and gay men
in the Black church.[2]

Were you raised Episcopalian?

No. I wasn't raised in any church.

Oh, really. How interesting! How did you get to seminary?

I felt really called to it. From the time I was very young, I was a pre-
cocious, spiritual kid. I wasn't raised in the church, mostly, I think,
because both my parents were. My father was raised in the Baptist
Church in the South and my mom in the Congregational Church in
Washington, D.C. Like a lot of kids, they didn't have great experiences
in church. When we came along, they didn't want to make us go to
church and they had long left the church. But I had a natural spirituality,
and I was also looking at doing social justice work, which was very
much connected to me through faith commitments. I went to Bryn Mawr,
which isn't a Quaker college but is in the midst of a lot of Quakers, and
I picked up on a lot of social justice through Quakerism and hung out in
Quaker meetings a little bit. I was also really attracted to the ritual and
liturgy of the Episcopal church. What's ironic is the first Episcopal
church I went to and really loved was a very conservative Anglo-
Catholic parish (*laughs*) in Rosemont, Pennsylvania. It's one of the leaders of anti-everything. I learned only in the end—I wasn't a regular
parishioner there; I went for holidays and so forth—that they were
opposed to women's ordination, which shocked me.

I wasn't raised in church, but I was attracted to and pursued the connection between religious life and social justice. I was actually headed
towards law school and made a change when I went to work for the
Quakers in Washington, D.C. I was a lobbying intern on the Hill doing
domestic economic justice work for the Friends Committee on National
Legislation. Then I did a little work for the National Council of Churches
and for Church Women United for two years and discerned that I did not
want to go to law school; I wanted to go to seminary. So, there's nothing
in how I was raised that would put me where I am. There's got to be
something about the Spirit in there.

*After being on the faculty at Episcopal Divinity School (EDS) for two
years, are you pleased to be back in a parish?*

Yes. It's hard for me, because I was spoiled when I was at Union in
terms of doing academic work and also working at St. Mary's for three
years, at St. Anne's for a few years, and at the Cathedral of Saint John the

Divine for about a year. I was able to do my parish-based, community-based work and also study and write. Doing both was a lot easier when I was a student than when working full-time. I miss being able to do both. While I'm enjoying parish work, I'm also trying to figure out how to continue to do scholarly work. I will probably teach again, either teaching while I'm working in the parish or teaching full-time, but my career will probably go in and out, both parish and academia.

What kind of work do you see yourself doing or wanting to do academically?

A lot of things, everything (*laughs*). I get pigeonholed a lot to talk about sexuality because I'm an out lesbian who's theologically trained, ordained, and willing to talk about it. I am very interested in the wholeness and multiplicity of issues around justice and how we do that kind of whole-justice work theologically. My doctoral dissertation addressed that, but my constructive work in it wasn't as strong as it needed to be, and I think it's getting stronger. So, I would probably do more constructive work around what form theology would actually take in faith communities committed to justice for the totality of creation. That's a piece of it.

I'm also very interested in looking at religion in the African Diaspora more broadly than what gets represented in religious studies around people of African descent, which is really Christianity—period. I want to look at the different layers and expressions of religion in the African Diaspora in this country and in the Caribbean. I want to learn how to make ethnographic films on religion.

My big interest is in religion and politics, in what motivates people to do change work. I've done work with undergraduates on religion and social change, hopefully showing people how religion can be relevant and useful for positive social change because now we're seeing a lot of the right-wing activity, and they're very successful in doing their own kind of change work, but it's not necessarily what I would consider to be positive or progressive.

Why do you think the right wing is successful?

I think they're really well-organized politically in terms of understanding how to do grassroots organizing in profound ways. Getting people to vote, to write letters, and to develop the political machine around that activity do matter. They also articulate their theology and use of the

Bible so much more effectively than liberals or progressives. That's a real weakness that we have. What's really interesting about working in a parish, particularly this size where you do a lot of adult education, is seeing where people's theological and biblical knowledge was stunted. What they learned in Sunday school as children is a lot of what they operate out of as adults. I'm talking well-educated people. People don't know about biblical criticism or about different expressions of liberation theology.

I'm interested in parish-based education that gives people the tools for change and for critical thinking about their own faith, because I've found in parishes a lot of internal conflict around being Christian, especially for gay people. Where does that come from? From being a kid in the church and not learning anything different, from not developing your own critical thinking around these issues. How can you "talk back" to the scripture when you weren't taught how to as a child? Parish-based education is about doing scholarly work with people to heal that. How do you work with people who got really messed up about religion as kids, still want to continue it because they sense there's something empowering and important there, but don't know how to begin to interrogate their own faith because we were taught to obey, not to interrogate? For me, developing critical-thinking skills around faith commitments is very important and fascinating.

Can you say something about what you mean when you say "faith commitments"?

It is knowing, first of all, what you believe and why you believe it and, then, how that motivates you to act in the world. A big concern of mine is how to reflect theologically on our political work. What commitments are you making out of your faith, out of what you believe? For example, if I believe that God intends for there to be peace and justice for all of God's creation, then I want to use that belief as a primary category or principle out of which I would do my political work. So, because of that belief, I need to be concerned about Headstart Programs in a community other than my own, since God intends peace and justice for all three-year-olds. To see that as important and be engaged in doing something about it is a faith commitment. It's about relating actions for justice in the world to my belief.

I'm concerned with faith commitments because my own journey has always connected faith, religion, and spirituality with social justice. It's my connection with church. I don't understand any other way. I'm not totally sure how I got that way. Maybe it was from reading Thomas

Merton[3] when I was twelve. But getting people to make those connections helps us to sustain our justice work and faith during incredible setbacks and disappointments. What sustains you when you're going through a Lambeth convention when people are voting on the worthiness of your being as a gay person? There's a spiritual root there that's really important. It keeps you motivated, keeps you going, keeps you alive.

Why do I stay in this work? Well, I think there's definitely a calling from God. It's not because I'm richly rewarded with praise every day. I can't remember whose quote this is, but "The point is not winning; it's being faithful." Trying to move people there. The other thing is that Christianity is a set of many ideas that are to be interrogated. You can question this stuff, you don't have to believe me. When I preach on Sunday, you don't have to believe a word I say. From teaching at EDS and in other settings, I've seen that people do need to articulate what they do believe. You find lots of people who can say what they don't believe; that's easy, a child can do that. Mature faith requires people being able to say what they do believe, and that is something that evolves and changes.

Are you surprised to hear that your essay in Cone and Wilmore's anthology, Black Theology,[4] *has been pivotal for a lot of people, including Jackie Grant and Kelly Brown Douglas? Sometimes we do something seemingly small and don't realize the impact or power it has to change the way people think and act.*

Yes. It's interesting, because Kelly's book on sexuality starts off quoting that essay,[5] which I wrote as a paper for a class *(laughs)*. A lot of people have turned to that. That's why I probably need to do more academic work and writing. People do get charged by small things like that. I preached for Stonewall 30[6] this year at the Cathedral of Saint John the Divine in New York, and I've gotten a lot of feedback about that—and it was a five-minute homily! I do have a sense that the essay I wrote was important, particularly in church circles and for womanist scholarship, because it was really a challenge to womanists about sexuality.

What was it about All Saints in Pasadena that attracted you or that attracted them to you?

I think they were attracted to me because I'm sort of a complete package for them. First of all, I was not very satisfied with my position at EDS. Being on the faculty kept me from doing community work. I met

Ed Bacon, the rector of All Saints, at the last general convention very briefly and then got a letter from him saying he was trying to recruit people for some positions. He wasn't recruiting me specifically at all, but the description was to do peace and justice work in a large parish, and that description looked really interesting to me. I had done this type of community organizing work in the church before in small, poor parishes in Harlem and in the Bronx, and I thought it would be a good experience for me to work somewhere that had a lot of resources, real access to money, and a very large congregation. I said I was interested, and Ed was very excited about that. They really wanted a person of color, and I am the only person of color among the clergy staff. They wanted someone who is an out lesbian; I come with a partner and a child. I think we're an attractive set for them. My partner also works here; she's in charge of children and family ministry. She is an ex-Presbyterian, having resigned her ordination in the Presbyterian Church because of its anti-gay position, and is now pursuing ordination in the Episcopal Church. Mary and I have been together for twelve years. So, we come as a lesbian family, we've got a great kid, we have a lot of good experience, and we are well educated.

Were your earlier parishes predominantly Black Episcopalian congregations?

St. Mary's in Harlem is. St. Anne's in the South Bronx is predominantly Latino—Puerto Rican and Dominican, and the older part of that congregation is West Indian and African American. Both of those churches have Spanish and English services.

Were you were out as a lesbian when pastoring those churches?

Not to the extent that I am here. When we were hired and introduced to the congregation, we were both brought up with our daughter: "Here is Renee and her partner." At St. Mary's, it wasn't as discussed. I wasn't ever closeted—I came out in college when I was nineteen—but there wasn't the same kind of focus on our sexual identity. Mary also worked at St. Mary's and was there before me. She ran the Sunday school. We were always together and were seen as partners. We took our daughter back to St. Mary's to be baptized. They talked about us both being parents to Helena. I think for them it wasn't as big a focal point as it is here for us to be a lesbian couple and be out. And the same with St. Anne's. I worked for Roberto Morales, and he knew us as a lesbian couple and that was fine with him. He sponsored me for ordination, and again nothing was hidden, but it also wasn't a big topic of discussion like here.

I want to pursue something with you, if you don't mind. The pastors I've interviewed often say something along the lines of, "Lesbians and gays have always been in our congregations, but it's never been made a big point." They say that church is about being part of the community and not about flaunting any particular difference. They're candid in admitting that there may be a bad side to this in terms of silencing or making some people less visible, but the community takes priority over the individual. Am I hearing that correctly?

I think that's true. And I also look at the economic class of those parishes. Louis Barrios started a lesbian/gay ministry at St. Anne's, where we had an incredible group of Black and Latino people who did not want to go down to the Lesbian/Gay Community Services Center in Manhattan, because it wasn't their neighborhood, but who would come to something in the South Bronx. Louis is a Black Puerto Rican, very pro-gay, a very radical guy, just incredible. I'll never forget the first meeting we had. There were forty to fifty people who turned out—all kinds of gay, lesbian, and transsexual people of varying camps. And it was no big deal for the church. I think they had greater concerns about other issues: violence against the children, drugs, getting enough food. These were much more paramount, and there was definitely a different thing about community. I mean, All Saints is economically secure. I'm sure there are people here who are not, but for the most part we're talking about upper-middle-class and wealthy people who don't have to focus so much on basic survival issues and can get into the politics of sexual identity in a different way.

What I see in white churches—and I think it's true here, too—is that a lot of people go for where they feel most marginalized, where they feel most victimized; and here, for example, I don't see a lot of struggle against racism, particularly among the white gay community. As I see it, they couldn't care less. There's one church here in California that's predominantly white gay men, and you've got to ask yourself, "Why aren't there any gay and lesbian people of color there?" I don't think they're really all that interested in race. Some of what I'm very concerned about is how people deal with multiplicities of oppression, internalized oppression. How do you really have a church or a community that is fully inclusive, where one oppression isn't more important than the other? I see that dynamic at work also where you may have lesbian and gay people of color just being there, relating as people of color, and not feeling welcome when white gay people are in a prominent position.

Can you say more about the multiplicity of oppressions?

It's interesting particularly if you are a person of color and gay or lesbian and you go into a faith community of color where sexuality is either ignored, vilified, or downplayed. You're there as a person of color. Or if you go to a predominantly white church where you can be gay and out, but people aren't necessarily paying attention to your race. It says to me those major bodies are not paying attention to the complexities of oppression and identity or even celebrating what is in their midst. That's where people get stuck—in between. Within the gay community there is a community of color that is lesbian and gay; but when people talk about gay people, they're really talking about white people. I think that if someone really wants to connect as a gay man or a lesbian to the broader lesbian and gay community, you have to be concerned about racism and classism, and folks aren't doing that very well. They have not been able to do a simultaneous struggle working on different oppressions and identities. That's why we always have oppression, because people can't root it out and see its multiple roots.

It seems, then, that lesbians and gay men of color have a set of experiences that make them the ideal or the most equipped community builders, and you're one of them. Do you see you and people like you moving into those kind of leadership positions?

Yes and no. Part of my burden in life is to be that kind of "bridge person." I hate it and get tired of it after a while, but it's also true that real change will never happen unless people are willing to follow this type of leadership. I have been speaking about it for years and trying to work on it here, and people just say, "Yeah, yeah, yeah." They can kind of intellectually get it, but people don't want to actually work on the places where they engage in or perpetuate oppressions. I think that folks are reluctant to look at where they contribute to oppressions. White gay people go right to "I'm oppressed as a white gay man," but they're not going to look at how they contribute to racism. I have to tend to my identity of being middle class; I need to look at how I contribute to classism and to what's happening with poor people. That's important for me. It doesn't take away from whatever experience and pain I have as a Black lesbian, but I have to own up to it as well.

There is a unique role for leadership, and I find there is also incredible resistance all the way around for people to be guided by that leadership. Some people are interested in it, and yet they can't get beyond feeling guilty about who they are. I'm really concerned in the Episcopal Church about pushes for same-sex blessings and so forth that are not attached to continuing discussions around gender oppression, racism, and classism. To me, not having that kind of discussion makes the gay issue moot. What kind of discussion are you having when you're not able to talk about justice for all people? I think that lesbians and gay men of color do have a unique leadership role, but there has to be a receiver for the information; and what I've experienced is a lot of resistance right now. That may change, but it's going to be a real struggle and people like me get tired. I go in and out of being willing to talk about it. People ask me to speak and lead workshops all the time, and I do when I'm not feeling totally exhausted.

Where do you find hope? Are there examples in the church of people getting off their butts and really tending to these things?

I think people are doing the work in little places here and there. There are individuals who are trying to get it and to do that work. That's one of the reasons I can still stay in the church for now. There is some movement and willingness to listen. But what happens is that people panic, like what's going to happen in the Episcopal Church is a lot of panic around same-sex blessings in our general convention. People will get galvanized around this one issue without looking at the multi-layers of it. Progressive, liberal people have not learned to strategize and work for justice in a comprehensive way. The Right has, but progressives and liberals get into a defensive stance really quickly and are not able to do the kind of proactive coalition building that needs to happen in a serious way. Some people are getting it. I'm thinking about a leader like Elizabeth Kaeton at the Oasis in New Jersey, who I think has really great politics.[6] She's a white woman who understands racism. There are these little pockets of people saying, "Hey, wait a second; don't forget this other part of the problem."

In our church the leadership is definitely getting older, and there is a moment now where younger leaders and leaders of color who are progressive people have a opportunity to come in, step up, and say we need to have a different vision and a way of working that involves real coalition building. They also need to be very deft at working with issues of identity.

The conservatives in the church are fighting real hard not to change and, instead, to move backward, to pretend that cultural diversity, gender, and sexual orientation don't matter. I mean, all discussions around gay ordination to me are silly with the number of gay people who are actually ordained. We're having these retro discussions, and some people are just saying, "Wait a second, the train has moved ahead here." We need to see where we really are and to work with the realities of who and where we are, which is that the Episcopal Church is global and diverse in its sexual orientation, race, and class. We need to recognize and build a globalized community and respond out of that reality rather than the reality of the Episcopal Church in 1952.

So, my hope is in there being an open historical moment right now. I think the next five or ten years is going to tell us a lot about where we're going and whether or not the church is relevant. And the relevancy is going to be around how open and honest we're able to be. It's an integrity issue about who's already in the room that we're not acknowledging. I think that's where we are. I see hope in that, and I feel a lot of danger in it, too. I'm just looking and trying to do my contribution without getting clobbered.

Do you think the Episcopal Church is better positioned than some other denominations to be open to that?

Yes, maybe. I don't know a lot about other denominations. I think our polity—our diocesan structure—gives us an opportunity to do that, even though some people think that makes us more conservative. We have a general convention that gets together to talk about things for the national church, but bishops in different dioceses can do things differently from each other. There isn't one ruling body, as in the Presbyterian Church where the rules came down saying if you're gay and ordained after 1972 you can't be ordained anymore, you're not legal, which is why my partner left in protest. The bishops in our dioceses can decide who they're going to ordain, and whatever the national church says is not necessarily binding. Most people don't understand, for example, that the anti-gay position taken at the international Lambeth convention this year is not binding on the church. It may be upsetting, but it doesn't have legislative power. Some people will say that bishops are just part of and conforming to the hierarchical system. There is hierarchy there for sure—and there are anti-gay bishops—but I think the hierarchy provides for a kind of flexibility that other churches don't necessarily have.

You talked about helping people to see religion as a formation for social change, social justice, and political engagement. How can and does a eucharistic tradition like that of the Episcopal Church do that?

That's a big question (*laughs*). Briefly, when we gather together as a communion, when we've heard the Word and we're gathering together at the table, why are we there? We're being formed together as a community of people. We're sharing something, and something happens when we're all sharing it. You make Eucharist with a community; you don't do it in the privacy of your own home. You do it in a gathering of people. So, first, there is this gathering of people who have a common experience and hopefully have come to the table, reconciled with each other, after confession. But, secondly, you don't keep it in the church. This is my big thing. You don't stay in the building; you actually go out into the world taking the experience of having communion with each other and with God.

The Eucharist is really important to me and is why I'm Episcopalian and not something else. It is a very powerful symbol of people who may not have been reconciled all week but come together as a community and then take from the table that communion out into the world. It gives you an anchor, a heart, a center, a way of connecting with people. You are relating to your sisters and brothers in that faith community, and people begin to unpack that, to think about who is around them—gay, straight, Black, white, Latino, Asian, men, women, right-wingers, left-wingers. Everybody is coming to the table together to share in that act of making the Eucharist and communion with God. What's the metaphor? This is the dress rehearsal for the kingdom of God. That's what that is. And a lot of people aren't awake to that, which is why you've got to preach about it, touch people by it.

The other thing, which is something I learned from Cone, is to look around, see who is not at the table, and ask why. That's the reason that one piece of my theological methodology is self-reflection/self-criticism—not in a way to beat yourself up but to notice who is not there, who is silent, who is present in the church but not coming forward and why. How is this community constructed in a way that anybody is being left out or made silent? That symbol alone can be a much larger symbol in the whole world. It's a very powerful symbol about presence and absence, silence and speaking.

Do you think that lesbians and gay men may have to do more work on issues which are not specifically gay-related, for example, a gay minister working on homelessness as an openly gay person but not because it's a gay issue?

Yes. I think it needs to happen. That's exactly what I'm talking about in terms of being able to handle a multiplicity of justice work. Absolutely, because that's the only way I do coalition building. It can't just be about me me me. If my issues are paramount over yours, all I'm going to worry about is my same-sex blessing. It's also theologically incorrect, in terms of justice work, to be concerned about only one area of justice. I think you have to be able to work on all areas of justice work without any expectation of "I'm going to get something back for me personally." What you get back is the fact that you worked on a justice issue and that's what you're called to do—period. If you're a gay person working on homelessness or antischool violence, you're supposed to be doing that. That's what we're called to do.

The good thing, what we don't expect, is down the road. Non-gay people will say, "Well, working on hate crimes against gay people is in fact a justice issue." So, the same is true for straight people. They need to be working on these issues from a fact of human rights, human justice, justice for all creation. It's not just about my little pot of gold that I have to hang on to. We all have to be working on issues that don't necessarily directly affect us but do in fact affect us all as human beings. To get out, meet people, make friends, find out what the issues are, do some organizing and strategizing around a whole multiplicity of issues will take us really far. It also helps us to understand where and how these issues are connected. You're not going to find homophobia and not find sexism, and you'll probably also find racism. They almost always travel together.

What do you think makes you a good pastor?

I think a lot has to do with my ability to see a lot of things at once. I think a lot of it has to do with who I am as a person with multiple dimensions, that I can be empathetic around that. I have learned about shades of gray, that I don't believe that either you are all good or all bad. People make mistakes and people do things better. That has to do with having had to grow up to be able to see shades of gray. I can be sympathetic and empathetic and I can give people a break, because I know that that's life. From all my experiences of integration, of loss and celebration around just who I am and the communities that I've worked and walked in, I'm able to accept a lot of life. Trying hard to resist perfectionism for myself and other people . . . I think that is what helps me to be a better pastor. I'm still working on it.

PART IV

Reflection and Prophecy

Chapter 16

Rev. Dr. James H. Cone

*J*ames H. Cone is the Charles A. Briggs Distinguished Professor of Systematic Theology at Union Theological Seminary in New York City. He received his Ph.D. from Northwestern University and is an ordained minister in the African Methodist Episcopal (AME) Church. He is the author of many books, including the groundbreaking *Black Theology and Black Power* in 1969 and the definitive *A Black Theology of Liberation* in 1970. His more recent work includes *Martin and Malcolm and America: A Dream or a Nightmare?* in 1992 and *Risks of Faith: The Emergence of a Black Theology of Liberation, 1968–1998* in 1999.[1] Professor Cone's area of research and teaching is Christian theology, with special attention to Black theology; the theologies of Africa, Asia, and Latin America; and twentieth-century European-American theologies. He is generally credited as the first scholar to develop systematically a theology based on the African American experience of oppression and quest for liberation.[2] For many years Professor Cone has been an active participant in the Ecumenical Association of Third World Theologians (EATWOT), an organization with members from Africa, Asia, Latin America, the Caribbean, and racial minorities in the United States.[3] He is listed in *Who's Who among African Americans.*[4]

Personally and professionally, when did you first come to see that lesbian and gay issues should be recognized and integrated into your work?

I recognized the issues before I could do something with them in my work, because doing so required more than what I knew in my personal life. I had yet to read about the issues and acquire the language for scholarly discussion. There were some graduate students here during the early 1980s who brought me closer to it. An M.Div. student by the name of Macky Alston did an independent study with me on gays. I was the director for his study, and that's when I first got into the literature. But Dan Spencer, a doctoral student and one of my teaching assistants, was the main person. Dan had been here as an M.Div. student, and we had worked together then in terms of his own liberation, commitment, and identity. When he came back in the Ph.D. program (1990) and we worked together, I realized it was absolutely necessary for me to include material on the gay and lesbian experience. Dan was the first one to provide the bridge for my gap between personal and academic knowledge. Dan was the sophisticated guide. He knew the literature, knew gay history, and gave me key works to read. So I began to stumble along and to make lesbian and gay issues a part of my classes. Before then I knew they were important to me, but I didn't quite know how to get hold of them because I was so involved in Black theology.[5]

I also knew about the connection between gay and African American issues because of James Tinney.[6] He and I were close friends. He was just about the first gay African American minister to address this issue openly and publicly. I used to go and see him at Howard University—he was there before he died in the early '80s—and also to support him in his ministry. He also spoke at Union. We have all had experiences of dealing with gay and lesbian people from the time when we were small. And I've always had close friends who were gay, but we didn't talk about it that much. The Protestant chaplain at the first school—Philander Smith College in Little Rock, Arkansas—where I taught was gay. He didn't talk about it, but everybody knew and he was my closest friend at that time. But it's one thing to have close friends and remain silent about it; it's another thing to begin to address it openly, and that began to happen for me in the late '80s and early '90s.

Sometimes that situation where everyone knows but it's not spoken about is looked back on negatively. Do you think it's possible that it in fact laid a foundation or that there was something positive about that situation?

I think it's positive to me personally. I'm not sure it's positive for the social implications, because it's like being racist and being silent about it—knowing it's there and not talking about it. But I think it can be positive in personal relationships by providing the opportunity to know people you love who are gay. Even though we didn't talk about it, these relationships enabled me to know what I ought to be doing that I wasn't doing when the issue became really public. At Union Seminary it's hard to ignore what's going on around you. And that happened to me with the feminist movement, with the gay movement, with other people-of-color movements. You're almost forced, if you have any human sensitivity, to say where you stand. I think my early positive experience enabled me to feel more surefooted about where I should be. And yet, to me it wasn't difficult to know where I should be standing. I never, ever thought I shouldn't be standing there. And I felt that way with women, too, but I didn't always have the language and the knowledge in order to speak in a graduate-school setting. I remember when I first started stumbling through and trying to talk about gay issues. It was not easy to find and use the language in such a way that the people who embodied that experience would know that I was serious.

You said that Dan Spencer was important as the person who could help you begin to find the language.

Yes, he gave me the literature. I said, "Dan, look, I've got to address this." He was my teaching assistant. He actually gave me a bibliography to read about the history. So, I read the literature. I needed to learn something about the history. When did the issue emerge? When did the silence begin to be broken? What's the nature of the historical development of the movement? I started to realize the impact of World War II and the Civil Rights movement, the significance of the Stonewall Riots[7] and of AIDS. It gave me a sense of "Now I know where I am." I could see parallels with the Black Power movement and its language of militancy versus the conservative NAACP approach. I was able to find the language because of the similarities, but at the same time I wasn't a part of that experience in terms of its movement, so I still had to find my way into it in a way that I felt very comfortable talking about it. And that took a little while, about three or four years, before I knew where I was standing and could teach about it.

What were the early years of doing this like?

Oh, I was stumbling (*laughs*). There was one lecture I remember in particular. I was using James Baldwin and some other people to try to find the language; and by the time I finished that lecture, one student—a gay man—stood up and said to me, "You don't know a damn thing about gay people." He just came at me with all the hostility I could imagine. The only thing I could see as comparable was me getting mad when some white man tries to talk about Black people and doesn't know what he's talking about. There were about seventy people in that class. I let him finish, and that's when I knew where I had to stand. I said, "Look, you may be right and I may not know what I am talking about, but I know what's in my heart. And if you don't see what's in my heart, then you don't know me, because in my heart I am exactly where you are. I'm not trying to talk about gay issues just because you're gay and I want to express solidarity with you. I talk because this is a part of my humanity, and nobody is going to keep me from struggling with defining who I am, because I am connected to you and everybody else in this class. And each of us has to find a way to communicate with each other. I know I'm just stumbling here, but if you can't see my heart, then I don't know where your heart is." And it was at that moment that the spirit broke through for me and also with that class, and he really became a very close friend after that. And I think students after that began to see that I was serious.

You mentioned Dan Spencer. What is it that makes him a person who can bridge the gap?

Dan is quite the smart one. Dan is interested in other people. He's interested in African American history, in women's issues, in people of color, in a broad range of different people's concerns. His capacity to understand Black history or Black theology, his willingness to dialogue, and his sense of knowing my desire to do the same make it easier for me to bridge with him, because he is so genuine about his humanity and about his connection with other people. I felt that before I knew that he was gay. And I felt it even stronger afterward. When you meet somebody who is reaching out to others and who knows that others are connected with him—not because he wants to help them, but because our humanity is interconnected and what happens to others happens to you indirectly or directly—it's not hard for you to feel solidarity and empathy with him. Dan was that kind of person from the start, someone who was not just locked up in what he was about: his people, his group. Rather, he was involved with what it means to be human. That's the kind of person who can bridge the gaps between people, between difference.

Can you say more about your own background and experience that made you a likely candidate to bridge gaps, especially the one with lesbians and gay men?

I think there is something in the history of African Americans that's deep, that's embedded, that enables them to have solidarity with other people who are also hurt and wounded. Because of a history of slavery and segregation, it's easier for them, if they open up to the sensitivity to it in their culture, to make that bridge. So, I think it comes from Black religion, Black culture. I don't ever remember not feeling solidarity with people who are hurt. I don't care what color they were. I was taught that, and I've taught it in my community.

I grew up in the South in a small community, and we were taught that nobody else should experience hurt without you being there sharing that hurt. My mother couldn't understand why people were oppressing gay people. She was not sophisticated, but she just knew it was not right to be hurting people like that. People had a right to define themselves. I never heard her say a negative thing about anybody in that way. I remember once a woman got pregnant and was not married. I was a little kid, about seven or eight, and I said, "Well, you know what she's been doing"; and my mother looked at me and said, "You don't know nothing." She said, "There are others who ain't pregnant, and they been doing more than she's been doing." She corrected me in a way to say that I had no right to make any kind of judgment on this young woman. And she would do that in any setting. So, for me to reach out to people who are suffering or to say a word on their behalf is natural for me. I don't ever remember being converted to it.

Now, I must admit that I haven't always seen soon enough how not to lose my own identity and also embrace the language of all-inclusiveness. In a graduate-school setting, it's tougher to find that balance when the discourse emerges out of the movement itself and not from your own direct involvement with the people in it. You have to study it. It's more than just going on the basis of your own instinct, even though the natural instinct is to embrace "the other," especially the one not treated well.

Some who come out of the Black tradition of empathy for oppressed people can't or won't make the connection, the jump, to include gay people.

That's right. One of the reasons why they cannot make it is because the religion that Black people have is also one that is strongly influenced by the language of conservative white evangelicals, who are strongly anti-gay, who are literalists, fundamentalist types. As long as Blacks were segregated from white evangelicals, not worshiping with them, Black people were not as literal in their interpretation of the scripture. You didn't find

Blacks debating science and trying to prove truth against science, as with creationism and evolution. That debate never happened in the Black church. There has always been a belief in "Yes, the Bible is true," but not in the sense that you have a fixed set of doctrines that have to be tested out against science. With the emergence of the Civil Rights movement, white conservatives decided that a token Black presence in their community was positive politically. They don't want to be seen as racists. So, now you find conservative leaders, such as Jerry Falwell and Ralph Reed, recruiting Black ministers.[8]

Some Black people, because they've been shut out of white religion, sort of rush over to the side of white conservatives, because their language is so familiar. Blacks don't have sophisticated theologians to tell them that everything that *looks* like truth is not *really* the truth. So, when they join the community of white conservatives, the only thing they watch out for is racism. You don't have to tell them about that. Blacks can discern and are suspicious of racism, but not homophobia. We lack a tradition of critical theological inquiry and, as a result, don't know what questions to ask. White Christianity alienated African Americans from their own Black experience, and thus they are easily swayed to become virulently anti-gay. White conservatives point out things in the Bible that are anti-anything, except racism, and some Blacks go along and turn out to be far more reactionary than the white conservatives whom they join. That is largely due to their separation from their own Black tradition of solidarity with the oppressed of any group. I read in the newspaper about an AME pastor in Florida who saw the Klan marching against gays, and he said, "If I knew that was the only thing they were marching against, I'd march with them."[9] So blinded. His own anti-gay feelings have been so internalized. And that's been at least partly influenced by the religious right, which now is accepting and recruiting Blacks into its ranks.

Could you give me an example of the similar language of Black pastors and white evangelicals?

The language has to do with spirituality, the focus on Jesus as the sole savior, on salvation, on the Bible, on being able to show you what's right and wrong by pointing to the Scriptures. The one thing Blacks can't be swayed on biblically is the acceptance of slavery, but they will be swayed by the so-called anti-gay passages—like citing Sodom and Gomorrah or Leviticus, pointing to the Bible and saying, "That shows it's so." And they've adopted that kind of evangelical spirit and feel of certainty. It's the kind of certainty that, I think, poor people especially want, and their daily life does not provide it. Conservatives give them that certainty. They don't find it in a more progressive approach where intellectual sophistication and resources sustain you in considering many possibilities. If you don't have much, you can still know the Bible is there and Jesus is there. So, that book—the Bible—acquires a sacredness that provides the kind of certainty you won't get anywhere else.[10]

Most whites don't need that certainty, because their life in this world is not as vulnerable. But people in Harlem need it. They don't know where their rent is coming from, they have to worry about police abuse, they have a lot to worry about, so when they go to church they say, "This is one thing I can count on. The Bible says this." I see Blacks using this little bit of certainty in an individual sense—to hold onto something, so they can survive in this troubled world. But white conservatives are not facing that kind of a situation at all. All they want is control of the world. They have political power and want more of it. You don't see Black conservatives searching for that. They know they can't get that. They want just enough power to be able to find meaning in life, and the Bible, Jesus, and the worship context itself become a center of meaning for them that enables them to have it. In finding that meaning, they will adopt language and attitudes very much like the white conservatives, even though they are not the same. They're not responding to the same experience that gives birth to their spirituality.

Now, the other side of that is that some African Americans are in leadership positions with some social and political power, and they can and have used it to express support for lesbians and gay men. Some people think that African American clergy may have more credibility on gay issues, because they are perceived as having deeper faith and more genuine spirituality than white clergy.

That's why I feel a responsibility to speak. I know the Black church context, and I always try to bring up the subject when I speak in that context. Sometimes my doing so elicits heated debates, and other times people just don't bother to respond; but for the ones who are gay, it may provide a kind of space for them to begin to articulate their life and place in the church. I think we should use our power for freedom and use whatever influence we have in a very positive way. I know that there are more Black gay and lesbian students here than in other seminaries, but there are also quite a few Black students who are not quite vocally anti-gay, but certainly not gay-supportive. They won't say anything in my classes when I speak on gay issues; but privately I have talked to some of them, and they are influenced by the white conservative approach, even though they don't want to acknowledge it.

I feel it's my responsibility to speak. Therefore, when the Black and gay people-of-color caucus held a meeting about the Black church and homosexuality two weeks ago in the chapel, I felt I should speak, not just because they asked me to, but I also thought I should identify and let people know where I stand. I think on all issues dealing with human life and suffering, we are obligated to take a stand. I just regret sometimes that I didn't do it more quickly, particularly about women. It was about 1975, I think, before I realized I should speak up for women's issues, not that I had said anything against women, but I hadn't come out in support of women's issues the way I should have. And about gays I should have spoken out sooner, and I ask myself why I didn't. As I said before, part of it has to do with not having the language to do so, and part of it has to do with not wanting to detract from what I was doing in my own particular community. But, you know, fighting for justice anywhere always empowers a struggle for justice everywhere. So, it is never disconnected, it is always interrelated. Only after you see those connections will you really be able to understand what your own struggle is about.

Do you tell your students that you should have come to it sooner? Just as I think there is power in your speaking for the lesbian/gay experience, there is also power in your saying that this is something that you had to stumble and work through. It's not just that students have to "get it"; it's more that they have a process with which they can work through issues.

Right. And I talk about that process for myself, particularly dealing with women, gays, and other people's struggles as well. I think it's very important for public figures to say when they were wrong and when they should've spoken out and didn't. And I tell my students that. I talk about that a lot, because I use my own earlier texts in my classes so they see for themselves. I left the sexist language in the twentieth anniversary edition of *Black Theology and Black Power* just so they can see it and know what it was, to see the movement of my change and to talk about it. I wrote about the need to acknowledge mistakes and changes in my theological perspectives in *My Soul Looks Back*; and I also talk about it a lot in class as a teacher, because we need to realize that we aren't suddenly given the truth or that we always had it. Doing theology is a process of growth and development where you learn from life and from other people. And if you really believe that, then you can't possibly stay the same.

I like the way Malcolm X put it. He says, "My life is a chronology of changes." And that's what mine is. We are obligated to talk about those changes and how we got there. What bothers me sometimes is theologians don't talk about their own process. They talk about where they are now, but not about how they got there. It's important for students to know that development takes time.

I'm teaching a class right now on Martin and Malcolm with white, Black, and Third World students. I told them my job is to create a context in which they can talk freely about their true feelings regarding the issues that are raised. They can differ and they can learn from each other. And everything is permissible as long as you do the hard reading, are really committed to truth, to justice, to life, and really want to learn from others. We don't have to have everybody thinking the same way. It would be a boring world if we did. Teaching theology is about giving voice to people and helping people find their voice. It's not about my voice. My voice should elicit theirs. It's a process for the purpose of bringing their voices out.

Gay experience tends to get universalized as white, and a lot—probably most—of white gay people don't understand what it is to be African American and gay. Do you have any advice or any observations about what's wrong there and what has to happen for the gap to be bridged?

I say this not only to white gay people and lesbians: I think we're all obligated to make connections with other people we love and care about. So, I know who you love by who you make connections to. If the gay movement is primarily white, and it's been that way for a long while, that means they love white people. They don't mean to say that they hate Blacks, but they love white people and they aren't bothered that Black people are not around. That's pretty typical of white experience in the world generally. In America whites have never felt that they needed Black people, but Blacks have grown up knowing that they are a minority in this society. Therefore, their well-being is connected to white people. So, we naturally reach out to other people. Whites don't naturally reach out to anybody. Gays may be an oppressed group within the white community, but they don't see that connection with Black people. The same thing happened with the women's group. They were mainly a white group of women with very genuine issues and concerns but who didn't make connection with Black women an urgent matter. When they were confronted with this and embarrassed by it, some tried to do something about it to get rid of the shame. And I'm sure lesbians and gay men will do the same.

Now, I don't mean all individuals are that way, but the great majority are. So, most white movements are just that, *white* movements, because they tend to define the issues and then invite everybody else in to join the issues they've defined. You see, whites are not interested in creating an agenda or movement with other people, because whites have been in charge of this society and in the modern world. So, it's natural to think of white people in charge. It's just the way things are. It's been that way for five hundred years. So, a white person doesn't have to think that he's superior, he just acts that way. I think it's unexpressed, unarticulated. To see it in the gay community is not surprising. It's in every white context, including the church. Where white people are involved in significant numbers, they are running it.

So, what kind of message or what kind of hope do you give to African Americans who are lesbian and gay? This is a tough thing they're dealing with.

Yes, it is a tough thing. I do think that hope is always derived from struggle. There is no hope without struggle. You have to struggle in a way that life becomes meaningful. It's not about winning. It's about finding, searching, struggling for truth and for life and for justice. And doing that in a way that there is joy in that struggle. So, I think Black gays and lesbians are going to have to know that the struggle in their own Black community and in the gay community is going to be tough. Because the gay community is primarily white and the Black community is primarily heterosexual, how to be a part of both and each of those is hard, but you have to find a way of struggling as every oppressed group has to find.

I think the struggle should always be connected to other people who are not quite like you. I know when a struggle is genuine by what it connects itself with. When I see a struggle that's turned in on itself, I know there's something wrong with it, it's demonic, and it's going to self-destruct. What's kept the Civil Rights and Black Freedom movement alive is that it has been connected to many other movements. It spurned other movements and has been connected with other movements. When you talk about freedom, Black people are right there in the heart of defining what struggle is about in the modern world. And I am very proud of that. The women's movement, the gay movement, other people-of-color movements, almost every kind of movement you can think of in America has fed off of the African American movement. They found their language in that movement and in such things as the Civil Rights bill and Voting Rights bill. So, I look back and I say, "We gave the foundation for a lot of stuff here."[11] And other movements fed off that foundation and achieved their own independence, their own language, their own identity. While other movements didn't remain locked into our way of talking about freedom, they were influenced by the Black struggle for justice. We gave strength to their struggles. And that makes me really, really, really proud.

Can you give an example of a movement that has become so fixated on itself that it becomes demonic?

In thinking about my own community, extreme examples would be the kind of nationalism that is exclusive, rigid, and doesn't have the capacity for change. One of the great things about Malcolm X that made him so different from most people in the Black Muslim community is that he could change and did change.[12] He was one of the most popular speakers on college and university campuses, debating professors and engaging students. He was invited to Harvard three times. That in itself tells you what kind of person he was. He could learn. He could really debate. They're not going to invite you back if you're just going to be closed-minded and not really engage in dialogue. So, I think when a movement ceases to look beyond itself, it's on the road to being demonic. It will become what it is fighting against. The gay movement opens itself up for embracing racism when it doesn't reach beyond itself. Anytime you have an all-white group, that's a danger because it turns in on itself. You have to know that humanity is broad and diverse, and you need to be making those links outside yourself.

From what you were saying earlier about the Black movement as a foundation and source for other movements, it would seem that lesbian, bisexual, gay, and transgendered people who come out of the Black tradition would be an especially important resource for the gay movement, if it is truly to benefit humanity.

They would. Even when whites learn from us, it's hard for them to acknowledge it. There are so many fields in which this is true: music, sports, the freedom movements. We have made a distinctive contribution, but whites don't like to acknowledge that. That's why it took jazz so long to find a legitimate place in the art world without people having to ask if it really belongs there. And I find that reluctance also when most white writers appropriate our language of freedom, justice, and spirituality. I think it's hard to be in America and not be influenced by Black people, but acknowledging that influence seems difficult for white people. I think that if the white gay movement will just turn to Black gay people, it will have a resource and power that is deeply connected with an oppressed group that provides ways to make connections beyond itself. You can't grow just with your own experience. Only when you make connections beyond yourself will you grow. You'll grow by reaching out to others, who make you think about things you haven't thought about before and make you address issues you haven't addressed before. They make you ask questions you haven't asked before. It's no use staying within your group talking about the same things over and over again, going around the same circle, going nowhere. So, I would want to emphasize how important it is for any group to move beyond itself in order to become itself.

Have you seen the gay movement or gay people doing things that make you think that we're onto something that others could learn from?

Oh yes, I've learned a lot. I've learned a lot from people-of-color struggles, particularly in the Third World context, a lot from the women's movement about gender, and a lot from the gay movement, especially as it focuses on sexuality and the body. I remember it suddenly came to me one day when I was lecturing. I was talking about anti-gay attitudes and violence in the church and I said, "Here's a movement that makes love its center, and the church itself claims to be about love. And yet, since the church is so hostile to gays, it can't possibly be about love." Here you have body, spirit, all the dimensions of love at the center of a theology, at the center of a movement, and the church is rejecting it, even though the church itself claims that love is at its center. What a contradiction! Focusing on love and reading about it in gay and lesbian theology and experience really helped me to love my body a lot more, helped me to see the connection between pleasure and God, the deeply sacred part of my being and of our interconnectedness in this society. It helps me to like myself as a bodily human being with all the pleasures and feelings that I have when I'm connected with another person and to see my own passion, bodily passions connected with my own spiritual theological passions. To me, I think if you're not passionate about something you can't care that much about it. So, to have my theology passionate, engaging, and deeply felt, that can't be disconnected from my bodily passions, my sexual passions and love; and I see it all as one. The whole of life is like an orgasm. I love this life. And being able to embrace that openly and to talk about it and to think about it and to love myself definitely comes from reading about and learning from gay and lesbian people.

Chapter 17

Rev. Dr. Emilie M. Townes

An ordained American Baptist clergywoman, Emilie M. Townes received her Doctor of Ministry from the University of Chicago Divinity School and her Ph.D. from Northwestern University. For ten years she was a faculty member at Saint Paul School of Theology in Kansas City, Missouri. As professor of Christian social ethics and Black church ministries, she edited and authored five books that have developed the emerging field of womanist theology.[1] Kelly Brown Douglas, author of *Sexuality and the Black Church*, credits "womanist ethicist Emilie Townes" with being "vocal about the need to address matters of sexuality":

> Fueled by the potential for HIV/AIDS to virtually destroy Black families and communities, Townes urges the Black community to break the death-dealing cycle of "sexual repression"—that is, being sexually active yet refusing to speak about sexual matters. She says such sexual repression is indeed killing the community as it allows for misunderstanding the relationship between HIV/AIDS and homosexuality.[2]

At the time of the interview, Rev. Dr. Townes had recently arrived in New York City to begin her new position as professor of Christian ethics at Union Theological Seminary.

How do you see the discussion of homosexuality, homophobia, and the issues of gay men and lesbians happening in seminary settings?

I think there's a public and a private conversation. At a school like Saint Paul, which did not have an official nondiscrimination policy across the board around issues of sexual orientation, it was understood by the faculty, in admission processes, and in all other ways that we functioned as a school that it was unacceptable to discriminate against issues of sexual orientation. That was the public stance of the school, but it was an "understood" stance, because it's a United Methodist Church seminary and has to abide by that denomination's *Book of Discipline*.[3] While I was there, the school would not make an official statement, would not declare itself welcoming and affirming, but would do so by practice. So, in classroom discussions almost all of the faculty, if not all the faculty, made it clear that it was unacceptable to practice any form of discrimination against gays and lesbians—verbally. It couldn't control the body language, but at least verbally there were no attacks allowed.

The private conversation was much more diverse and a lot less certain. There was at least one lesbian who was harassed. We never found out who was doing it, but the school did put out a very clear statement against it. Her mailbox kept disappearing. Her name would be removed, her mail would be taken out, and the other mailboxes would be rearranged as if she didn't exist. Finally, the director of student affairs just said that we've got to say something because this is unacceptable. When the student first came to Saint Paul, she was very out but became less so in her time there because of the harassment she received from some of her student peers. So, on the private level there was a lot of acting out amongst the students. I don't know of any instance that happened with faculty being privately discriminatory. The faculty never quite figured out how to get a handle on addressing the issue other than by making as many clear statements as we could within the classroom and around informal settings that such forms of discrimination were unacceptable.

Even at liberal or quasiliberal institutions like Saint Paul, where the faculty is clear that such forms of discrimination are not acceptable, I think the long and short of it is a very mixed bag when a school is bound by denominational polity. It also depends on how the administration views the role of the seminary. Some United Methodist seminary presidents do not see the seminary's role as prophetic, but simply as following the *Discipline*; others view the seminary as a place to take on a prophetic role; and some others sit in the middle. I think that's probably where Saint Paul would be classified—somewhere in the middle.

Are there lesbian and gay students who are out and organized?

Not organized, but we had a number of UFMCC[4] students who were very out, almost by nature of their denomination. What you run into at a school like Saint Paul is a lot of part-time students, and most of the gay/lesbian students in recent years were part-time. So, they weren't really interested in organizing much of anything; they were just trying to get out. So, there's no gay/lesbian caucus, nothing like that.

What about course content? Did you and/or colleagues try to introduce material on homophobia and homosexuality?

I know that Tex Sample[5] and I did, and we're both gone now. I'm not sure about others; I believe so. I know that Donna Allen, who is an instructor of homiletics, introduced that kind of material.[6] I think perhaps the majority of the faculty may well have waited until the issue came up in conversation. I think there are some attempts made in the Introduction to Ministry course taught by one professor. If I'm not mistaken, there was some course content that had to do with issues of heterosexism and homophobia. But there's not a entire course on these issues, certainly.

Do you yourself have a sense of what you think are good resources for introducing the issue in course content?

You know, there's a lot of books out there; and what I get frustrated with is that when one uses these resources, it allows students to objectify the issue and hold it at a distance. And so what I tended to do is, if I used a reading—which was rare actually—I would do much more work in terms of personal experience. "Where are you on this? What has been your experience in dealing with gays and lesbians? What have you heard?" So, students would have to deal with what they bring into the classroom and not objectify from a distance. I have found that to be much more helpful, and I also do that in the context of talking about a host of other forms of oppression, so that students have a sense of how dangerous it can become if you start to ghettoize forms of oppression as opposed to recognizing clearly that they are linked, have similar mechanisms that trigger and fire them off, are held together by similar sets of assumptions, prejudices, hatreds, and fears, and that it's not unusual to have a person or a group who's experienced one form of oppression commit another form of oppression on another one. I'm much more interested in trying to help students understand the intricacies of evil, so that issues of homophobia and heterosexism are placed in a conversation while drawing out the distinctions that come from them.

Do you see the links and distinctions being made well with that approach?

It depends on if any given student really wants to be changed. I discovered several years back that I can't make them change (*laughs*). It was a hard, bitter pill. And then I remembered that nobody was able to make me change either when I was a student. I had to be ready and open for it or be so overwhelmed in misery that it had to happen. So, yes, by students who are really opened and engaged in trying to understand what God has called them to and—because Saint Paul is a school that concentrates on preparing people for parish ministry of various sorts—what the world is like that they're being asked to minister. "Given what you're going to face in a parish, can you really be a pastor to the majority of people in your congregation or the communities from which they come or the city or town that the church sits in?" If they're interested in that, then, yes, I've seen students who have been previously fairly conservative or not actually having even thought about the issues—which always just mystifies me—coming to say, "Oh," making some "Ah-ha's," and seeing where they have made some missteps and miscues and how they need probably to rethink how they do what they do. But there are some students who are simply surviving seminary to go and commit ministry. And there's not much that can be done with them other than try.

Sometimes I find that the more conservative students, if they are willing to be open, get into these issues in a more genuine way than liberal students who seem to think they know where they should be already.

That's true. I think the flip side of that is both liberal and conservative students who are so certain they don't think they need to do anything other than refine what they already know; they're very hard to get at. Saint Paul's in the last couple of years has taken an increasingly conservative turn among the student body. And there's a genuine mean-spiritedness that has developed at the school around a lot of issues of diversity. Gay and lesbian rights is just one of them. And so, I wonder what's happening with those students who say they follow the Bible, but then when you ask them exactly where their behavior is condoned, they're really hard-pressed, they really resort much more to cultural and social mores as opposed to really examining what scripture has to say. So, for me it became rather puzzling.

Any sense of why that tendency is occurring?

I think that some of what is happening is that—at least at Saint Paul, and I've heard this rumored around in some other schools—a lot of the students were coming not out of any religious tradition or formation but really out of having a strong conversion experience of some sort. And "strong" is a much more ambivalent word than I intend it to be, because the strength doesn't mean a bowl-you-over, struck-by-God experience. Often it's just finding a church that actually let them be who they are; or they were at a place where they had no other alternatives, so they tried this church down the street and it worked. And they translate that experience into a call to ministry. What often happens with that is these students, and this happens to liberals as well, have no religious foundation. They've not had the Sunday school experience or any sort of formation, so they don't have a sense of history or tradition or understanding that these issues are not new in the life of the church. What they come with then is a lot of their own preconceptions about what is right and wrong that haven't been formed in a faith tradition of any sort. And usually that gets to be really dangerous. It's almost as dangerous as when your faith tradition does form you, because they tend to religiosize their own moral principles as opposed to examining where these things come from. That dynamic among the conservative students means they start justifying their phobias and hatreds for a variety of groups, because it hardly ever is just gays and lesbians; they tend unfortunately to cast a fairly wide net.

A lot of those folks are now entering seminary, and I think part of it is sort of "turns in the church." I tend to be doubtful of cyclical views of history, but we do seem to repeat ourselves around the turn of any century in the churches. We tend to get much more conservative as a church across the denominational spectrum and we tend to hunker down because we don't know what this new century is going to hold and we tend to get protective of our own interests. I saw that dynamic as I studied the turn into this century, and I am noticing how much we are playing into that once again as we get into 2000 and beyond. Some of it is just fear, but some of it is just genuine evil and hatred. There is no other way to put it. Some folks have just decided they don't like other folks based on their sexual orientation, and they'll use any means necessary to justify that hatred or they won't even think it's a matter that they have to justify.

Why do you think you have been able to be one of the people who has stood up to the issue of homophobia in the church and to ask the difficult questions?

It makes a difference when your favorite uncle dies from complications from AIDS and it's very clear that he doesn't want the church he was raised in—at least the pastor there—to do his funeral and that he does want you to do it. He didn't trust the pastor to put him away in a dignified way without judging him. I think that is really the most simple answer I can come up with. There was something wrong with that whole scenario. My aunt called and said to me, "He doesn't trust them to put him away right." This was a small Black AMEZ [African Methodist Episcopal Zion] church in North Carolina where my grandmother was one of the pillars of the church; the kids were in the church all the time—every day almost, in fact—so much so that all of them are churched out now (*laughs*). They say they got a storehouse early on. So, this is a church where he was well known and well loved, and he didn't trust that church to put him away with dignity. That is just wrong. That actually got me looking. Beyond the emotional level of that, I was also starting to work on issues of people of color and AIDS and I began to see the links with the church's silence on that. So I got pissed off, to put it mildly. I think that's what led me there.

Did he surmise on his own that the church would respond that way?

Oh, yes. Two of my aunts, who are his sisters, were his primary caretakers. They had been charged with that by my grandmother, who at some level knew what was going to happen years before he was diagnosed. He wasn't even diagnosed HIV-positive; he was diagnosed as full-blown AIDS. It had progressed so far. I just have a sense that watching that happen—even from afar, because they were very clear that they didn't want me to come down to take care of him—that he knew and he was very clear with them. If I'm remembering the words of my aunt who called, she said, "Your Uncle Pete wants you to do the service. He doesn't trust them." Yes, he knew. He had been an AIDS buddy in New York for a number of years before he got sick and had seen enough of what happens with religious communities and families.

What do you see as the link between womanist theology and that experience? One part of Alice Walker's definition of "womanist" is the loving, either sexual or otherwise, of people of one's own gender.[7]

Well, that's the interesting thing about Alice Walker's four-part definition and womanist thought in general, because there's not a common agreement that all four parts of the definition are necessary to be a womanist. It depends on whom you talk to. I think that the four of them have to be held together, because each one has its own particular set of challenges and gets at the different parts of the diversity of African American life. That's the problem of using a writer who wasn't intentionally writing for posterity on this issue—and Walker's more surprised than anybody that this has taken hold and she's also very suspicious of the organized church. I believe she understands herself to either be pagan or neopagan,[8] although she herself was raised in the AME [African Methodist Episcopal] church and her mother was one of the pillars of the church who later became Seventh-Day Adventist. So, she waited until both her parents were dead until she announced that she was no longer a Christian—as most good Black girls would (*laughs*). But she wasn't writing for a systematic anything. She was writing a definition, because her editors wanted to know what "womanist" meant. It wasn't a toss-off, but it really wasn't meant to be systematic. So now, those of us in the religious disciplines have the rather delicate job of trying to look at four parts of the definition that were never meant to be a methodology and to turn it into a methodology. For me, I think all four parts just need to be there.

What are the four parts of the definition of "womanist"?

The first part is the mother/daughter dialogue and gives the history and context in terms of little Black girls who want to know everything, be and act grown, and be serious. So, there's some contexting of Black women's experience and the way wisdom is passed from generation to generation. The second part of the definition starts getting into issues of the diversity of the community in terms of sexuality and sexual orientation, colorism, issues of geography in the way in which the North and the South often get pitted against each other even in the Black community. The third part of the definition is the looking at the self—"Loves herself. *Regardless*."— and runs through a number of negative stereotypes and turns them on their head in terms of loving roundness and food when the larger culture says stay away from food and be pencil thin. And then the fourth part of the definition is a critique of white feminism—"Womanist is to feminist as purple to lavender."—really trying to push at the way in which a feminism that only deals with issues of sexism is incomplete feminism for far too many people and certainly for far too many women. Women's experiences are much more diverse than what happens with sexism.

Having those four parts in place for me is a way in which I try to hold myself accountable to what I have to look at within myself and places that I don't like to go or don't like to admit or don't actually welcome a lot of people into; and, I think, in some ways it helps me be a little more accountable to the diversities found in African American life. So, it becomes very natural for me then to talk about issues of sexual orientation and sexual discrimination and heterosexism and homophobia, because I'm simply trying to be true to the methodology I've adopted and to the reality of Black life where we like to hold a lot of that stuff at a distance and not be accountable to one another or remain silent in a lot of instances in faith communities when we know exactly the amount of diversity sitting in the room.

So, I think those are parts of why I've been able to do that. But I think that may be the more intellectual reason, and the emotional reason of just watching what happened to my uncle—who actually had an excellent death because his family was able to keep him at home through almost all of his decline and he was able to die in his own bed, but then to turn around and not be able to be buried out of the church he grew up in—I think that actually fuels me more than the intellectual side.

It strikes me that womanism is a methodology that's not inappropriate for lots of people to use in terms of theological inquiry. Those four parts really are a very effective check for whatever one's experience may be.

I tell students all the time, "No, you can't be a womanist, but you can certainly use the methodology, just like I'm not Tillich or Niebuhr, but I do find what they did in part very helpful in my own work. So, the point is not that you get to appropriate a word which really is specific to a particular social location, but that the methodology being used is one that can be very helpful from where *you* stand. You can walk into your stuff, don't steal mine." I think that can be very challenging for folks, because what I hear from time to time from students from varieties of backgrounds is, one, a sort of romanticizing of the Black experience, which gets very wearying, and then, two, this deep yearning to have an experience that they can call their own. So, having to remind them that they do have one; they grew up in a family system of some sort in a town somewhere or varieties of towns and places. "That's where you start." There's almost always an initial reluctance to take that on. I have to push a little more and ask, "Why are you practicing forms of self-hatred?" And depending on who that student is, it leads them into a variety of inquiries, some of which really is having to look into the self-hatred that they do carry around. Class injuries tend to crop up almost as much as injuries around sex and sexuality. "So, take the methodology and really examine your own life and then start with that set of experiences and know that better than you've ever known it before and then you can start to make connections with others."

One hears from Black lesbians and gay men that not being able to be in the church of their origin is like being cut off from their people. That kind of link to community doesn't seem to be as strong for white lesbians and gay men—maybe because we think of the whole world as our community and don't have a sense of a particular community that nourished us. Do you have any advice for people who do want to stay within a church tradition but feel trashed or conflicted by it?

Well, I think more and more people in more and more denominations are finding ways to build community within community. It's not just a Reconciling Congregation movement for United Methodists or the More Like movement for Presbyterians;[9] several denominations have a caucus of some sort that meets regularly and tries to do whatever it can. But I think those forms of community-making within your local church are hard to sustain if you're getting an onslaught of nastiness every week either in the worship service or in some of the other activities of the church. So, what I have found to be much more effective is finding churches that are open—whether they say they are publicly or not, that are open to the diversities of the people in the neighborhood or the people in the city—and not settling for whatever it is you find closest by you or what you know best. It may mean experiencing other worship styles and other understandings of mission and service to the community—and that may not be a bad thing to learn and to engage in. It may be that's a part of where your faith journey is necessarily taking you—outside of your comfort zone or your zone of common knowledge to a new place. It's a new way to experience God in community. I think finding that community is most important.

It used to catch me up short how surprised students were and continue to be when I start to talk in class about the power of community, because most of them have not experienced it. They don't have a sense of community; they may have a sense of family—and that's loaded for a lot of folks—but not a group of people whom you are not biologically related to but are committed to for a lifetime. Finding people who are willing to build and craft that with you, I think, are some of the ways that I know Black gays and lesbians stay in the church and stay healthy; and there are others who are really unhealthy because they just internalize, internalize, and internalize, and then they become very dangerous people when you meet them out on the street. But I would say, "Find those folks who are seeking to understand that your sexuality is not a problem, but a gift from God, another piece of the fabric of creation and nothing more than that." Those who do are finding groups of people more and more and coming together for something larger than just self.

The downside of strong U.S. individualism is that we've become far too individualistic as a culture. When you get that individualistic guide in you, it's hard to begin to think about forming bonds of friendship, loyalty, and love with folks beyond the romantic or the biological. It's simply because it's the way we survive best as human beings when all is said and done. So, I think those are pieces of what can be helpful. I think it's very hard to do if you've not spent your life doing it, like a lot of Black folk have. But I also have noticed that the Black community is fragmenting and fraying as it's now starting to take off on this individualistic flair from the larger culture. That is troubling.

You're saying originally or historically Black people have had the experience of making community and that gays and lesbians, especially white gays and lesbians, by focusing on the self and trying to find acceptance just for their sexuality, don't have the experience of making community.

Not in an ongoing and rigorous fashion, because instead of banding together for issues of common survival and common good—and I know that's a really dangerous phrase, but in the best sense of "common good"—what often happens, if you don't have the experience from day one that you're in deep doo doo just by virtue of who you are and where you were born, is that coming together takes on "What can I get out of it for *me*? How can I find survival mechanisms for *me*?" It doesn't get translated into how can *we* get together and figure how *we're* all going to survive and bring a whole bunch of people along with us. It's that old notion from the Black women's club movement[10] of "lifting as we climb" that, I think, can be so helpful from African American experience: as you succeed, you bring others with you. This is not something you do by yourself; it's a communal act. And so, when you get that sort of ethos in your background, either spoken or unspoken, it's hard to leave something like the church, because when you were younger the church was the one place where you heard that you were worth something when everyone else was telling you you weren't. For girls it's a little more of a mixed bag. Depending on what kind of church you were in, girls were either allowed or not allowed to be full participants. I was lucky; I was raised in a church where girls got to do everything that boys got to do in the worship service and in leadership. There are a lot of Black folk who were not that fortunate. But coming from that kind of experience, I've seen what happens and I know what happens when you live your life for something more than just yourself and your family. I think that is a piece of it. So, it's more than just self-survival. It really becomes issues of survival of the whole community and really trying to be serious about the length and breadth of that community, as opposed to picking and choosing, like some folks would rather do.

It seems as though Black lesbians and gay men may have the history, tradition, and skills to be the ones who can make the new communities instead of looking for someone to accept them.

I think the rise of the Unity Fellowship Church, Carl Bean and what he's trying to do with that is a prime example of what can happen—"Had enough, not going to give up the church, just going to go and create a new one."[11] Now, it's got its own set of problems, but at least its their set of problems as opposed to problems being imposed by others.

What do you see as their problems?

I think they're still trying to figure out their theology, which could be a bit of a problem in and of itself. I've been to two or three services at the Unity Fellowship Church in Seattle, and it's a very theocentric denomination. They don't talk much about Jesus officially, but I had to chuckle because when they started the opening praise and sing-spiration time, all these folks sitting in this room were coming out of very strong religious traditions of some sort or another and all I heard were "washed in the blood of Jesus" songs. That says to me they've got some work to do, because it was sort of funny. I said to myself, "Now, wait a minute, this is a theocentric denomination where you don't talk much about Jesus at all. God is love. But I'm hearing all these old songs to Jesus about being the lamb of God and getting washed in his blood." I think that's something to contend with. I think they also have to figure out how to train and keep their clergy alert. I was talking to the pastor of that church who spends most of her time doing pastoral care, which she is not trained to do; and it is just wearing her slick as she is tries to do the make-up work in order to continue to be helpful to her congregation. I think they're still in the midst of figuring out how to do those kinds of things.

Do you see a movement at all of gay people being ready, not just to address their own problems and their own needs, but being ministers for all people?

I think that's person-specific. I don't see it as a movement. I wish it were, because that would signal that we've come a lot farther along in how we relate to each other in this country than we have. If folks were allowed to be just who they are and say, "This is part of who I am, but here's another part of who I am, and all the parts make me up and I've got a variety of gifts." So, I think there are some folks out there who do that. I think the majority of folks either choose or are slotted into positions where they are not allowed to. And so, I don't see much of a movement.

Do you have a sense at all of there being any kind of critical mass or a small body of African American clergy who are moving ahead on lesbian and gay issues in a way that they weren't ten years ago?

Not a critical mass, but a small body. I think of folks like J. Alfred Smith in Oakland at Allen Temple Baptist and Emanuel Cleaver in Kansas City, who was also the mayor for a number of years and on the city council. There are some women, like Yvette Flunder in San Francisco,[12] who are pastoring and very clear that their churches are open for everybody. There's a small, small number—to be sure. It never hurts that a lot of these churches are influential pastorates and people pay attention to things that come out of them. I'm hopeful from that beginning that more can emerge.

What is your hope or vision for lesbian/gay/bi people in the near future? What do you think lesbian/gay/bi people should or need to be doing?

I think it's going to get worse before it gets better. I don't know how much more worse it's going to get, because we've gotten pretty bad, but I'm really concerned about the amount of rage in our culture that's now being acted on in a variety of settings. And it's more than the shootings at Columbine High School[13] or the guy, I forget his name, who started shooting white folks on the Long Island Rail Road.[14] It's more than that, because there's a level of violence that's now acceptable in our culture and that we seem to want to blame everybody but ourselves for. I have to shake my head at the amount of blame-shifting that went on around dealing with the guys who killed their peers at Columbine High. It was easy to pick on the entertainment industry. But not much was said, that I had heard, about what values did their parents transmit and where were they getting this stuff from, the impact or the possibility of impact of white supremacy groups and access to that information, even if they may not have been formally a part of it. Somebody had to teach them that; it doesn't grow out of the air.

That kind of violence seems to be permeating our lives these days; and when you put issues of sexuality, heterosexism, and homophobia in that mix, I see more problems ahead than I see the light at the end of the tunnel. And actually I'd be suspicious of any light I'd see at the end of the tunnel; at this point I'd be afraid it might be an oncoming train because we've become a culture of mean-spiritedness in so many ways. So, when looking at issues of sexuality and sexual orientation and those of us who live them out every day—because everybody's got a sexuality of some sort—it becomes much more crucial for me to ask, "How do I start to really take hold of the culture we've created and been handed and start to reshape it?" Can gays and lesbians do that? It's possible. We've had social movements before that have reshaped the landscape of the U.S. Will it happen? I don't know.

I don't know if we have the energy or the insight for any group in the country right now—beside those folks who are already well organized and more than capable of pulling off mess—to go ahead and do it. But I would like to think that before it gets any worse than it is that they'll be some folks who will say, "We've probably gone about as far as we need to let things go without starting to say enough is enough and then doing something about it." I think a lot of us are saying, "Enough is enough," but not very many of us are actually doing much about it. So, my hope is somebody will start the movement and the rest of us—if we're not the one—will join in and really start working like hell for justice. It seems like to me that's all we got left.

You've done research on Ida B. Wells, who led much of the antilynching campaign in the late-nineteenth and twentieth centuries. Is she a possible model for what needs to be done at the current turning of the century?[15]

The one thing to keep in mind about Wells is that she was a Lone Ranger and she never trained anybody else how to do what she did. If we can learn anything from Wells it's don't do it that way, because a lot of momentum was lost when she died suddenly. She had this very great knack for alienating everybody she came in contact with. If people weren't moving fast enough for her, she would just do it herself. In her autobiography there are several times when she goes, "Strange to say. . . ," and then recounts how somebody is upset with her after she's decided they were moving too slowly and she went ahead and did what she thought needed to be done.[16] She didn't get that that might be problematic. We need people like her, but I think the majority of us need people like her who also train us how to do some of the things she did.

Last year Dwight Hopkins[17] at the University of Chicago put together a conference that I participated in. Part of the conference was Cornel West,[18] Jim Cone,[19] and myself sitting with high school students who'd read our work over the year and letting them ask us questions. First of all, all three of us were like, "You're reading our work and you're in high school?" Especially Cornel. Jim and I were giving Cornel all sorts of grief, "Cornel, you think they understood all the words you use?" But they got it, which was really a sign of hope. One of the students, one of the young men, asked, "Who will be the next leader and how will we know him?" Jim and I looked at Cornel and said, "That's your question." Cornel just looked at the young man and said, "You and everybody in here are the leaders. You're the people who are going to do this." Then all the kids' eyes got real big, and Cornel just kept at it. He said, "We're not going to have this one-person-as-leader anymore; it's going to take all of us working together." And then we proceeded to talk about that for a while. I think some of the kids became convinced that they could make a change, that they could be a part of it. Others of them were scared shitless. And some of them were like, "It's just not me," and they checked out, which is about the range of emotions you would expect. So, I really do think looking for the lone heroic figure for how we're going to do justice these days is very counterproductive. We're going to have to step up to the plate as individuals, then come together as communities, and do it ourselves, because it's not going to be one person out there anymore. It's too easy to pick them off, and they do it with regularity. I've always been amazed, it's always the good people who get killed. So, the more you have, they got to use a lot more ammo.

Chapter 18

Rev. Dr. Kelly Brown Douglas

*K*elly Brown Douglas is associate professor of theology at Howard University Divinity School in Washington, D.C. Her scholarship and publications have played a significant role in developing the emerging field of womanist theology.[1] Her first book, *The Black Christ,* surveys the portrayal of Jesus from early slave testimonies to the Civil Rights and Black Power movements.[2] Her second book, *Sexuality and the Black Church,* provides a long-awaited discussion of Black sexuality and critique of homophobia and heterosexism.[3]

Rev. Dr. Douglas received her Ph.D. from Union Theological Seminary and is an Episcopal priest. She was among the first Black clergy to call for the Black community to take seriously and respond to the HIV/AIDS epidemic.[4]

Were you nervous about being the first scholar to address in a systematic and thorough way sexuality and homophobia in the Black church?

It's funny, because initially I had no thought about being nervous at all. It was just something I felt I had to do. As I said in the book, but want to emphasize, it was a topic that called me and that burst forth from me, given what was happening in my life and also given that I just never understood the intensity of homophobia in the Black community. I simply couldn't grasp why people whom I respected on other levels had such homophobic and heterosexist attitudes, why I couldn't change them, why they thought those attitudes were acceptable, or why they would say to me, "Well, you know it takes time." My response would always be, "Well, you know, that's what white people said, 'It takes time to get rid of racism,' but you don't accept that. If it's wrong, it's wrong; and if you're talking to the people who are being hurt by it, it's already been too much time." I never understood the intensity of those feelings, and I didn't know what to do about them. So, that was boiling or brewing for a long time; and then as life and circumstances came together, it was just something that I had to do. The right time came to do it.

In doing it and even in making the conscious decision to write this book, I never thought once about the risk to myself professionally or about what people would say, until people found out I was writing it. Then they said, "Oh, better you than me." Scholars didn't want to broach it and were saying to me, "Glad *you're* doing it." I really was surprised. They said, "Well, you're going out there now; you're sticking out your neck now." But I never felt that. I don't know if people's responses made me nervous, but they made me more aware of what I was doing and more aware that this really is a topic that people are afraid to broach in the Black community. So, I became more acutely aware that it was a difficult subject and said to myself this book can either be a bust or get a lot of clamoring. It could be put out there and then go away quietly, which I didn't want; or it could at least create and promote discussion, which is what I wanted.

Can you say a little bit about what it's like to work with students on the issues of lesbians and gay men?

The year before this book came out, while I was in the process of writing it, I taught a course on sexuality in the Black church, and I'm teaching that same course this year. In the context of all the courses I teach, this one has been the easiest for talking about these issues, though it's interesting that both times the students come in almost ready to pounce with, "You're not going to change my mind." They tell me on the first day, "You know, certain things are just sinful; and we'll hear what you have to say, but you're not going to change my mind." Then I say to them, "What are you talking about?" And they say, "You know, homosexuality. I don't know if I can go with you there, Doc." I say, "You know, it's interesting because this course isn't on homosexuality; it's on sexuality. In fact, we won't be getting to the issue of homosexuality until about mid-point in the course; so, why are you equating sexuality with homosexuality?" We start out by deconstructing sexuality and their misunderstandings of it; and I try to assure them that, though they may have a lot of fears and anxiety connected to various sexual issues, by the time we get to homosexuality perhaps they won't feel the same way, or at least they'll be asking different questions or have a different response. By and large, the first time that's exactly what happened. The students didn't put up the same barriers that they do in my other course, where it's just a topic in Systematic Theology, where I've not paved the way to get there.

In your other courses you have a gay component that's one among many others?

Exactly. In every course that I teach I do gay and lesbian theologies or philosophies, whatever I'm teaching. It comes up in the middle of the course and is one of the most difficult issues I deal with besides biblical infallibility. The students shut down almost right away. But in the sexuality course, I start by deconstructing sexuality and getting them to understand what it is. I start by saying, "Someone tell me what sexuality is." And they equate it with sex. So, we do a deconstruction of that and then we talk, much as I do in my book, about the way white culture has impacted Black sexuality. And then this year for the first time I had a psychologist of religion come in, and we had them begin to do personal sexual histories, which is another layer.

We do the social construction, white culture, the Christian church, Black culture, and then the personal. It's the personal layer—the repression/projection stuff—that really causes them to have some of the reactions they do. This week they're in the middle of doing their sexual histories, sexual autobiographies, and the responses to it have been tremendous. For instance, one student said to me, "You know, I know what you're saying about all this repression and personal stuff, but the bottom line for me is that homosexuality is a sin. That's what my church teaches and that's where I'm going to end up." I said, "You know, we don't adopt ideologies or even enter worship communities by happenstance. They usually are things we take on that are compatible with something about us. So, you didn't come to the ideology first; something led you to that particular ideology." Then all of a sudden the student was quiet, and at the end of the class the student said, "I've been sitting here thinking that I remember when I was little, people used to talk about this gay man on my street all the time and say how terrible he was. I think you're right. I thought that about gay people before I even went to my church." And I say, "Ah, keep moving, keep doing that."

My experience in this course is that I've at least gotten them to a different point of wrestling with the issue. Even if they've not really made the full leaps, I've gotten them to a different point of wrestling. But I have had students leave and spread rumors about me.

Spread rumors that you are a lesbian?

Exactly. Like, "Why's she teaching this course; she must be gay." I always say that for those of us who are heterosexual to claim to be heterosexual in the midst of talking about homophobia and heterosexism—you know how people say, "But I'm not gay"—is privilege. I've just grown to understand, "So be it; I'm not going to claim that privilege by saying, 'I'm not gay. I'm just talking about this, but don't put me there. I'm not the sinner.'" Some students try to press me, "Well, Doc, what about you?" And I press them back, "Why is this important? If you found out one or the other, what would that mean in how you respond to what I say?" And then they don't want to go there. Each time I've taught a course with gay content, some students come out convinced I'm bringing the issue up because I'm gay and they proceed to let everybody know that (*laughs*).

You mentioned people who seem really solid on all issues except this one. If people do make the shift and begin to connect the issues, what helps them most?

I used to think that I could just draw the parallels between homophobia and heterosexism and racism and that they would simply see them and make that shift. But I've since come to believe that I can't do that, because they quickly begin to talk about the differences between being gay and Black—false differences though they may be in some sense, they begin to make those distinctions. I'm beginning to think that you've got to do two things: first, to put sexuality into a wider context and help them to understand that issue in general, and, secondly, to help them understand sexuality in terms of who they are as Black people in particular. When people can really relate sexuality more to who they are personally or existentially—to their own experiences—then I think they can begin to make those connections.

When all else fails, I say to people, and it usually makes them pause, "If you can't figure your way out of this issue and you can't figure what side to get on, look who's lining up on the other side." I say, "Do you want to line up as a Black person with the Pat Buchanans and the Jerry Falwells and the David Dukes of the world? If you're over there with them, something's wrong with where you are." And oftentimes that jars them. I say, "If you can't figure it out theologically or biblically, look at who is with you." They'll at least get back in the middle and be ambivalent.

I think what I'm really coming to understand with the issue of homosexuality is that sexuality is something human beings are uncomfortable with anyway and something we don't understand. We don't understand how we come to express our sexuality the way we do. For instance, white people know, "If I rub up against Black people, I'm not going to become Black," and men know, "If I rub up against women and let them sit next to me in the job, I'm not going to become a woman." But what we don't know is what causes us to express our sexuality the way we do on many levels. We're very uncertain about sexuality anyway; we don't know enough about it. So, I think people are more fearful about this issue, because they know sexuality is tenuous.

I often hear many Black students say, "Why do they have to be so radical about it; why don't they just be quiet?" And I say, "What could be more radical than running around the streets saying, 'Black power'? The real issue is, 'What's going to happen if you begin to open the door and give persons permission to be who they are? What happens if you open the door and say it's not a sin? What happens if this gay guy becomes your friend and you like him? Will that change you?' because we're so uncertain as to what goes into who we are as sexual beings?" So, I really do think it's that fear of sexuality that's the bottom line. Then the other stuff gets layered on. I try to tease out all those issues and try to open the students up on all those levels. Sometimes we make movement.

I know in your book you talk about your cousin Lloyd and also about Renee Hill's critique of womanist theology as two influences on you. Do you think your training in liberation theology also made you more likely to step up to this issue? Do you think you're generally someone who has the courage or is pushy enough to wade into areas that other people avoid and are afraid of?

I don't know. I try to think about why I do the things I do or say the things I say, because as you know it would be easier to shut up. I often say, "Kelly, why can't you just ignore it and life would be easier?" (*laughs*) But from when I was little—and I talked a little bit about it in my relationship with Lloyd—I never fit the norm. I was a girl who didn't like "girl things." I liked boy things. I liked sports, as I still do. I never saw the sense of dolls; still don't. I liked to read, would rather watch a football game any day than whatever else little girls were supposed to do. So, I was labeled the tomboy. I was very bright and not, as we used to say, one of the fly girls or pretty girls. I wore my little glasses, had braces, and was smart. That doesn't make you one of the most popular girls with the guys. I knew what it was like to feel like the nerd, and I compensated by being very bright and popular in a different way. But I always took up for the underdog. I always tried to befriend the kid who got teased, and I think that's because I knew what it was like to be teased.

I remember—and I don't know if it was a dream or real, but it doesn't matter because it had the same impact on my life—that one day I saw these two little kids. We were driving downtown with my parents. I was seven or eight, and these two little kids were walking across the street, little Black children. It was pouring down rain. These kids were not properly dressed for the rain, clearly dirty, clearly poor; and I cried. I said to myself, "One day I'm going to come back and get these kids." I had an acute awareness of the fact that while we were by no means rich, we were privileged; and there were these poor Black kids. Seeing children suffer always made me very sad. So I cried; I was always a very sensitive kid. People used to call me "crybaby." I cried most of the time when I would hear that people got hurt. As I charted my journey, I knew I was going back to get those kids. When I was little, I said, "I'll grow up, they'll stay little, and I can come back and get those same exact kids." At first I thought I was going to become a schoolteacher; that's how I would go back and get them. My life journey—consciously or unconsciously, as I look at it—has been going back to get those kids. I took many turns, ended up where I am, and it's put me back at doing what I wanted to do in the beginning.

So, I don't know. I think it's because of my own life experiences, because I knew what it was like to be teased, to be called a nerd and a tomboy, and it made me feel bad for others who would be teased. I remember when my neighborhood middle-class school began to bring in kids from a poor section of town. It was the first time I ever saw little AFDC and welfare lunch tickets. These kids, of course, got teased. I remember one kid in particular was always dirty, and that was the kid with whom I became friends. I was not raised in a nonhomophobic home, and I remember very early on that we would call certain boys sissies and say certain girls had something wrong with them, called them funny. I'm no better than anybody else; as a kid I would be party to that. Then as I got a little bit older, I would just stay quiet and not say anything. And now, as I said in my book, I don't have the excuse of childhood. You have to say something, and I can no longer be party to silence because even remaining silent is being party to that. I remained silent for far too long and saw people that I loved hurt by that stuff. I think it's a life journey and that who I am led me to do what I am doing.

When I came to do graduate study with James Cone, I was looking for a way to help. As an undergraduate I had been a psychology major, and we had learned to help people cope with their environment. I said, "It's unjust to help people cope with an unjust environment; I need something else." That need led me to the reading of Cone's *Black Theology*[5] and going to seminary. So, that's the trajectory I've been on, which is not to say that there are some days that I wish I wasn't on it, because life could be easier (*laughs*). And, I think that's what it is that helps understand why I've stepped up to the issues of lesbians and gay men. When I'm silent, when I don't say anything about what I know is wrong, I'm just compelled to speak.

I always tell people that I don't have the whole truth, but I do know that God doesn't intend for anybody to be treated other than as a child of God. I just have to believe that; and that's my fundamental principle— that everybody is to be treated as human beings, as gifts from God, and that we are to create a world, create the space for that to happen in—that's what I live by. So, I don't care who the person is or what the issue is; what's important is, "Are they being treated as a child of God and given the space to fulfill all their potential as one of God's children?" That's what I live by; and so, I tell people, "You know, I may not get all the nuances of the theological argument right, but I just know in my heart that it's right. That's what guides me. And the reason I think that's right is because I know what it feels like to be treated differently, and it's not good. God wouldn't want that for any of us." That's what pushes me forward, maybe foolishly sometimes.

Do you think there's going to be a turning point when lesbians and gay men will become more identified or visible in the Black church—and if so, how is it going to happen?

I think it has to happen, but how is that to happen? I think the church is going to have to face the crisis. What's brought this issue to the forefront clearly is AIDS/HIV and the epidemic in the Black community. People can no longer run away from that issue, which means they can no longer run away from the issue of sexuality. I think that something is going to have to force the issue of greater gay openness and visibility in the Black community, the way AIDS/HIV forces the discussion of sexuality. I simply don't know what that will be. But as long as we can ignore it, I think we and the church will. It has gotten along thus far doing that. I think that it's not going to be so much the keying in on the gay and lesbian issue as it's going to be another issue that's going to force it to come to the forefront, like the more general issue of sexuality—perhaps women's issues, perhaps clergy abuse, or even the issue of teenage sexuality. I think those issues are really becoming very significant and will be detrimental if they aren't faced in the Black community. Those other issues are imposing upon the life and death of the Black community and are forcing the discussion of sexuality, and I think it's the forcing of the discussion of sexuality that is going to cause us to take another look at the issue of homosexuality. It's going to be through that door that it is going to be opened up. I think it will, because the sexuality issue has to be opened up. And of course there are places that are doing that.

Can you say where some of those places are?

For instance, Carlton Veazey of the Religious Coalition for Reproductive Choice has run three summer conferences at Howard on Sexuality in the Black Church, and they have been very well attended. They discuss issues from teenage pregnancy to homosexuality. I've participated in two of those. He does these summit meetings all over the country. I've been surprised by the response to it. So, that's out there. The issue is being opened up. People are discussing it.

There are people like the very well-respected pastor Jeremiah Wright.[6] His church is very significant in the Black community, and he's a very significant Black pastor. Jeremiah by his own admission was once "homophobic," but now he has changed. It's going to take people like Dr. Wright, whom other people respect, to begin to come out and say different things, as in fact he is doing. I think it's going to take more Jeremiah Wrights to come out and publicly renounce homophobia, and then you'll begin to see some change.

As a theologian, I can never divorce myself from the church. But I think a theologian has a different role than a pastor. We certainly don't have the same kind of influence in the church, and I don't think that we should pretend to have the same kind of influence that a pastor does. Maybe our role in the church in part is the way I see my task at Howard: I'm training these students to go into the Black church; and if I can just make a little impact on some of this leadership, then I feel that I'm doing my job. I really take seriously that I'm training these students, because there are Black lives at stake. They're going back into my community to enter my churches. So, at least when they come through the classroom, they won't leave saying the same old things with impunity. There will perhaps be a little voice saying, "Uh, wait a minute," and there have been students who have changed. I think our task is to create the conversation, to work with the leadership, just as I, as a womanist with other womanist scholars, empower Black women going through my classes and sitting in those pews—and that's why I continue to go to these little churches and do workshops and preach, because those women sitting in the pews will force the leadership to change. The bottom-line question is, "Why is the leadership going to change that which has been good to them?" They aren't. It's going to take the people sitting in the pews. When you empower them, they'll change it, and that is why I do the work that I do in and outside of the academy.

One of the pastors I interviewed, Rev. Larry Menyweather-Woods, in Omaha, said that your book is very important. He's been having sexuality classes for about a year and has wanted that kind of a resource for a long time. So, there's a link.

I'm glad to hear that. Especially with that book, I tried to write it in such a way that it is accessible to the Black church. That's whom I wrote the book for, so I'm pleased to get that kind of feedback. I tried to do it so it's scholarly yet accessible. You don't have to be a theologian to read it. It has gotten out there.

Can you say more about why you're hopeful and what you see as the future for this issue?

Maybe because I'm an optimist and believe in the good of humanity, I think there is hope. I really do think that we're going to come to a different place on this issue of sexuality. I think that it is the last issue to fall, not that all the other issues really have fallen, trust me. The reason I think that goes back to what I said earlier: sexuality in general is the issue we are most uncomfortable with and it will take a lot more work. I think we will get there, because, quite frankly, we have to. I don't know if it will mean that we will change hearts, but perhaps we will get to the place of at least being politically correct on this issue in the church. When we tend to any issue, it's usually because we have to. I think for the Black community we have to, because it's an issue of life or death. It's tied to so many other issues. So, I think we will. Begrudgingly maybe, but I think we will.

What's your advice to lesbians and gay men who feel alienated about being in the church and are thinking that they should leave it? What should they do in the meantime—before those changes occur?

Only they can make those decisions. I think that everyone has to decide for themselves. I don't think that anyone should ever subject themselves to a community that is dehumanizing and dehumanizes them. I don't think that we are meant to suffer; and I don't believe in any little redemptive suffering motifs, that we are meant to carry that cross. If that cross is too much to bear, if you're in a community that is not affirming, if it's destroying you, then you need to get out of it. You don't need to be anywhere you are being destroyed. I just believe that. On the other hand, people have to make that decision for themselves. Some people decide they can stay in it and find some community of support within it. If they can, fine. If not, find a community of support elsewhere, because there are other communities of support in other Black churches that will be more affirming. In every city there is a Black church that is affirming. So, my suggestion would be, "You know what? Don't be somewhere that is destroying you, because that is not what God calls us to. God doesn't call us to be destroyed and dismantled and to suffer like that." People should know that that's not what life is about, that there can be more supporting communities, and that you don't have to leave the Black church to find them. It might be hard, but you don't have to leave the Black church to find them.

Chapter 19

Dr. M. Shawn Copeland

Shawn Copeland is associate professor of theology at Marquette University[1] and specializes in systematic theology with attention to method, theological anthropology, liberation and political theologies, and African American religious experience and culture. She received her Ph.D. from Boston College and formerly was associate professor of theology and Black studies at Yale Divinity School. The author of many articles in books and professional journals and the coeditor of *Feminist Theology in Different Contexts* and *Violence Against Women,* she is currently conducting research in two areas: 1. African American critical thought and 2. suffering, solidarity, and the Cross.[2]

As a past executive director of the National Black Sisters' Conference, she was one of several people who began meeting in the 1970s to articulate a theology for Black Catholics and participated in the first meeting of the Black Catholic Theological Symposium in 1978. She currently serves as chair of the Doctoral Fellowship Selection Committee for The Fund for Theological Education and is included in *Who's Who among Black Americans.*[3]

What do you see in your theological tradition that provides a link to supporting and welcoming lesbians and gay men?

What in the Roman Catholic theological tradition provides a link to support and welcome lesbians and gay men? I think a key dimension for us is twofold: On a philosophical account, there is *one* human nature and we're all human beings; and on a theological account, we really are all creatures of the same God. This concern for the human person is, I think, the link. Granted, there is an appropriate criticism of organized and institutional religion to be made about not living up to this concern, but at the same time there is a very important way in which the primacy of the human person has been supported by the church, by our theological traditions, over against other claims of priority that come from society. So, the human person in an incarnational religious theological tradition is of paramount importance. I think that is our most fundamental resource. Now, it is also true we are having trouble understanding the human person, but that regard and that commitment to life is our most valued resource.

In your work how do you bring out that tradition to understand humans better? How do you work with the troubles we have?

In my own case, it is probably obvious why my own theological interest started out with concern for the human person. I belong to a racial group that's completely despised in the Western world. Blacks fare no better in the United Kingdom than they do in Canada or the United States or France or Germany. And I'm a woman; and women in a real way don't fare very well through history. So, when I reflect on my own processes, I have noticed my own work and interest tending toward theological anthropology—how we understand theologically the human person. And I suspect it started for me when I was a child. I remember being about twelve when I went to summer school one year because I had nothing else to do and took a course in world history. I was quite amazed to learn about the Sho'ah, about the extermination of the Jews, about Hitler's Final Solution. I am an only child, and my grandmother had a great influence in my upbringing. She used to say to me frequently, "Everybody can't like you." If you're an only child in a household of adults who dote on you, that's an important lesson. There's a problem there, of course, because you may grow into a person who wants everyone to like her in later life. But, what struck me in that world history class was the connection for me between the personal and the political. I thought to myself, "What can happen to you, if you're in a social situation in which people don't like you or a government doesn't like you or people in power don't like you and indeed hate you, is that they can exterminate you." For me at twelve this was a shocking realization, that the world really was not as friendly as my own little segregated neighborhood and my own encounters with people of different races and different cultural backgrounds.

I can say now what I was actually recognizing was a certain sheltered experience I had had; but it also meant that when I began graduate school I wanted to work on this realization. So, I focused for quite some time on the political, because I was looking at systems. But as my teaching has developed in the last seven or eight years, I've come around to teaching courses that concern the human person quite directly and also the human person's role in the social order—in the political and economic and technological order—and how the human person has both contributed to and been a victim of social suffering. This has also meant that I have become interested in writing about and trying to understand identity, difference, and solidarity. So, trying to understand difference and at the same time holding us accountable for one human nature has increasingly become a sharpening focus in my work.

I haven't taken on a direct analysis of the situation of lesbians and gay men, and I don't have a list of isms against which I'm willing to enact my theological practice, although anti-Semitism, heterosexism, or homophobia are all concerns that I'm certainly willing to bring up to anyone in a conversation, because it is simply not tolerable in a very elemental Christian perspective to kill people because of their difference.

If a student approached you to try to find the link between the issues for women, for African Americans, and for lesbians and gay men, how would you help her or him?

I would not want my first appeal to be that of rights. I think that human rights in the kind of liberal society in which we live is not necessarily the best mode or strategy. I am not opposed in any way to human rights or to—in our modern political context—political or civil rights, but a commonsense understanding has us thinking of rights as a status, a property or entitlement. People think that when someone else asks for rights they're trying to take something from "me." I think that understanding immediately sets up a negative relationship of tussling over what we think are limited properties, in other words, that there only so many rights to go around and you can't have any more than I have. If you seem to be getting too many then that must mean that I'm losing something. So, in that sense I would not want to take that approach.

What I would try to do is go back to the situation that I described. I'd like to try to make a broader appeal, that is, to try to figure out how we can talk about difference of varying sorts as expressions individuated in the matter of the human person. In other words, there's one human nature but it becomes individuated in different ways in each person. In this sense I would want to return to the question of our being creatures from a theological perspective. I would want to talk about making an appeal to the human person as prior to social formations, and I would want to support ways of thinking about the human person and about forms of difference we already have in, let's say, Trinitarian thought. For example, we can speak about difference in God, God manifests the divine being in three persons, there are distinctions and differences of mission and approach, but there is a profound unity. I have a very classical theism. I do recognize a kind of patriarchalization of God, but in some ways I'm a very traditional theologian. So, my approach would want to be that difference is an inherent part of Christianity; and I would want to reinforce a notion of the human person always as sacred, and not just a notion, but the human person as a sacred reality.

When you see people working on issues of identity and difference, what is a frequent stumbling block when it comes to sexual orientation?

That's a good question. I was having a conversation with a colleague around this issue to a certain extent. We were talking about the way in which culture forms people around sexual mores; and we were suggesting that Americans, people who live here, particularly European Americans, have a heavy dose of Anglo-Saxon and Anglo-Irish culture in working out their formation. There is a way in which much of organized Christianity reinforces some of those mores, a way in which we are almost pruriently caught up in questions of sexuality. We both want to know and don't want to know. So, there's something about our cultural formation interacting with religious formation. I think, for instance, the French are very different about matters of sex and sexuality. For example, and this is not about homosexuality, but think of the very striking differences between Bill Clinton's experience and that of Francois Mitterand. There is Mitterand in his coffin being slowly lowered into the ground. In front the wife and two sons stand; beside them stands the daughter, and behind her stands the mistress, her mother. While this is happening in a little village, at the Cathedral at Notre Dame in Paris, the Cardinal Archbishop is celebrating the Eucharist at Mitterand's memorial. And then we've got the response to Clinton in the United States. What a juxtaposition! I'm not suggesting that adultery or extramarital sex is something to be lauded. It certainly isn't. And Christianity enjoins chastity on all Christians regardless of their sexual orientation. So, neither of these people are acting in a chaste manner inside their relationships; but there's something here that's cultural, also.

I think there is something about homosexuality that awakens a certain amount of fear in people. I may be heading down a Freudian road here, but is it that people are afraid of their own sexuality, are they afraid of a loss of control? I think people are afraid of what is different. One of the things that happens to us when we talk about difference—and I've said and written about this before—is that our language undermines our discussion. We want to value difference, but if you go to a thesaurus and look up the synonyms for "difference," they are very negative. There are very few positive synonyms for "difference." How can we affirm something as positive which our language tells us is negative? So, that struggle occurs in our discussions. In our country we also seem to have a kind of prurient interest in both exploiting homosexuality for heterosexual purposes and at the same time not wanting to know about homosexuality to protect heterosexual purposes.

So, I think one of the elements here is cultural formation and another is psychological. It's fear. We don't know how to account for homosexuality in the psychological sense. Even if the American Psychological Association now insists that homosexuality is not a disorder or a disease, even if we want to recapture Freud's sense that sexuality is not clearly differentiated in people until much later in their lives and that perhaps we all begin life in some form of undifferentiated sexuality, we don't know how to account for it. And I think because we don't know how to account for it, whatever is outside of whatever is considered normative is to be feared, is to be held at arm's length against a certain boundary. Often, people in Africa, China, or Korea will say, "Oh, homosexuality is an American thing." It's not. It's a human orientation, one of several human sexual orientations. So, to talk about how we deal with difference, it seems to me— to sum up—we're talking about cultural formations and about personal responses to one's own development and sexuality.

Do you think homosexuality provides an opportunity to examine our theology in a way that is good for the church and for Christians? Does it bring forth some of what we need to consider if we are really going to take ourselves seriously as Christians?

A lot of theologians, myself included, can be concerned about issues or questions that emerge in our society, because whether we are focused on historical theology or social ethics or biblical studies or systematic studies we do live at a particular place in the world and at a particular time in history and it seems to me we cannot ignore the concerns of other Christians. That's part of our responsibility. How could any of us ignore the experience of Matthew Shepard—a young man pulled out into a desert, a faraway place, and left on a fence, beaten and bludgeoned and dying?[4] This is modern-day crucifixion.

So, for me the question of homosexuality from my point on the theological spectrum is bringing up questions about "the Other." How do we respond to the Other? How do we respond to whoever is considered the stranger? The Judeo-Christian tradition insists that we be hospitable to the stranger. Whether you're reading the Hebrew Bible or the Christian Scriptures, that's very clear. Do we violate this? Of course, we do; and I think most of us do so out of ignorance and out of fear, and again I may be heading down a psychological road, but from my perspective it is sin, clear and simple, to treat the Other as if the Other had no right to exist—and I'm using the word "right" in the theological sense that none of us has any rights to live except those rights given to us in relation to the Creator, in terms of our own creatureliness. In this way the destruction of the Other is unintelligible. It is irrational; it is chaotic. The destruction of the Other is a form of the surd, the absurd. It has no intelligibility whatsoever. And yet that sort of unintelligible behavior characterizes our performance in the world more often than not.

Do you remember when you first thought that you needed to relate to lesbians and gay men as the Other in an accepting way?

I think by meeting people as a young woman in college. I met people who I know now, and I knew to a certain extent then, were struggling with their own sexual identity. I met women who were beginning to identify themselves as lesbians. These were people who were just like me. They were human beings. They were trying to get their homework done. They were happy and unhappy, just like me. They wanted to get out of whatever we could get out of and wanted to do whatever we could do, with generosity and courage. So, I think for me it was simply encountering other people as human beings and fellow travelers, if you will, on the road. I don't have a specific experience. It is not as if there was a specific person who finally said to me, "I am a lesbian," but more of general engagement with others. I don't know that I have any special sensitivity to people, but I certainly can recognize, as I said about my experience at twelve, that when people consider you to be an Other and don't like you, their response to you can be your death. It certainly wasn't a way I wanted to live or to which I wanted to contribute. And it's not simply about moving beyond intolerance. I don't like the word "tolerance" very much because it quickly, as Bernard Lonergan pointed out,[5] devolves into being able to tolerate anything. My grandmother used to say to me, "If you can't heal bodies, heal souls." So, it seemed to me that I ought to try to engage other persons compassionately in conversation, in friendship, in intellectual relationship—whatever; it was our role and task as a human person, as a Christian.

Do you in your own work as a theologian find yourself relying on or drawing on lesbian and gay theologians or writers, such as John Boswell[6] or Audre Lorde?

Of course, I've read John Boswell, but I haven't done a purposeful reading of lesbian and gay authors. Audre Lorde is someone whose work has a great impact on me because of the topics she writes about. I'm more interested in people's ideas than I am in their sexuality; and I recognize that that's both a snare and a delusion. You can too easily say someone isn't writing about what you're interested in, but when you simply read what it is they've have written, you may find they're very well writing about what you are interested in. So, yes, I'm reading Audre Lorde because she writes so well about the erotics of power and about difference.[7] And I'm reading Adrienne Rich because she writes so well about women and honor, what it means to tell the truth.[8] What she has to say about living truth and living lie transcends any sort of sexual specificity. Her examples are drawn from her own experiences, but they have a universal character.

I find that I can use Lorde's writing in just about any class, and just about any student can somehow connect with her.

Exactly. That's the point. It's the old saw. Do Black writers write protest novels or propaganda novels or do they just write novels? They reflect on their experience. Does their experience have any universal value? Absolutely. They're human beings. Gay men and lesbians are writing novels and all sorts of things that can have a serious and true impact, because very frequently people are raising universal issues. Are there some bad gay writers? I'm sure there are. There are plenty of bad writers in the world.

The Catholic Church seems to get criticized a lot for not being good on gay and lesbian issues, yet some of the people who have advanced the discussion of homosexuality most significantly have been Roman Catholics, like John McNeill[9] and John Boswell. And now we also have the bishops' pastoral message, Always our Children.[10] *So, maybe the attacks overlook the good, however small, that's being done. Do you see things happening either locally or within Catholicism more generally that are good for lesbians and gay people?*

I think increasingly on Catholic university campuses our lesbian and gay students have been importuning us to really respond to their situation. Gay men and lesbians have always been in Catholic colleges and universities and always will be there, so their presence has to be met with real compassion and real interest; and we have to figure out how to do that. We have here an effort to create a gay/straight alliance—that's not its actual name—whose purpose would be educational. I'm not sure that it's going to happen, because people often become afraid that any group that has the word "gay" or "lesbian" or "homosexual" in it will be about "recruiting" (put that in scare quotes) gays and lesbians. There's the concern that if the university approves such a group it also sanctions so-called "recruitment," which is not at all the purpose of these young people.

The Catholic Church struggles over a lot of issues. We've got a lot of people. It's a global church. There are hundreds of cultural traditions and mores swirling around trying to inculturate a Christianity that is old and ever new. This is a particular challenge for us. We have to figure out ways to respond to our students, because the Matthew Shepard case was a startling one. Here's a person the age of some of the students I teach who winds up brutally murdered, and what does that say to them? How do we assure our students that the places in which we teach them are safe places? And how do we assure the parents of these students that their sons and daughters can be safe? If the pastoral message from the bishops—and I haven't read it yet; only caught some excerpts—says anything, it says that we must continue to love our children. One of the dimensions of love is protection and safety.

This also means we've got to inform and teach other students who are nongay and nonlesbian that someone else's sexual orientation is not an incrimination or an indictment of their own and that in the world where they live they will begin to find that many of their friends, in fact, turn out to be lesbians and gay men. I have a certain sense that there is increasingly among college youth an acceptance of this. I might be too sanguine, but I sense a kind of acceptance in which other people are allowed to be themselves and students may be more accepting of difference than we were or are. They may take their acceptance a bit too much for granted and may need to understand that many people in this country and around the world have suffered incredibly at the hands of Western civilization in its advance toward progress, and the church has been a part of that, but that we still can accept, we can embrace, we can still meet the Other face to face without violence being a part of that encounter.

I used to teach at Marist, a Roman Catholic college, and now I'm at Wesleyan, which is secular and very liberal. I found at Marist an openness to and struggle with uncertainty that was raw and real, while at Wesleyan there's more of an expectation that people simply should and do have the right position. Did you experience anything like that—in reverse—in your move from Yale to Marquette?

That's an interesting question. Our current struggle here concerns approving a gay/straight alliance and may be an example of that. Catholic universities have also responded to gay and lesbian students by saying that the chaplaincy is one place for you to gather. I think there is something to that, something positive in our own Catholic context that allows or encourages that readiness to accept and support—and this is my point about how all of us are formed culturally in our responses to sexuality, and in a certain way Catholics have a further formation that comes from the church.

The church's recent desire to emphasize the goodness of marriage and procreation of children is a response to never having emphasized it much in history, because we've preferred the celibate life, whether in men or women, to marriage. Any Catholic high school graduate of the '50s or so can recall those catechism pictures in which there stands the priest or the sister and underneath is written, "Single life is good, married life is better, but the best is the celibate life—the priesthood or religious life." To emphasize the goodness of marriage, I think, is a response of the Second Vatican Council to that casual approach historically to marriage.

So two things are operative here. One is that a procreative and marital emphasis, which might be seen as excluding and denying gay people, is not really at the heart of the church's history. The other is that the church itself is always struggling, in this case over issues of sexual identity. And there may be something positive in this Catholic context that lends itself to university chaplaincy responding to lesbian and gay students in a way that provides them a space and also facilitates their reflecting on their own struggle for identity in the midst of the swirling life that all college students have and the particular needs of our young gay and lesbian students. I think that that's part of the tension and the mix, because Catholics so live out of our church, we so live out of that kind of relationship. We're a funny church, because we all have an individual personal relationship with the head of the church who doesn't know that we exist (*laughs*)—I mean that in the best and humorous sense—and yet he does know we exist. So, we're funny people like that. We want to be known and to know; and that's a blessing, a gift. But it's also a tensive gift. We struggle with one another quite a bit.

As Roman Catholics I think we need to remember to struggle with one another in more charity in the really positive sense of that—"loving the Other." The parable of the prodigal son is not about the son; it's about the father. In a certain way our struggle is not about who's right and wrong, it's about recognizing that God is involved in this and that God, in a certain way, is trying to tell each of us something in any struggle. And the "something," I think, is about love and compassion for the Other on both sides, one brother for another in the case of the prodigal son. In the story of the Good Samaritan, one person already injured by exclusion is loving another who's been wounded and struck down perhaps by his own people. So, the wounded help the wounded in a certain way. And believe me, I don't want to go off on Henri Nouwen and *The Wounded Healer*[11] (*laughs*), but I think there is something to that. We're learning something about God being involved in that.

So, yes, for me there is a certain tensive quality about all of this for Catholics; and I think there can be something good that can come out of it, because all young people today need some guidance and direction on how to live their lives. Margaret Farley has been quite outspoken in writing about mutuality in same-sex ethics.[12] What's required in a heterosexual relationship, the kind of regard and respect for the other, is equally required in a same-sex relationship. Because we are, I think, both prudish and prurient at the same time, we tend to think of what's different as bad and exotic; so, we imagine homosexual relationships as wanton and opportunities for debased sex, whereas the demand of the relationship is real for anyone involved in it.

Do you think that the issues for Black lesbians and gay men are different than those of white lesbians and gay men? Does lumping all gay men and lesbians together do a disservice to them?

If we've learned anything from Black feminists or "womanists," if we've learned anything from Hispanic/Latina feminists or mujeristas, if we've learning anything from Asian feminists, it's that we have to account for differentiation.[13] That analysis really taught us all that there's no universal woman. Women are concrete in particular and have social context. I think the same is true for gay men and lesbians. There's a social context. As we found out in the women's movement, racism transcends gender; and I suspect racism transcends sexual orientation. Some African American lesbians and gay men, whom I know, have had that experience with white gay men and lesbians. I also think that some of that has been broken down in maybe the last decade. But I also think that gay men and lesbians need to look more carefully at issues among themselves and that we all need to participate in that examination in as much as we can all learn from various critiques.

For Black gay men and lesbians there are a range of issues. I don't know them all; certainly, I've read a lot of Audre Lorde and a number of other people who try to explore some of this. I think that one of the things that we all need to remember about the African American community is that one of the areas in which we've been wounded is sexuality. The legacy of deep scarring and the use of Black women and Black men sexually for several hundred years by slave holders impacts us today. So, the African American community—and this is a gross generalization—really struggles not to imitate European American life but to live its own life; and part of that life is a certain code of ethics and behavior. Now, even as I say that, that can be shocking for some people because they have come to assume that Black people are simply sexually loose and casual. I suspect that that image is reinforced by some of the gangster rap, which thankfully has begun to recede on the cultural scene today, although it's left a residue.

It seems to me that African Americans display all the kinds of human fears as other people do; and because we're human, we will. It's fear of difference, it's worry about your child, "What will happen to my child—who certainly is Black—when people find out that he is gay? He's going to get it from every side." The fears of every parent, which are ingrained in them for centuries, emerge at a time like this. One of the ways in which those fears strike us is a kind of anger. You're angry at the situation to which your child has come, and some of that anger unfortunately is deflected toward the child.

So, yes, while we're no different from other human beings, I think that there are some ways in which our differentiated social and cultural situation make us respond to this issue in the ways in which we do. But let me not ignore free will. People can and do respond to their children with love, enthusiasm, and support. There are wonderful examples of that. I think our responses in the end are as varied as any other group of people, and at the same time Black gay men and lesbians really are attempting to provide new information for our community about ourselves. In other words, they're reading back to us how we behave toward them, they're calling into question our rejection and our fears; and I think that's very healthy and important. I'm not trying to paint a rosy picture of the African American community, but I do think there's a dialectic developing. There's a learning going on and an encouragement for that learning.

I think what I hear you saying is that because the African American family has been under assault for so long, parents may respond to their gay children by trying to protect them. And the response of gay children may be to feel a desire and obligation to be part of that family in a traditional way.

That's true, but I think that the response on the parents' part is also to support gay and lesbian relationships. There are plenty of Black mothers and fathers who do just that.

Yes, you said there are wonderful examples. Can you share one?

I'm very careful about talking about people, because people suffer in so many ways. But I'm thinking of a mother of a friend who really has supported her tremendously both in her work and in her relationships. The mother of her partner is saying, "I always wanted my daughter to marry someone in the church and look, she did." There are plenty of opportunities of this kind of support, we just don't know about them. This is another issue, isn't it? We're frequently not able to allow people to be out. And that's hard, because then it doesn't provide models for people like my students.

They don't see healthy, strong, committed relationships, and they need to see heterosexual ones, too. It's not as if heterosexuals are ideal examples of how to carry on sustained committed relationships. Look at the heterosexual divorce rate. We have people who have serial marriages; they may not be polygamous, but there are serial marriages. This is true also among gays and lesbians, but the fact is that it does happen among heterosexuals. Look at the abuse of women in heterosexual marriages. It's not that gays and lesbians don't abuse one another in their relationships. Some do, but heterosexual marriage as we look around is not necessarily providing us with ideal examples of how to live. And where we have opportunities, where gay men and lesbians live committed relationships, we need to see and recognize them.

There are plenty of examples of people who are caring for each other; and we have plenty of examples in public life of people who abandon their partners at illness. Look at Bob Dole. During his first wife's illness, he divorced her. Margaret Farley's work on same-sex relationships and on commitment has been a challenge to everyone who wants to live a godly life, a life that has God in it and that keeps that relationship as a beam that moves through all of what we do, how we feel, and how we behave toward one another.

Do you have any advice for lesbians and gay men, any words of encouragement for those who are trying to find a place in the church and having some difficulty doing it?

I had a student—and this is advice I give myself, so I'm not trying to speak in a way that I wouldn't speak to myself—who wrote me a little note at the end of a reflection paper. It said, "I would just like to know what you think about the church and how the church deals with women." And I responded by explaining how the questions that she'd raised in the paper were important. What I would say to lesbians and gay men is that the questions you have raised for us are tremendously important. And I think they ought to become our questions—not "your," but "our" questions. And I think we all need to focus, not so much on the rules and regulations, although they are needed features of social connections, but—as I also said to my student—on God. That may sound pie-in-the-sky at a certain level and I recognize that people may respond to it in that way, but God is not implicated—although we may attempt to implicate God—in our choices and decisions to reject others because they seem different. There is one God who is one just judge of all. It seems to me this is where we need to fix our attention if we identify ourselves as Christians living in such a way that our living reflects Christ living in us. Again, I am not being naïve about the impact of socialization or the way in which we want to legislate people out of their sexual orientations or "cure" people of their sexual orientations. I certainly don't condone any of that. I do believe that all of us need to look beyond our own poor strategies and look someplace else, look to someone else, someone Divine.

Chapter 20

Rev. Dr. Yvonne V. Delk

*I*n 1974, Yvonne V. Delk became the first Black woman to be ordained in the United Church of Christ (UCC). From 1981 to 1990, she was the executive director of the UCC's national Office for Church in Society; in 1991 she became the first woman and the first Black executive director of the Community Renewal Society, an interfaith mission agency in Chicago. She has served on several boards and commissions of the World Council of Churches.[1]

Rev. Dr. Delk received her Doctor of Ministry degree from New York Theological Seminary. Her work, along with that of Sojourner Truth, Harriet Tubman, Ida B. Wells-Barnett, Mary McCloud Bethune, Anna Julia Cooper, Fannie Lou Hamer, and Shirley Chisholm, is anthologized in *Can I Get a Witness? Prophetic Religious Voices of African American Women.*[2] She is included among *Ebony* magazine's "America's 15 Greatest Black Women Preachers" and in *Who's Who among African Americans.*[3]

In the early '90s I did a national survey of lesbian/bisexual/gay people within the UCC. One of the questions I asked was, "Which denominational leader do you think has been the most supportive and encouraging?" You were most often named.[4]

That surprises me and encourages me to do more. I thought there were other folk who were a lot more involved and active than I was, but I'm pleased and honored.

Why do you think you've been a person who has been sensitive to the concerns of lesbians and gay men?

I really think at the core of my being, knowing the reality of what it has meant to grow up African American and female—and also in the Red Light district of Norfolk, which places the class issue right in the midst of this, too—created in me a sensitivity to the issues that gay and lesbian sisters and brothers were dealing with. Struggling in this society for my place to be, to stand, and to speak has created in me an openness and a responsiveness to others who are trying to do the very same thing. Having come out of a struggle of oppression into a place of liberation has made me very sensitive to the issues of others who are struggling. Second, I came out of a deeply spiritual, faith-based context. The church and my faith have been deep foundational affirmations for how I live my life. My faith perspective and beliefs have led me to make the connections between the different issues of injustice and oppression, and many of the attitudes and realities that gay and lesbian sisters and brothers have been dealing with have been deep justice issues.

A lot of people write off the church as a place that is hopeless in terms of lesbian and gay issues, and yet you're saying it's because of your religious background and faith commitment that you've been able to step up to the issue.

I was born into a church tradition that spoke very deeply to the sins and evil of racism in our society; it was the church that first named that evil as clearly as possible for me. For me it was my local Black church—Macedonia African Christian United Church of Christ now—that my momma and daddy brought me and my six sisters and brothers to on Sunday. In that place the faith perspective of who we were as persons created in the image of God stood over and against the cultural, social, historical, and economic perspective. I grew up in a strong faith tradition that affirmed me as a daughter of God and created in me a powerful sense that nothing and nobody can, once you have been named in the image of God, name you in a lesser way. I grew up with that message in my Sunday school, in the preaching that I heard over and over, in the choir messages, and in Wednesday night prayer meetings. The reality that the Gospel of Jesus Christ affirms you in a powerful sense as a child of God was so deeply ingrained in my psyche that it became one of the foundational affirmations of what I believe. I read the Bible and found stories that would reiterate that message—from stories in the Old Testament of the Hebrew people being delivered out from under slavery and oppression to stories of the new image of who we could become in Jesus Christ who created a new community across the lines of race and class and gender. I grew up with that, and it was a part of what helped me to understand what it meant to be a part of the household of Jesus Christ. Walls were brought down, bridges were built, and tables were set up where we could in fact begin to encounter each other—not in the way of the society or the culture, but in a new way of understanding, which was the community of faith.

When you've been baptized into that understanding, when you are nurtured Sunday after Sunday in that kind of context, it ingrains in you a sense of hope about what the church can be at its best. That's not to say that the church is not flawed by a lot of human understanding and society's understanding. Sometimes we bring our understanding of what it means to be human from our nationality right up into the church and use that as the gospel rather than the gospel that is there. It's not to say that our church is not broken by some of the same realities that we struggle with in society, but it also brings a powerful sense of hope and openness to become the new. And for me it's been one of the major places in society that I continue to have hope for and in. It's why I stay in the church, because even as I look at all of the other institutions that are out there, I still feel that there is a great hope in the religious institution when it allows itself to be shaped by the gospel of Jesus Christ and not simply by our own understanding, to really become a place where renewal, justice, and true human community can take place. At sixty years of age I still feel and believe that.

When you were talking before about examples from your past where walls have broken down, barriers have been overcome, and people have really dealt with issues, is part of that your experience of being Black and a woman within the church?

Yes. No matter how many steps you take forward, you encounter the reality of all of the prejudices and all of the negative ways of thinking that people bring into the church. So, to be African American and to be female in the church of Jesus Christ, I have had to walk up against many walls. I've hit those walls many times, but it's also been in the church that I have encountered the spirit and the power of people to reach beyond those walls for a new place. I have encountered folks not being content to simply stay in locked places, but to reach to really become the new creation in Jesus Christ. For some people it takes longer than others, but it's been in that setting that I've been excited about the possibility for the new.

It's not a coincidence that many of the leaders in the civil rights struggle came out of religious institutions. It's not a coincidence that the

Black church created itself and struggled within itself to become something other than the closed institution of the white church on the issue of race. It was born out of the struggle for justice and for wholeness, even though the same Black church wrestled with women in it and wrestles now with understanding gay and lesbian sisters and brothers; but it has been in that place that they have been willing to wrestle and struggle.

So, yes, I speak as one who has been deeply shaped by the religious institutions that I have been a part of; and those have been the Black church, the United Church of Christ which I've been part of for most of life, and lately the World Council of Churches in which I've had the opportunity to serve and to look at how faith communities connect across boundaries. It is in religious institutions that I have experienced both woundedness and the most hope.

Many lesbians and gay men have felt that the wounds have been so deep that we should leave. Perhaps we're at a point now of realizing that the wounds are deep for lots of people and they are not a reason to leave but to stay.

I keep remembering and I love this story from Henri Nouwen[5] where the people were asking, "Where is the Messiah?" And the Word is, "The Messiah is at the gate." So, the people go to the gate and all they see are wounded beggars. They come back and say, "We went to the gate, and we didn't see anyone who looked like a Messiah." So, the Word comes again, "Well, go back, look more carefully, and at the gate you will find a lot of beggars, but one is different, one who will be wounded and bandaging her own wounds, but with the other hand she will be bandaging the wounds of the others."

I grew up with the notion that the Christ we serve is a wounded Christ, not one who has it all together in terms of one strength, but strong in different ways than we think of. So, when I have moved through the struggles, pain, and wounds that I have had to move through, I've looked at them as a part of what it means to be a part of the community of Jesus Christ. If you are looking for a place in which there are no wounds, maybe the church doesn't hold the answers. It is the place of woundedness where even the Christ figure takes on the wounds of the world; therefore we take unto ourselves the wounds of the Other. It is another reason why the gay and lesbian issue is my issue, because I connect out of that space to the wounds of my sisters and brothers and in many ways walk as a part of the wounded healers in the midst of the world that we are part of. So, I'm not looking for perfection in the church; I'm looking for that place where we can open ourselves up and share our wounds, our pain, and our struggle, but in that to find the places of healing, hope, renewal, and the community that allow us to wrestle and struggle with each other.

Many times when my momma and daddy and all of us would go to Macedonia, it would be hard times. I remember my mother in the prayer meeting sharing some of the pains of having been through the week or my daddy talking about some of the indignity of going through the week; they were able to share the pain and the struggle. Others in that place met them with pain and struggle, but they also met each other with hope and a sense of affirmation that together we can walk this road and be renewed by the Word, together we can keep on keeping on. It was a marvelous sense of community in the midst of the woundedness, pain, and craziness of the world.

As you look back on the last thirty years in the UCC or in the church more generally, what do you see as the hopeful signs around lesbian/gay issues? What's taken place that you could never have imagined would take place?

I remember the time I first saw Bill Johnson.[6] Only Bill can tell the story of his relationship and encounter with his church, but it was a magnificent symbol for me when Bill Johnson stood up in that Synod[7] in 1972 and affirmed who he was, named himself as a gay man in this denomination. He pressed hard for a place in this church, which was so difficult in the beginning, and began to open up some possibilities for others. I never thought I would see the first Association[8] ordain a person who openly named himself gay, but it stood up and said, "Okay, we affirm this person in his calling as a member of the household of Jesus Christ and that is the predominant reality we will live by, and we do not necessarily judge him by what his sexual orientation is." I really thought it would be almost impossible for a gay or lesbian sister or brother to receive a call. And while the doors have not opened up as much as we would like, it's the beginning doors that allow you to begin to step forward and break down some of the walls that continue to block us.

In 1980 when I was the affirmative action officer for the UCC, it was clear that gay and lesbian sisters and brothers were beating their heads up against the wall trying to get access to positions in the denomination. We had named equal employment opportunity for a number of groups—on the basis of race, gender, and the differently abled—but we had not named sexual orientation. When that language was finally approved through the executive council, we were able to add those words. I felt we were making some breakthroughs just by the sheer naming of it and having the first meeting with several of our gay and lesbian sisters and brothers to ask, "Now, how do we make this real, how do we take this and enable some doors to open employment-wise?" That's what we were working on at that time, "How can the gifts of gay and lesbian sisters and brothers who have prepared themselves for ministry be received in this church?" So, that was a beginning step; and I think that the UCC Coalition for Lesbian/Gay/Bisexual/Transgender Concerns[9] has done some marvelous work to educate us, to press some of the critical issues, and to keep them before this church in a critical way, ending up most recently with, I thought, a very strong word from president Paul Sherry.[10]

It's been a hard issue for a variety of reasons, but I have been very hopeful each time a person stands. The first person I saw stand was Bill; for others it may have been other people. He stood in that strong way, walked through this church and up to that stage and named himself as clearly as he could as a person within the household of Jesus Christ and as a part of the United Church of Christ who was offering gifts to this church. I watched him and another gay man walk to the communion table at Synod to participate with people who were coming from all over to receive communion. His holding the hand of a gay brother and walking down the long aisle to that communion table symbolized for me the presence of Christ in them and the ability of the Word to flow through them and to take unto themselves the broken body and the new covenant. After they had communion, they embraced each other. I'm sure people were gasping. For some folk that was probably a very hard moment; for me it was an opening of a door and of some space for us to move through. To watch the variety of ways that some doors have opened since then has been very, very significant for me.

Recently, just before the last two Synods opened, the Urban Ministries Network[11] has been offering a worship time called, "Is It Well with Your Soul?" We began to offer out of the brokenness of the urban scene and out of the fact that so many of us who are working in the urban reality find ourselves broken in spirit and body. We're dying of heart attacks, high blood pressure, cancer, stress, racism, homophobia, classism, and sexism. All continue to eat away at us; so, the question is, "How do we move to healing and wholeness in the midst of the day-to-day brokenness?" We wanted to create a worship setting where we could bring folk together who had experienced brokenness in some way. The Coalition for

Lesbian/Gay/Bisexual/Transgender Concerns has been active, as well as the Council for Racial and Ethnic Ministries and the Coordinating Center for Women—all of us in that place found ourselves opening ourselves up to the Other, to receive from the Other, to be embraced, loved, and affirmed by the Other. I think we have to figure out new ways to come together in places that allow us to be touched by the Other. I've been very moved by our ability to step outside of and break down the negative, stereotyped ways of what I call looking at the Other as the stranger to be feared rather than as the sister or brother who is a gift from God.

How have you dealt with the people who have either been against or had trouble opening those doors? What finally allows them to open up?

One of the more difficult parts of this journey is trying to figure out how to unlock deeply locked minds on this subject. For a number of people, the locked-in nature has to do with biblical and theological affirmations they've developed over a period of time. I can't tell you how many times, especially in the African American church, that people just say that the Bible says that homosexuality is evil or wrong or sinful, even when I talk about how there are other things in the Bible that would cause us to question whether or not we can live with that Word. I talk about the Word as it relates to women and to people of color, especially to Black people, and that if we only did proof-texting of the Bible there would be a lot of people we would not welcome into the community of Jesus Christ. Even when I try to deal with them on biblical grounds, I find that people are often very stuck, but I still feel we've got to do biblical work. When we find that folk are really critically struggling with the Bible and that's their reason for saying, "We will not invite into the household of Jesus Christ people who are gay and lesbian," then we've got to do biblical work to open that door. But that's only a piece of it. Biblical work is one part; the other piece has to do with a deep fear.

I often preach sermons on overcoming fear of the Other and looking at the world with different eyes than we have looked at it in the past. People construct a way of being, believing, and deciding what's good and evil based on laws. As long as they can live with that law or their preconceptions, then they can deal. Unraveling that makes them fearful that anything and everything goes, that they'll have to live in a world without walls, where nothing will be valued or sacred. It's partially the fear of the Other and partially the fear of accepting almost anything. You have to try to get at the fear where people are and to try to work with people in terms of whether they are going to live their lives out of fear or hope. I do that by talking about gifts.

When I was the affirmative action officer, I tried to help folk understand this is not just about numbers and quotas, which was their big fear. And I said, "Of course, we don't want quotas; the church of Jesus Christ is not built on quotas, and therefore we need to have a different set of understandings about what it means for us to be a part of the household and to be an inclusive community. I don't want that just to mean we count and say how well we're doing. The faith and the commitment to Jesus Christ breaks all of that down; and we've got to come up with a new reality with which to look at the world, at who we are, and at who ought to be at the table." So, I tried to move outside of a numbers game by talking about gifts and about the church and the community that we can create through faith. I tried to erase the boundaries that we've built up around fear and to create another vision of a church that celebrates the gifts of all folk, where the gifts would be enriching and renewing us. Then our churches would be growing and overflowing; we would have vibrant communities able to reach out and speak to some of the issues that we're dealing with in our society. The church would have life and energy that would really affirm what it means to be a vibrant, faith-based presence in the midst of the world that we are part of. So, I try to paint those kinds of pictures, to offer that kind of vision of who we could be in our fullness.

As executive director of the UCC's Office for Church and Society during the '80s, I got called upon to speak almost everywhere and anywhere: conference meetings, association meetings, women's meetings, youth meetings. I was a voice all over the place (*laughs*). The words that I was able to bring impacted the way the church opened itself to becoming Open and Affirming.[12] Each time I spoke I made a decision that the vision I would paint would always be a church that was Open and Affirming as it related to gay and lesbian sisters and brothers. People would often come to me and say, "We thank you, we appreciate the fact that you named that, that you included that as a part of your vision. So, we're going to take that back to our churches, and we'll start struggling and fighting for that in our churches." I feel that a number of those churches became Open and Affirming churches because I was willing to stand and to say this is my vision, my image, my affirmation of the sisters and brothers who ought to be included at the table. I stood in enough places and I really believe that vision took root in the minds of some folk who were previously shut down.

I came to the national offices of the UCC in 1969; and during the '70s and '80s I was involved at one level or another working on justice issues and Christian education. In the 1975 Synod, I think, "Women in Church and Society" was named the number-one issue; and the church was really going to be critical in its commitment to eradicating sexism in the church. A women's inner-staff team was created; women from the different national instrumentalities and offices formed a team to look at how we could move the commitment taken in Synod throughout the life of our church. Five of us were working together, a powerful team. We would go around to Conferences[13] and deal with a number of women's issues; but we had not clearly named the issues as they related to gay and lesbian sisters and brothers in the church, until we were at this wonderful consultation on women's issues in California.

A lot of women came to look at the issue from a variety of perspectives. We had already planned to address the issue of women from a racial perspective, an economic perspective, in terms of language, and a variety of other things. Each of us on the women's inner-staff team had a particular orientation that we were really going to open up and talk about. I knew I was going to talk about race. Susan Savelle was to talk about language. The night before the event was to take place, Susan called the team together and said something like, "I've been wrestling for a long time, and I have decided that tomorrow when we do our presentation I will name myself and talk as a lesbian woman." Susan had not come out publicly as of that moment, but on this occasion she had decided to. Well, the other four of us who were on the panel struggled with that for quite some time that night trying to decide, "Is this the best thing; is it going to take us away from everything else we were planning to do?" But Susan was so clear she felt called to do it that we basically said, "Okay." How can you say no to someone who felt as called as that, even though you might be anxious about what would happen?

This was another breakthrough moment in my lifetime in the church on this issue. The place was packed; we moved through the panel; and then Susan did her presentation. She stood in that place and shared out of the deepest part of her being who she was and how there had been a scream building up that she had to let out. She had been unable to name it before, but now today she was going to be free because she could name this and let her affirmation of who she was come to the surface. When she named that, you almost felt like there was a hush that moved through all of those women who were gathered. After the panel finished its presentation, there was a time for people to respond. And I'm telling you, people lined up at the microphone, and while I thought folks would be very upset, which is not to say there weren't some, for the most part she had opened up in women in that place a space that allowed them to respond. She gave permission, and it wasn't just lesbian women who responded. Mothers of sons and daughters who were gay or lesbian came to the microphone to talk both about their joy that she had finally named it in a way that allowed them to open themselves up, to name it for themselves, and to say what they were feeling and to be in dialogue about that. We had to reconstruct the workshops afterwards because so many people wanted to keep talking about the issue.

What it did for me was make me realize I had to name the issue. As a heterosexual woman I named it differently than Susan, but I named it. I tried to name it in a way that people would have permission to talk about it, open themselves up, and begin to look at some new possibilities for it. That was for me what I call a "world-changing moment" in the midst of the ways in which we had been doing things in the church. I will always be indebted to Susan Savelle for her decision to break rank with everything we had planned, and to really be able to say, "In this place I will stand and share who I am." I felt that the wind and spirit of God moved all through the place and so many others were then opened up to begin to talk and to reach in relationship.

When you said you named it differently than Susan, how did you name it?

Susan stood as a lesbian woman and named what it had meant for her to not be able to say who she was, to keep it a secret, to be in the closet, to hide her identity. She stood there as one who was now able to say, "I am a lesbian woman; I affirm who I am as a lesbian woman; and I want this church to celebrate and affirm the gifts that I have." There is something powerful about being a lesbian woman naming it in that particular context that opened up other women who were lesbian as well.

I stood as a heterosexual woman who had been very homophobic. That's the other piece of my life that I also have to admit. Up until and moving into the '60s, I probably was about as homophobic as anybody I remember, because I grew up with people who had always looked negatively on folk who were gay or lesbian. Throughout high school I heard all the negative stuff about anybody who was different, all the harmful, hurtful words used to define anyone who was gay or lesbian; and even in the church that affirmed me so strongly as an African American woman of faith created in the image of God, when it got to this issue, I also heard the negative words with scriptural references supporting them. I must say that I was homophobic.

It was a wonderful, opening, affirming relationship with Jan Griesinger that first made me examine my homophobia. I met Jan when she and I were both in Cincinnati in the '60s. We got a chance to sit at the table with the all-male ministerium, because there were no UCC women pastors in Cincinnati. We were not ordained at the time, but we were commissioned as directors of Christian education, so they had allowed us to sit with our commission status at this table. She and I bonded right away because we had to protect ourselves in the midst of a very male-dominated situation. We were always pushing justice and women's issues, so we became good friends very quickly. Jan was married, and I used to go over to their house all the time. When I left Cincinnati and Jan went back to school to get her degree for ordained ministry, we remained friends. Jan would visit my family in Virginia, and I would visit her family in Illinois. Everybody in my family loved Jan, and everyone in Jan's family loved me. I remember that day in Ohio when Jan called me and told me she wanted to talk. We met for dinner, and she said she wanted to share something. What she shared was that after her divorce and going to school, she had found herself being very drawn to a woman. She had come to understand this as love and had decided she was going to make a commitment to this woman. Well, I'm telling you, I felt like I wanted to go across the room. Jan had been a wonderful friend, but I wanted to say, "Well, now, this changes everything!" But understanding who I was, Jan continued to reach towards me. She helped me to understand where she was in this relationship and what it was for her to make a commitment to a woman. She didn't leave me; she stayed with me while I continued to ask my questions, to talk about how I felt, to talk about my fears. So, more than anybody else, Jan Griesinger's presence through that relationship of love and caring helped me to make my first major step outside of my homophobic tendencies. I continue to have to do that day for day for day.

So, at that women's consultation in California I stood up to speak as a heterosexual woman who had been very homophobic. I could say, "I have been in that place where you are or where you may have been, and I am continuing to struggle." I felt if I spoke with the same kind of authentic openness that Susan did and people saw that what I was offering was real and not just politically correct, if you will, that it was really coming out of my spirit and affirmation of faith, then I could still reach people. Different than Susan—who was white, female, lesbian, coming out—Yvonne Delk, African American woman of faith, had once been homophobic and had the tendency to fly back over into that camp.

When you talk about people and their fears, you know what you're talk-
ing about.

Yes, I've been there, and I know exactly what I'm talking about.

What advice do you have for lesbian and gay men about what we need to
do in the church from this point on?

First, I would say don't give up on the church, on the faith community
that is there. I still believe it has great potential. Every now and then I see
it coming in wonderful visions where we are all together affirming, lifting, encouraging, engaging in acts of justice, doing what it means to be
the household of Jesus Christ. When I see and feel it, when I'm in those
places where it takes place, I know what a powerful community that can
be. It's a place we can both receive gifts from each other as well as be sisters and brothers on the road to dealing with all the realities of life that we
need to deal with. It is a table that allows us to come together affirming
our faith and being a part of the household of Jesus Christ. So, first of all,
I wouldn't give up on the religious community, on the household of Jesus
Christ. I would continue to reach from within it for where we can really
be sisters and brothers on this journey together.

Second, I think it's important to continue to name the issue out of the context in which they experience it. You have to name it. One of the things I've
said about racism all my life is that I will name it. I will never allow folk to
silence me on the issue or how I see it, because we have such a great proclivity to engage in denial as it relates to what is really going on in this society. In order to counteract denial you've got to name the reality. So, I
encourage them to continue in as many ways as possible to name the issue,
both the ways in which folk have been victimized as well as the gifts that are
there, give us hope, and enrich the lives of our church. People are accustomed to having us name how we've been wounded, victimized, and broken
by the reality of this issue; but on the other side is naming how we are called
to be the new community with the gifts we bring and what they can mean
for our lives together as a whole people seeking to be God's people in the
midst of the world that we are part of. So I would name both: the injuries
and the gifts.

Third, I would say continue to look for those places where we can
build some bridges. As we reach to become a multiracial, multicultural
church and talk about what it means to be inclusive of all, we have to
be sure we have named ourselves Open and Affirming as it relates to

gay and lesbian sisters and brothers, to make sure the justice issues relate to gay and lesbian sisters and brothers. It was very interesting to me recently to see Jerry Falwell, who is not one of my favorite people, sitting with two hundred to three hundred gay and lesbian sisters and brothers; and while he still thinks that scripture speaks against them and that the religious community has done nothing to harm them in any way, he's not willing to live with the violence against gay and lesbian sisters and brothers. So, they gathered with him and came to that table on the issue of violence; and I believe irrespective of what Jerry Falwell says, he's not going to be able to stay as rigid in his condemnation of gay and lesbian sisters and brothers as he once was.[14] My advice is to keep looking for the tables that will allow us to begin to build connections, communities, and a sense of being together in the midst of the journey in front of us.

Finally, I would say—and this is the hardest part, at least it's been the hardest part for me—if you can, take and use Martin King's words, "You've got to love them." I can remember in my heart the lynchings, the horror of the slavery, the middle passage, the second-class citizenship, and all the horrible experiences we've had to endure, and then for Martin to say you've got to love, because love can win in a way that hating cannot. So, the question is how to function from a place of love when you've been judged—and a lot of what gay and lesbian sisters and brothers are dealing with has to do with having been judged and the absence of being loved—how to be in that place of love that allows you then not to demonize the Other, because if I demonize those who are oppressing me and create out of them something less than human, I will have taken on the role of oppressor. And so, I stand on the ground that is most affirming in terms of being able to build a new world. We're getting ready to move into the new millennium, and I really do believe that our ability to understand what it means to love and to create open tables will take us further than we've been in the twentieth century. I'm so rooted in the faith community, because it is the place that allows me to wrestle with that understanding of what love is. And that is not to mean that I will not fight the injustice. I will. But it does mean that I will not demonize you, because when I demonize you I lose hope. When I demonize you, I've created a wall of enemies and given over to the power and principalities that will take us in the direction that I don't intend to move in. My advice is to hold on to the love ethic and to allow that love ethic to lead them to places which will open up even more tables, more newness, and a more inclusive society that we can be a part of.

Now, I know that none of that is easy. As one who's never found it easy, I have also felt that every door you bring down, every wall that comes down, every bridge you build takes you to a new place where it is possible to reach for the kind of world God intends. It's worth it.

Notes

All of the notes below are the work of the interviewer and not of the people interviewed. The notes are intended (1) to document and provide additional information about various statements, events, and references in the interviews; and (2) to suggest further reading about the topics discussed and the issues raised in the interviews.

ACKNOWLEDGMENTS

1. James Baldwin, "James Baldwin: A Rare Interview with a Legendary Writer," interview by Jere Real, *Advocate: National Gay Lesbian Magazine,* 27 May 1986, 42–46.

INTRODUCTION

1. Garth Kasimu Baker-Fletcher, Xodus: *An African American Male Journey* (Minneapolis: Fortress, 1996), 35.

2. By capitalizing "Black" when referring to African Americans, I adhere to the advice of Mary L. Foulke and Renee L. Hill, "We Are Not Your Hope for the Future: Being an Interracial Lesbian Family Living in the Present," in Robert Goss and Amy Adams Squire Strongheart, eds., *Our Families, Our Values: Snapshots of Queer Kinship* (New York: Harrington Park, 1997), 243, who write, "In resistance to whiteness as a cultural norm, Black will be spelled with capital 'B' throughout this essay."

"The Black church" is a general term that refers to Protestant denominations with predominantly African American memberships, such as the African Methodist Episcopal Church, African Methodist Episcopal Zion Church, and National Baptist Convention U.S.A., as well as to African American congregations within predominantly white religious bodies, such as the American Baptist Churches in the U.S.A., Roman Catholic Church, United Church of Christ, Presbyterian Church (U.S.A.), and United Methodist Church. See Reginald Glenn Blaxton, "'Jesus Wept': Reflections on HIV Dis-ease and the Churches of Black Folk," in Eric Brandt, ed., *Dangerous Liaisons: Blacks, Gays, and the Struggle for Equality* (New York: New Press, 1999), 128 n. 29; Barry A. Kosmin and Seymour P. Lachman, *One Nation under God: Religion in Contemporary American Society* (New York:

Harmony, 1993); and C. Eric Lincoln and Lawrence H. Mamiya, *The Black Church in the African American Experience* (Durham, N.C.: Duke University Press, 1990).

3. See Gary David Comstock, *Unrepentant, Self-Affirming, Practicing: Lesbian/ Bisexual/Gay People within Organized Religion* (New York: Continuum, 1996), 189–93; Renee McCoy, "Who Will Be There for Us?" *Open Hands: Journal of the Reconciling Congregation Program* (spring 1987): 14–15; Craig C. Harris, "Cut Off from Among Their People," in Joseph Beam, ed., *In the Life: A Black Anthology* (Boston: Alyson, 1986), 63–67; James T. Sears, *Growing Up Gay in the South: Race, Gender, and Journeys of the Spirit* (New York: Harrington Park, 1991), 47–70; and John Blake, "Gays & God: Hostility Rules among Black Congregations," *Atlanta Journal and Constitution,* 31 May 1998, sec. A, p. 19.

4. For various discussions of the pro-and anti-gay aspects of the Black church, see Victor Anderson, "Abominations of a Million Men: Reflection on a Silent Minority," in Garth Kasimu Baker-Fletcher, ed., *Black Religion after the Million Man March: Voices of the Future* (Maryknoll, N.Y.: Orbis, 1998), 19–26; Karen Baker-Fletcher and Garth Kasimu Baker-Fletcher, *My Sister, My Brother: Womanist and Xodus God-Talk* (Maryknoll, N.Y.: Orbis, 1997), 259; Blaxton, " 'Jesus Wept,' " in Brandt, ed., *Dangerous Liaisons,* 102–41; Keith Boykin, *One More River to Cross: Black and Gay in America* (New York: Anchor/Doubleday, 1996), 123–211; and "Gays and the Million Man March," in Kim Martin Sadler, ed., *Atonement: The Million Man March* (Cleveland: Pilgrim, 1996), 16–17; Harold Burris, "AIDS in the Black Community: An Interview," *Open Hands: Journal of the Reconciling Congregation Program* (summer 1988): 10–12; Michael Eric Dyson, *Race Rules: Navigating the Color Line* (Reading, Mass.: Addison-Wesley, 1996), 77–108; Sam Fulwood II, "Black Ministers Break Silence, Discuss AIDS," *Los Angeles Times,* 11 November 1991, sec. A, p. 1; Lynell George, "Breaking Barriers That Keep Them from the Church; Documentaries: Sylvia Rhue Explores Spirituality and Homophobia among African Americans to Get People Talking about a Sensitive Subject," *Los Angeles Times,* 15 April 1996, sec. E, p. 1; Manning Marable, *Black Liberation in Conservative America* (Boston: South End, 1997), 36–43; Cheryl Gay Stolberg, "Epidemic of Silence: A Special Report; Eyes Shut, Black America Is Being Ravaged by AIDS," *New York Times,* 29 June 1998, sec. A, p. 1; Emilie M. Townes, "The Price of the Ticket: Racism, Sexism, Heterosexism, and the Church in Light of the AIDS Crisis," in Susan E. Davies and Eleanor H. Haney, eds., *Redefining Sexual Ethics: A Sourcebook of Essays, Stories, and Poems* (Cleveland: Pilgrim, 1991), 67–73; Renita Weems, "Just Friends," in Gary David Comstock and Susan E. Henking, eds., *Que(e)rying Religion: A Critical Anthology* (New York: Continuum, 1997), 351–56; Cornel West, *Race Matters* (New York: Vintage, 1994), 119–31; "On the Future of the Black Church," interview by Paul Ruffins, *Prophetic Reflections: Notes on Race and Power in America,* Beyond Eurocentrism and Multiculturalism, vol. 2 (Monroe, Maine: Common Courage, 1993), 73–80; and Evelyn C. White, "Critics Say It Is Out of Touch: Identity Crisis for the Black Church," *San Francisco Chronicle,* 12 January 1994, sec. A, p. 1.

5. As quoted by Blake, "Gays & God," *Atlanta Journal and Constitution,* 31 May 1998, sec. A, p. 19.

6. See James S. Tinney, "Struggles of a Black Pentecostal," in Michael J. Smith, ed., *Black Men/White Men: A Gay Anthology* (San Francisco: Gay Sunshine, 1983), 163–72; George Chauncey, *Gay New York: Gender, Urban Culture, and the Making of the Gay Male World, 1890–1940* (New York: Basic Books, 1994), 254–56; and Adam Clayton

Powell, *Against the Tide: An Autobiography* (New York: Richard R. Smith, 1938), 57–59, 206, 209–20. See also as quoted by Sara Rimer, "Group of Leading Blacks Urges Campaign on AIDS Awareness," *New York Times,* 23 October 1996, sec. A, p. 16, Henry Louis Gates, chairman of Afro-American Studies at Harvard, who says, "In part because of a traditional homophobic tendency in our culture, in part because of our ignorant stereotypes about H.I.V. and AIDS, our people, our leaders, our culture, have long been in denial about AIDS in the black community."

   7. Comstock, *Unrepentant, Self-Affirming, Practicing,* 6–7, 243.
   8. See Sheila D. Collins, *The Rainbow Challenge: The Jackson Campaign and the Future of U.S. Politics* (New York: Monthly Review, 1987).
   9. See the following results from Pew Research Center for the People and the Press, "The Diminishing Divide . . . American Churches, American Politics," Washington, D.C., 25 June 1996, 20–21, 31, 33, 51–52:

Society should accept homosexuality
Total	46%
White Mainline Protestants	52%
White Evangelical Protestants	25%
White Catholics	52%
Jewish	79%
White Non-Religious	66%
Black Christians	47%
Black Non-Christians	56%
Hispanic Catholics	55%
Hispanic Non-Catholics	50%
Mormon	34%
White Other	48%

Favor allowing gay marriage
Total	28%
White Mainline Protestants	27%
White Evangelical Protestants	13%
White Catholics	31%
Black Christians	25%
No religious preference	45%

See the following results from Lyman A. Kellstedt, John C. Green, James L. Guth, and Corwin E. Smidt, "Grasping the Essentials: The Social Embodiment of Religion and Political Behavior," in John C. Green, James L. Guth, Corwin E. Smidt, and Lyman A. Kellstedt, eds., *Religion and the Culture Wars: Dispatches from the Front* (Landam, Md.: Rowan & Littlefield, 1996), 174–92.

Against gay rights
Mainline Protestant	27%
Evangelical Protestant	48%
Black Protestant	31%
Conservative Non-Traditional	38%

Liberal Non-Traditional	13%
Roman Catholic	24%
Orthodox	54%
Jewish	11%
Non-Judeo, Non-Christian	14%
Secular	24%
Average	28%
Average religious groups	31%

10. Comstock, *Unrepentant, Self-Affirming, Practicing,* 191–92.

11. See William Sloane Coffin, *The Heart Is a Little to the Left: Essays on Public Morality* (Hanover, N.H.: Dartmouth College Press, 1999).

12. See John Shelby Spong, *Here I Stand: My Struggle for a Christianity of Integrity, Love, and Equality* (San Francisco: Harper, 2000).

13. See Jim Dyer and Mark Hornbeck, "Special Report: Catholic Church; Gumbleton Wears Mantle of Liberal Hero, Pariah Priest," *Detroit News,* 28 March 1997, sec. C, p. 1; Peter Steinfels, "Bishops Protest Vatican Advisory Condoning Anti-Homosexual Bias," *New York Times,* 2 November 1992, sec. B, p. 11; and Richard L. Smith, *AIDS and the American Catholic Church* (Cleveland: Pilgrim, 1994), 51.

14. See Tex Sample and Amy E. DeLong, eds., *The Loyal Opposition: Struggling with the Church on Homosexuality* (Nashville: Abingdon, 2000); Tex S. Sample, "Should Gays and Lesbians Be Ordained?" in Sally B. Geis and Donald E. Messer, eds., *Caught in the Crossfire: Helping Christians Debate Homosexuality* (Nashville: Abingdon, 1994), 121–31; and Kate Beem, "Local Group Opposes Move of Conservative Methodists," *Kansas City Star,* 24 February 1996, sec. C, p. 2.

15. See Jane Adams Spahr, Kathryn Poethig, and Selisse Berry, eds., *Called OUT: The Voices and Gifts of Lesbian, Gay, Bisexual, and Transgendered Presbyterians* (Gaithersburg, Md.: Chi Rho, 1999); Virginia Culver, "Lesbian Evangelist Speaks Out, 'Now the Country Is My Congregation,' She Says," *Denver Post,* 5 May 1995, sec. B, p. 1; Don Lattin, "Church Upholds Its Ban against Gay Clergy," *San Francisco Chronicle,* 9 June 1993, sec. A, p. 15; Nancy Bartley, "When Religion and Sexuality Collide: Some Fear Issue Will Tear Presbyterian Church Apart," *Seattle Times,* 22 May 1993, sec. C, p. 7; Gayle White, "Presbyterians Await Ruling on Lesbian Minister's Role in Church: Some Challenge Call to Serve as Pastor," *Atlanta Journal and Constitution,* 8 June 1992, sec. A, p. 4; and Don Lattin, "Presbyterians Hire Marin Lesbian Pastor: Denomination's 1st Openly Gay Minister," *San Francisco Chronicle,* 13 December 1991, sec. A, p. 2.

16. See Kris Culp, "The Disciples Vote: Discovering Politics," *Christianity and Crisis,* 13 January 1992, 406–09; Ronald J. Allen, "Kinnamon's Defeat and the Disciples of Christ," *Christian Century,* 11 December 1991, 1156–59; Chris Bull, "Christian Church Rejects Candidate over Pro-Gay Views," *Advocate: The National Gay & Lesbian Newsmagazine,* 3 December 1991, 17; Cecile Holmes White, "Disciples Choose Less Controversial Leader," *Houston Chronicle,* 2 November 1991, 1; James L. Franklin, "Gay Issue Defeats Kentucky Dean," *Boston Globe,* 31 October 1991, 40; Janice Bullard, "Church Leader Rejected for Views on Gays," *USA Today,* 29 October 1991, sec. A, p. 2; Peter Steinfels, "Split on Homosexuality; Church Rejects a Prospective Leader," *New York Times,* 30 October 1991, sec. A, p. 19; and Bill Wolfe, "Views on Gay Ordination May Cost Pastor Top Post," *Courier-Journal* (Louisville), 22 September 1991, sec. B, p. 1.

17. See Gustav Niebuhr, "Reform Rabbis Back Blessing of Gay Unions," *New York Times,* 30 March 2000, sec. A, pp. 1, 20; Gary D. Robertson, "Reform Rabbis Consider Sanctioning Same-Sex Unions: Resolution Would Allow 'Commitment Ceremonies,'" *Ottawa Citizen,* 26 March 2000, sec. D, p. 6; Michael Paulson, "Reform Rabbis Seen Backing Same-Sex Ceremonies," *Boston Globe,* 24 March 2000, sec. A, p. 1; Marilyn Henry, "U.S. Reform Movement May Approve Same-Sex Unions," *Jerusalem Post,* 19 March 2000, 1; Marilyn Henry, "American Rabbis Sign Pro-Gay Rights Declaration," *Jerusalem Post,* 19 January 2000, 4; and Charles W. Bell, "Reform Rabbis in Flux," *New York Daily News,* 22 May 1999, 22.

18. Audre Lorde, *Sister Outsider: Essays and Speeches* (Freedom, Calif.: Crossing, 1984), 43–44.

19. Ibid., 115.

CHAPTER 1: REV. TIMOTHY MCDONALD III

1. See the church's Web page at www.firsticonium.org, and in the *Atlanta Journal and Constitution* the following articles: John Blake, "High Ideals May Undergird a Pastor's Work, but Ministers—Like Their Flocks—Are Not Immune to Wrongdoing; Pulpit Temptations," 6 February 1999, sec. C, p. 1; Hollis R. Towns, "New Directions: Atlanta after the Million Man March; Message Has Crossed Religious Lines; Baptist Minister Respects What Farrakhan Is Preaching," 12 May 1996, sec. G, p. 4; and Gary Pomerantz, "Communities; The Well-Amplified Preacher," 20 September 1992, sec. E, p. 6.

2. Shirelle Phelps, ed., *Who's Who among Black Americans,* 8th ed. (Detroit: Gale, 1994).

3. See the following articles in the *Atlanta Journal and Constitution* for coverage of Rev. McDonald's advocacy and community work: Rochelle Carter, "Minister Vows to Stop Cafeteria Contracts," 11 March 1999, sec. JD, p. 8; S. A. Reid, "NPU-W; No Protests Pending Decision on Voting Rights," 11 March 1999, sec. JD, p. 10; "Ministers Denounce Scholarship Proposal," 1 April 1998, sec. B, p. 3; Rochelle Carter, "Black Groups Step Up Edison Opposition; Foot in the Door; Privatized Education Project Arouses Suspicion of a Future of Neglect for Inner-City Youngsters," 26 December 1998, sec. F, p. 1; Hollis R. Towns, "Clergy Group Focusing on Economics," 9 May 1997, sec. D, pp. 3, 5; Tracie Reddick, "Black Workers Find 'Tale of Two Cities,'" 12 May 1996, sec. G, p. 4; Rick Christie and Scott Shepard, "Race and the Election; Born-Again Politics; Stung by Fires and the 1994 Vote, Many Black Churches Are Taking a More Aggressive Stand; and They're Targeting the Fall Election," 6 October 1996, sec. G, p. 1; Macon Morehouse, "Group Plans Voter Drives, Ways to Help Black Kids," 25 October 1995, sec. B, p. 2; Mark Silk, "Religious Leaders Unite to Influence Public Policy," 12 March 1994, sec. E, p. 6; Ellen Whitford, "Anti-School Board Group Picks 9 Candidates It Says Can Pull Together as Team," 9 September 1993, sec. D, p. 12; "Helping Needy Often Means Learning from Past Mistakes," 19 April 1992, sec. D, p. 7; Charles Salter, "Georgia Activists Urge Senate to Reject Thomas Nomination," 11 September 1991, sec. A, p. 8; and Bert Roughton Jr., "The Games; Atlanta Plans for its Future; Activists Take on Olympics Program," 26 October 1991, sec. B, p. 3.

4. See John Blake, "Gays & God; Hostility Rules among Black Congregations," *Atlanta Journal and Constitution,* 31 May 1998, sec. A, p. 19.

5. See, for example, Timothy McDonald, "Chuck's Story: The First Iconium Baptist

Church," in J. Shannon Clarkson, ed., "Life Stories," in Letty M. Russell, ed., *The Church with AIDS: Renewal in the Midst of Crisis* (Louisville, Ky.: Westminster/John Knox, 1990), 159–60.

CHAPTER 2: REV. LARRY C. MENYWEATHER-WOODS

1. Brochure, "History of Mount Moriah Missionary Baptist Church"; Julia McCord, "Stigma Against Divorced Clergy Eases," *Omaha World-Herald,* 21 January 1995, sec. SF, p. 53; and Donnette Dunbar, "Joyful Noise; Many Pastors Embrace the Dramatic Style of Preaching Known as 'Hooping,'" *Omaha World-Herald,* 21 February 1998, sec. SF, p. 65.

2. In *Omaha World-Herald,* see Cindy Gonzalez, "Black Leaders; Response from Police Improves," 6 January 1999, 2; Cindy Gonzalez and Chris Burbach, "Black Leaders Voice Frustration," 21 January 1999, 6; Melissa Matczak, "Omaha's NAACP Group Backs School-Bond Issue," 28 April 1999, 13; C. David Kotok, "Anti-Violence Workshop Held for King Holiday Events across Omaha Seek Ways to Commemorate the Slain Civil Rights Leader," 18 January 1998, sec. B, p. 5; Jim Minge, "Diversity Aim of Program," 24 February 1996, sec. SF, p. 57; Jena Janovy, "North Omaha Plan Gains Support; Council Backs Funds for Renaissance 2000," 20 September 1995, 1; and Alva James-Johnson, "Ames Project Backer Tired of Waiting for Banks," 1 June 1995, sec. SF, p. 13.

3. Donnette Dunbar, "Black Churches and Gays; While Homosexuals Sometimes Play Active Roles in Congregations, Their Sexuality Is Often a Matter of 'Don't Ask, Don't Tell," *Omaha World-Herald,* 18 April 1998, sec. SF, p. 65.

4. For a brief summary of the emergence and development of liberation theology, see C. Eric Lincoln and Lawrence H. Mamiya, *The Black Church in the African American Experience* (Durham: Duke University Press, 1990), 176–82.

5. The Balm in Gilead is a national, nonprofit organization located in New York City. "The mission of the organization is to work through Black churches to stop the spread of HIV and AIDS in the African American community and to support those infected with and affected by HIV." See Web page at www.balmingilead.org.

6. First Corinthians 6–7 warns against extramarital sex and provides directions for marriage.

7. Kelly Brown Douglas, *Sexuality and the Black Church: A Womanist Perspective* (Maryknoll, N.Y.: Orbis, 1999).

8. For a brief definition, summary, and discussion of womanist theology, see Lincoln and Mamiya, *The Black Church in the African American Experience,* 301–4.

9. See Delores S. Williams, *Sisters in the Wilderness: The Challenge of Womanist God-Talk* (Maryknoll, N.Y.: Orbis, 1995); Diana L. Hayes, *Hagar's Daughters: Womanist Ways of Being in the World* (New York: Paulist Press, 1995); Emilie M. Townes, *In A Blaze of Glory: Womanist Spirituality as Social Witness* (Nashville: Abingdon, 1995); and Evelyn Brooks Higginbotham, *Righteous Discontent: The Women's Movement in the Black Baptist Church, 1880–1920* (Cambridge: Harvard University Press, 1993).

10. In Dunbar, "Black Churches and Gays," *Omaha World-Herald,* 18 April 1998, sec. SF, p. 65, Rev. Menyweather-Woods is quoted as saying, "The hypocrisy of the church is not being able to deal with who we are and the reality that in spite of ourselves, God can still use us. I've seen God use gay people just as he has heterosexuals."

11. See Gayraud S. Wilmore, *Black Religion and Black Radicalism: An Interpretation*

of the Religious History of African Americans, 3d ed. (Maryknoll, N.Y.: Orbis, 1998); "Pastoral Ministry in the Origin and Development of Black Theology," in James H. Cone and Gayraud S. Wilmore, eds., *Black Theology: A Documentary History, Volume II, 1980–1992* (Maryknoll, N.Y.: Orbis, 1993), 116–26; "Black Power, Black People, Theological Renewal," in James H. Cone and Gayraud S. Wilmore, eds., *Black Theology: A Documentary History, Volume I, 1966–1979,* 2d ed. rev. (Maryknoll, N.Y.: Orbis, 1979, 1993); *Last Things First* (Philadelphia: Westminster, 1982); and "Black Theology and Pastoral Ministry," in Earl E. Shelp and Ronald H. Sunderland, eds., *The Pastor As Theologian* (New York: Pilgrim, 1988), 30–67.

CHAPTER 3: REV. DR. AMOS C. BROWN

1. Larry D. Hatfield, "Brown Names New S.F. Supes; Black Minister, Gay Lawyer to Replace Migden, Kennedy," *San Francisco Examiner,* 21 May 1996, sec. A, p. 1.

2. Shirelle Phelps, ed., *Who's Who among African Americans,* 11th ed. (Detroit: Gale, 1998); and "The 15 Greatest Black Preachers," *Ebony,* November 1993, 156–64.

3. Bill Staggs, "Troupe Irks San Francisco Catholics," *New York Times,* 26 March 1999, sec. A, p. 14. For a chronology leading up to the event, see *San Francisco Chronicle:* Edward Epstein, "Sisters Receive Go-Ahead in S.F. for Easter Party; Supervisors Uphold Permit over Catholic Protests," 30 March 1999, sec. A, p. 1; Don Lattin and Elaine Herscher, "Catholic Weekly Spurred Protest of Sisters' Party; Editorial in New Newspaper Galvanized Readers to Action," 31 March 1999, sec. A, p. 1; and Don Lattin, "Archbishop Not Amused by Sisters; But Levada Seeks Talks to End Rift with the Church," 2 April 1999, sec. A, p. 1. For a report of the event itself, see Cynthia Laird, "Sisters' Easter Party Draws Big Crowd, Few Problems," *Bay Area Reporter,* 8 April 1999, 14.

4. David Tuller, "Black Support for Gay Rights Bill; Coalition Tries to Counter Opposition from Evangelical Clergy," *San Francisco Chronicle,* 5 June 1991, sec. A, p. 22.

5. See Martin Luther King Jr., *Why We Can't Wait* (New York: Harper & Row, 1964).

6. Rev. E. V. Hill, pastor of Mt. Zion Missionary Baptist Church in Los Angeles, has long been a politically conservative voice among African American clergy.

7. See, for example, Evelyn C. White, "Christian Right Tries to Capitalize on Anti-Gay Views," *San Francisco Chronicle,* 12 January 1994, sec. A, p. 6, who reports on how the Traditional Values Coalition's video, *Gay Rights, Special Rights,* is used to rally Black preachers and congregations against gay rights legislation.

8. See Lee Rainwater and William L. Yancey, *The Moynihan Report and the Politics of Controversy* (Cambridge: MIT Press, 1967), which includes the full text of Daniel Patrick Moynihan's "The Negro Family: The Case for National Action."

9. See Pam Belluck and Jodi Wilgoren, "Shattered Lives, A Special Report: Caring Parents, No Answers, In Columbine Killers' Past," *New York Times,* 29 June 1999, sec. A, p. 1.

10. Rev. Jim Mitulski is the senior pastor of Metropolitan Community Church–San Francisco, located in the city's Castro district. He has spoken out against anti-gay violence and for a more compassionate response to the city's homeless. See Cynthia Laird, "Marshall Forces: Vote for Pride Grand Marshall April 17," *Bay Area Reporter,* 8 April 1999, 17. For more information about the relationship between Rev. Brown and Rev.

Mitulski's Metropolitan Community Church–San Francisco, see Stephen Schwartz, "Gay Congregation's Rousing Welcome for New S.F. Supervisor," *San Francisco Chronicle*, 27 May 1996, sec. A, p. 11.

11. For examples of verbal opposition and physical threats to Rev. Brown see: Bill Lindelof, "Baptist Delegates Oust Pro-Gay Churches," *Sacramento Bee*, 7 January 1996, sec. A, p. 3; Marsha Ginsburg and Erin McCormick, "Death Threats Sent to Pastor; Supervisor Brown Fears Hate Group Targeting His Church," *San Francisco Examiner*, 23 June 1996, sec. B, p. 2; and Don Lattin, "Tepid Welcome for Baptist Leader; Rev. Lyons Was in Oakland to Raise Cash for His Defense," *San Francisco Chronicle*, 19 March 1998, sec. A, p. 17.

12. For chronological coverage in San Francisco Chronicle, see April Lynch, "Minister's S.F. Job in Peril; Gay Bias Cited," 29 June 1993, sec. A, p. 13; Marc Sandalow, "Jordan on Spot over Rights Aide; Mayor Is Being Asked to Choose between Blacks and Gay Groups," 7 July 1993, sec. A, p. 13; Marc Sandalow, "S.F. Pastor Refuses to Resign from Panel; Human Rights Commissioner Rebuked by Gays," 13 July 1993, sec. A, p. 18; Marc Sandalow, "Jordan Keeping Baptist Pastor on Rights Panel; Minister Says Gay Lifestyle Goes against Bible," 14 July 1993, sec. A, p. 1; Dan Levy, "New Move to Oust S.F. Human Rights Panelist," 30 July 1993, sec. A, p. 21; Dan Levy, "New Push to Oust S.F. Rights Panelist; Board Committee Goes after Controversial Minister Again," 5 August 1993, sec. A, p. 15; Dan Levy, "S.F. Supervisors Urge Ouster of Commissioner; Board Seeks Minister's Firing for Remarks about Gays," 17 August 1993, sec. A, p. 15; Dan Levy, "Jordan Asks Lumpkin to Quit, He Says No; New Statement about Gays by Embattled Minister," 21 August 1993, sec. A, p. 1; Frank Williams and Theresa Moore, "Lumpkin Relies on His Faith; Embattled Rights Panelist to Meet with Mayor Today," 23 August 1993, sec. A, p. 17; Dan Levy, "Lumpkin Fired from Rights Panel; Mayor Says Latest Remark about Gays Went Too Far," 24 August 1993, sec. A, p. 1; Don Lattin, "Religious Leaders React to Firing; Interpretations of Lumpkin Case Vary Even among Evangelicals," 25 August 1993, sec. A, p. 15; Clarence Johnson, "War of Words over Lumpkin; Gays, Blacks Try to Cool Tensions," 28 August 1998, sec. A, p. 1; "Federal Judge Backs Jordan in Firing of S.F. Commissioner," 19 November 1994, sec. B, p. 13; "Court Upholds Firing of Rights Commissioner," 5 April 1997, sec. A, p. 18; and Reynolds Holding, "Minister Fired from Rights Panel Loses Last Appeal," 2 December 1997, sec. A, p. 16. See also John Gallagher, "Troubled Alliance: A Hot Debate in San Francisco Complicates the Tense Relationship between Gay and Black Civil Rights Movement," *Advocate*, 5 October 1993, 24–27, 36–40.

13. Book of Leviticus 18:22, "You shall not lie with a male as with a woman; it is an abomination." 20:13, "If a man lies with a male as with a woman, both of them have committed an abomination; they shall be put to death, their blood is upon them."

14. In *San Francisco Chronicle*, see Edward Epstein, "S.F. Supervisor Blasts Billy Graham Remark; Evangelist Assailed for Comments on Gays," 30 September 1997, sec. A, p. 17; and Don Lattin, "Billy Graham Crusade Vexes S.F. Supervisor; Evangelist Asked to Oppose 209," 2 October 1996, sec. A, p. 14.

15. See, for example, the opinion-editorial by Rev. Amos Brown, "The Black Church Should Get Its Due," *San Francisco Chronicle*, 9 February 1994, sec. A, p. 21.

16. In *San Francisco Chronicle*, see Clarence Johnson, "Supervisors OK Symbolic Wedding Rites for Gays," 30 January 1996, sec. A, p. 1; Elaine Herscher, "10 Gay Couples to be Honored for Stability at S.F. Ceremony; Brown to Officiate," 20 March

1998, sec. A, p. 20; David Tuller, "S.F. to Marry 150 Gay Couples; City's First Civil Ceremony for Domestic Partners," 23 March 1996, sec. A, p. 1; April Lynch, "Gay Couples Joyously Exchange Vows in S.F.," 26 March 1996, sec. A, p. 1; and Elaine Herscher, "Exchange of Vows at City Hall; 190 Gay Couples Take Part in S.F. Ceremony," 27 March 1999, sec. A, p. 17.

17. For writings by Howard Thurman, see *The Search for Common Ground* (Richmond, Ind.: Friends United, 1986); *The Luminous Darkness: A Personal Interpretation of the Anatomy of Segregation and the Ground of Hope* (Richmond, Ind.: Friends United, 1965, 1989); and *Conversations with Howard Thurman* (San Francisco: Howard Thurman Educational Trust, 1987).

18. Clarence Johnson, "The New S.F. Supervisors; To Amos Brown, This Job Is Fulfillment of Destiny," *San Francisco Chronicle,* 28 May 1996, sec. A, p. 1.

19. Book of Deuteronomy 22:5: "A woman shall not wear anything that pertains to a man, nor shall a man put on women's garments; for whoever does these things is an abomination to the LORD your God." May and Metzger, *New Oxford Annotated Bible with Apocrypha,* 242.

20. For information on joint programs with Temple Emanu-El, see Gregory Lewis, "Jews, Blacks Form a Bond for Education," *San Francisco Examiner,* 20 January 1995, sec. A, p. 25; and Teresa Moore, "Building a Bridge of Learning; Tutors from Church and Temple Cut across Race and Class," *San Francisco Chronicle,* 29 January 1996, sec. A, p. 14.

21. For more information about Rev. Flunder and City of Refuge, see Don Lattin, "Liberal Protestant Group Embraces Offbeat Church," *San Francisco Chronicle,* 30 June 1995, sec. A, p. 25.

22. For an account of gay politics in San Francisco at this time, see Randy Shilts, *The Mayor of Castro Street: The Life and Times of Harvey Milk* (New York: St. Martin's, 1982), 153–68.

CHAPTER 4: REV. DR. MOZELLA G. MITCHELL

1. Mozella G. Mitchell, *New Africa in America: The Blending of African and American Religious and Social Traditions among Black People in Meridian, Mississippi, and Surrounding Counties* (New York: Peter Lang, 1994); *African American Religious History in Tampa Bay,* Religious History of Tampa Bay Project, No. 6 (Tampa: National Conference of Christians and Jews, 1992); as editor, *The Human Search: Howard Thurman and the Quest for Freedom: Proceedings of the Second Annual Thurman Convocation,* Martin Luther King Jr. Memorial Studies in Religion, Culture and Social Development, vol. 1 (New York: Peter Lang, 1992); *Spiritual Dynamics of Howard Thurman's Theology* (Bristol, Ind.: Wyndham Hall, 1985). For examples of articles, see "The Black Woman's View of Human Liberation," *Theology Today,* 4 January 1983, 421–25; "Bring Back the Children," in Allegra S. Hoots, ed., *Prophetic Voices: Black Preachers Speak on Behalf of Children* (Washington, D.C.: Children's Defense Fund, 1993), 42–43; "The African Methodist Episcopal Zion Church and the Actions of the Spirit," in Rena M. Yocom and William R. Barr, eds., *The Church in the Movement of the Spirit* (Grand Rapids: William B. Eerdmans, 1994), 101–3; "Religion and the Discovery of Self: Howard Thurman and the Tributaries of the Deep River," in William Scott Green and Jacob Neusner, eds., *The Religion Factor: An*

278 Notes

Introduction to How Religion Matters (Louisville, Ky.: Westminster/John Knox, 1996), 84–96; "Woman at the Well: Mahalia Jackson and the Inner and Outer Spiritual Transformation," in Emilie M. Townes, ed., *Embracing the Spirit: Womanist Perspectives on Hope, Salvation and Transformation* (Maryknoll, N.Y.: Orbis, 1997), 167–78; and "Discovering Christian Resources for a Theology of Interfaith Relations from the African Methodist Episcopal Zion Church," in S. Mark Heim, ed., *Grounds for Understanding Ecumenical Resources for Responses to Religious Pluralism* (Grand Rapids: William B. Eerdmans, 1998), 157–74.

2. In *St. Petersburg Times,* see: Jackie Ripley, "Woman of the '90s," 2 January 1996, sec. B, p. 1; and Stephanie Gonzales, "Love of Christ African Methodist Episcopal Zion Tabernacle," 27 February 1999, sec. B, p. 12.

3. Jackie Ripley, "Help Wells Up from Group," *St. Petersburg Times,* 22 October 1995, sec. B, p. 3.

4. Mozella G. Mitchell, "The Dynamics of Howard Thurman's Theology" (Ph.D. diss., Emory University, 1980).

5. In Ripley, "Woman of the '90s," *St. Petersburg Times,* 2 January 1996, sec. B, p. 1, Mitchell is quoted as saying, "Realizing the heart of the civil rights movement was happening in the church, I took a leave of absence [from teaching English at Norfolk State University] to attend seminary in New York for two years. I was ordained and appointed to a congregation, but not even being the only Black student in all-white college classes could prepare me for the rejection I would find in the church. At that time women ministers were rare in mainline Christian churches, and while the congregation accepted me, some of the people in positions of power within the church did not.

"Not to be deterred, I started my own mission in Norfolk. But it wasn't until I was writing the dissertation for my Ph.D. at Emory University that I got my first pastorate. . . .

"The resistance to me as a woman pastor still exists, though it has lessened somewhat. The opposition is less political but more concealed, coming now from some of the women in the church who are accustomed to a male figure.

"Because I knew as a woman minister I would never get a church big enough to support a full-time minister, I continued my academic career."

6. See, for example, Tracie Reddick, "Black, Gay and Under Fire; In Black Churches throughout the Bay Area, Ministers Are Pounding Their Pulpits against Homosexuality," *Tampa Tribune,* 14 July 1996, 1.

7. For a brief summary of the emergence and development of Black liberation theology, see C. Eric Lincoln and Lawrence H. Mamiya, *The Black Church in the African American Experience* (Durham: Duke University Press, 1990), 176–82.

8. See Emily C. Hewitt and Suzanne R. Hiatt, *Women Priests: Yes or No?* (New York: Seabury, 1973), and Carter Heyward, *A Priest Forever: The Formation of a Woman and a Priest* (New York: Harper & Row, 1976).

9. See Mozella G. Mitchell, "The African Methodist Episcopal Zion Church and the Potentialities for Social Change in the Black Community of Rochester" (M.A. thesis, Colgate-Rochester Divinity School, 1973).

10. See "Rev. Lyons Found Guilty of Racketeering, Grand Theft," *Jet,* 15 March 1999, 16.

CHAPTER 5: REV. IRENE MONROE

1. Andrew Goldman, Nichole Bernier, Lisa Gerson, Cheryl Bentsen, and Louisa Kasdon-Sidell, "The 50 Most Intriguing Women in Boston," *Boston Magazine,* December 1997; "Out 100: People Who Rocked 1998," *OUT Magazine,* January 1999, 58; and Kevin Maynard, "In the Life, Across the Country; The PBS Newsmagazine Braves the Homophobia It Documents to Celebrate the Lives of Gay and Lesbian Americans," *Advocate,* 17 August 1999, 105–07.

2. Michael Kenney, "Foundling to Fighter: Once Abandoned, Now a Gay Preacher, Irene Monroe Battles Farrakhan and Black Homophobia," *Boston Globe,* 25 February 1998, sec. D, p. 1.

3. Goldman et al., "The 50 Most Intriguing Women in Boston," *Boston Magazine,* December 1997; and Diego Ribadeneira, "Black Religious Leader Faults Church's Treatment of Gays, Women," *Boston Globe,* 30 May 1998, sec. B, p. 2.

4. See, for example, Irene Monroe, "The Unacknowledged Roots of American Slavery," *Boston Globe,* 15 March 1998, sec. C, p. 7; "Are You Living in a Tolerant or an Accepting World?" *Brown Papers: Women's Theological Center* 4.2 (June/July 1998): 8–11; *Encyclopedia of Homosexuality,* vol. 1, *Lesbian Histories of Culture,* 2d ed., s.v. "The Black Church" and "Womanist"; "A Garden of Homophobia," *Advocate: The National Gay and Lesbian Magazine,* 9 December 1997, 9; "The Ache Sisters: Discovering the Power of the Erotic in Ritual," in Marjorie Procter-Smith and Janet R. Walton, eds., *Women at Worship: Interpretations of North American Diversity* (Louisville, Ky.: Westminster/John Knox, 1993), 127–35.

5. Irene Monroe, "Louis Farrakhan's Ministry of Misogyny and Homophobia," in Amy Alexander, ed., *The Farrakhan Factor: African American Writers on Leadership, Nationhood, and Minister Louis Farrakhan* (New York: Grove, 1998), 275–98; guest ed., special double issue: "The Intersection of Racism and Sexism: Theological Perspectives of African American Women," *Journal of Women and Religion* 9–10 (winter 1990–1991); and Richard Newman, ed., *African American Quotations* (Phoenix, Ariz.: Oryx, 1998), 79.

6. See Gayraud S. Wilmore, *Black and Presbyterian: The Heritage and the Hope* (Philadelphia: Geneva, 1983).

7. Alex Ayres, ed., *The Wisdom of Martin Luther King* (New York: Meridian, 1993), 125.

8. Richard Allen was the founder of the African Methodist Episcopal Church. See C. Eric Lincoln and Lawrence H. Mamiya, *The Black Church in the African American Experience* (Durham: Duke University Press, 1990), 50–56.

9. Beverly Wildung Harrison is the Carolyn Beard Professor of Christian Ethics *emerita* at Union Theological Seminary and the author of *Making the Connections: Essays in Feminist Social Ethics* (Boston: Beacon, 1985), and *Our Right to Choose: Toward a New Ethic of Abortion* (Boston: Beacon, 1983).

10. Rev. Peter J. Gomes is the Plummer Professor of Christian Morals and the Pusey Minister in the Memorial Chapel at Harvard. He is the author of *The Good Book: Reading the Bible with Mind and Heart* (New York: William Morrow, 1996; Bard, 1998), and *Sermons: Biblical Wisdom for Daily Living* (New York: William Morrow, 1998).

11. E. Franklin Frazier, *The Negro Church in America* (New York: Schocken, 1964).

12. For more information see Larry B. Stammer, "SCLC to Honor Founder of Church

for Minority Gays; Group Says that Recognition for Unity Fellowship Should Signal Mainstream Black Denominations to Recognize People Who Lead Alternative Lifestyles," *Los Angeles Times,* 16 January 1993, sec. B, p. 4; and Joyce Shelby, "Gays Discover Unity—and Spiritual Home," *New York Daily News,* 22 June 1997, 3.

13. *Encyclopedia of Homosexuality,* vol. 1, *Lesbian Histories of Culture,* 2d ed., s.v. "Womanist," by Irene Monroe. For a brief definition, summary, and discussion of womanist theology, see Lincoln and Mamiya, *The Black Church in the African American Experience,* 301–4.

14. Others agree. See Renee Hill, "Who Are We for Each Other? Sexism, Sexuality, and Womanist Theology," in James Cone and Gayraud Wilmore, eds., *Black Theology: A Documentary History,* vol. 2 (Maryknoll, N.Y.: Orbis, 1993), 345–46; Kelly Brown Douglas, *Sexuality and the Black Church* (Maryknoll, N.Y.: Orbis, 1999), 1–2, 127–30; Delores S. Williams, "Womanist Theology: Black Women's Voices," in Judith Plaskow and Carol P. Christ, eds., *Weaving the Visions: New Patterns in Feminist Spirituality* (San Francisco: Harper & Row, 1989), 179–186; and interviews with Hill, Douglas, Emilie Townes, and Shawn Copeland in this volume.

CHAPTER 6: REV. DR. CECIL "CHIP" MURRAY

1. See First AME's Web page at www.famechurch.org.

2. See Nina J. Easton, "Power to the Pastor: Cecil Murray's First AME Church Is Action Central for a Wounded South Los Angeles," *Los Angeles Times Magazine,* 16 August 1992, 12; Cecil L. "Chip" Murray, "One Person on Fire," interview by Bill Yankes, *The Humanist,* November-December 1992, 11–17, 28.

3. Cecil L. "Chip" Murray, "Making an Offer You Can't Refuse," in Ignacio Castuera, ed., *Dreams on Fire: Embers of Hope: From the Pulpits of Los Angeles after the Riots* (St. Louis: Chalice, 1992), 9–15.

See Lou Cannon, "Bradley, Black Leaders Try to Head Off Violence; Tense Los Angeles Awaits Beating Trial Verdict," *Washington Post,* 28 April 1992, sec. A, p. 3; David Ferrell and Amy Wallace, "Rich and Poor, Black and White Voice Anger," *Los Angeles Times,* 30 April 1992, sec. A, p. 1; Amy Wallace and David Ferrell, "Verdicts Greeted with Outrage and Disbelief; Reaction: Many Cite Videotape of Beating and Ask How Jury Could Acquit Officers; Few Voice Satisfaction," *Los Angeles Times,* 30 April 1992, sec. A, p. 1; Cecil Murray, "Los Angeles Times Interview; Cecil Murray: A Voice of Reason in a Time of Troubles," interview by Robert Scheer, *Los Angeles Times,* 3 May 1992, sec. M, p. 3; Ronald W. Powell, "Minister Sees Opportunity to Resurrect L.A.'s Soul," *San Diego Union-Tribune,* 28 May 1992, sec. A, p. 1; Seth Mydans, "Conversations: The Rev. Cecil Murray; Walking a Narrow Line and Praying for Calm in Riot-Torn City," *New York Times,* 13 September 1992, sec. 4, p. 7; and Nina J. Easton, "Understanding the Riots—Six Months Later; Money and Power, Making It in the Inner City; The Churches' Roles; 'Real Progress Means Turning over Dollars in Your Own Community,'" *Los Angeles Times,* 18 November 1992, sec. J, p. 7.

4. Hugo Martin, "AIDS Sermon Surprise: Nine Black Churches Arrange Condom Handouts at Services," *Los Angeles Times,* 14 October 1991, sec. B, p. 1.

5. Shirelle Phelps, ed., *Who's Who among African Americans,* 11th ed. (Detroit: Gale, 1998); and "The 15 Greatest Black Preachers," Ebony, November 1993, 156–64.

CHAPTER 7: REV. MSGR. RAYMOND G. EAST

1. See the Web page for the Archdiocese of Washington at www.adw.org.

2. See, for example, Mary Beth Rogers, *Cold Anger: A Story of Faith and Power Politics* (Denton, Tex.: University of North Texas Press, 1990).

3. In *Washington Post*, see Jacqueline Trescott's articles, "Black Priests at a Crossroads; With the Rev. Stallings's Breakaway, Renewed Soul-Searching on Their Roles in the Catholic Church and the Parish," 8 August 1989, sec. B, p. 1, and "Silence of the Ministers; Will Black Churches Now Speak Out for Those with AIDS?" 9 November 1991, sec. G, p. 1.

4. See Keith Boykin, *One More River to Cross: Black and Gay in America* (New York: Anchor/Doubleday, 1996), 126–27, 131–32; DeNeen L. Brown, "Citing Spiritual Needs, Black Gays Confront Condemnation from the Church," *Washington Post*, 1 August 1993, sec. B, p. 4; and Vincent Young, "Refusing to Give Up and Die; Group for Gay Black Men Wages Holistic War on HIV," *Washington Post*, 3 March 1994, sec. J, p. 1.

5. Currently Elias Farajaje-Jones is professor of cultural studies at Starr King School for the Ministry in Berkeley, California. See Elias Farajaje-Jones, "What Is Multiculturalism?" *Communities* 90 (spring 1996): 33; *Bi the Way, Is Anyone Listening? Racism, Sexism and Homophobia*, University Lecture Series (Ames, Iowa State University, 1994, audiocassette); *In Search of Zion: The Spiritual Significance of Africa in Black Religious Movements* (New York: Peter Lang, 1990); "Breaking Silence: Towards an In-the-Life Theology," in James Cone and Gayraud Wilmore, eds., *Black Theology: A Documentary History, Volume II, 1980–1992* (Maryknoll, N.Y.: Orbis, 1993), 139–59; and "Politics and Black/African, Lesbian/Gay Identities" (panel discussion), *Gay Community News*, fall 1995, 4–8.

6. Disagreement about the need for and propriety of integrating liturgical, musical, tribal, and dramatic traditions from the African American experience into the Roman Catholic Mass led to the suspension of Rev. George A. Stallings Jr. by Cardinal James A. Hickey. Rev. Stallings started the independent Imani Temple in Washington, D.C. See Trescott, "Black Priests at a Crossroads," *Washington Post*, 8 August 1989, sec. B, p. 1.

7. The "welcoming church" movement seeks to help local churches declare officially that they welcome and affirm lesbian/bisexual/gay/transgendered people. Such movements are underway within many Protestant denominations. See "Welcoming Churches: A Growing Ecumenical Movement," *Open Hands: Resources for Ministries Affirming the Diversity of Human Sexuality*, winter 1993.

8. See Web page www.dignityusa.org, which states: "Dignity USA is the United States' largest and most progressive organization of gay, lesbian, bisexual, and transgender Catholics. We serve as a proactive voice for reform in the church and society including same-sex marriages, women's ministry, AIDS ministry, and enforcement of anti-hate crime legislation."

9. National Conference of Catholic Bishops, *Always Our Children: A Pastoral Message to Parents of Homosexual Children and Suggestions for Pastoral Ministers: A Statement of the Bishops' Committee on Marriage and Family* (Washington, D.C.: United States Catholic Conference, Inc., 1997).

10. See Jim Dyer and Mark Hornbeck, "Special Report: Catholic Church; Gumbleton Wears Mantle of Liberal Hero, Pariah Priest," *Detroit News*, 28 March 1997, sec. C, p. 1;

and Peter Steinfels, "Bishops Protest Vatican Advisory Condoning Anti-Homosexual Bias," *New York Times,* 2 November 1992, sec. B, p. 11.

CHAPTER 8: REV. ALTAGRACIA PEREZ

1. Dianne Klein, "The Next Los Angeles: Turning Ideas into Action; Human Relations; Will Los Angeles Create a Model of Vitality by Shaping Common Goals, or Will It Disintegrate into a Modern-Day Babel?; 'We Are in the Baby Steps Right Now,'" *Los Angeles Times,* 17 July 1994, sec. S, p. 8.

2. Allison Samuels, David Gordon, and Steve Rhodes, "The Lord's Foot Soldiers," *Newsweek,* 1 June 1998, 26–28. This article is part of a special issue on inner-city ministry.

3. Shirelle Phelps, ed., *Who's Who among Black Americans,* 8th ed. (Detroit: Gale, 1994); and Gustav Niebuhr, "Clinton Urged to Preach Compassion; Religious Groups Tell President of Caring for People with AIDS," *Washington Post,* 30 November 1993, sec. A, p. 8.

4. *Diocesan News Service,* Los Angeles, 20 May 1999, available from www.ladiocese.org. Four months later, Rev. Perez led and was arrested at a follow-up protest demonstration; see "25 Arrested in Protest at U. of Southern Cal.," *Chronicle of Higher Education,* 17 September 1999, sec. A, p. 53.

5. See Martin Luther King Jr., *Why We Can't Wait* (New York: Harper & Row, 1964); and James Melvin Washington, ed., *A Testament of Hope: The Essential Writings and Speeches of Martin Luther King Jr.* (San Francisco: HarperSanFrancisco, 1991).

6. See Peter Y. Hong, "Local Elections; 10th Los Angeles City Council District; Holden Seeks One Last Win in Final Race," *Los Angeles Times,* 4 June 1999, sec. B, p. 1.

CHAPTER 9: REV. DR. ARNOLD I. THOMAS

1. The More Light Churches Network within the Presbyterian Church (U.S.A.) is part of the "welcoming church" movement that seeks to help local churches declare officially that they welcome and affirm lesbian/bisexual/gay/transgendered people within the life of the congregation. Such movements are underway within many denominations, including the Open and Affirming Program within the United Church of Christ and the Disciples of Christ, the Reconciled in Christ Program within the Evangelical Lutheran Church in America and other Lutheran denominations, the Reconciling Congregation Program within the United Methodist Church, the Supportive Congregation Program within Brethren/Mennonite churches, the Welcoming and Affirming Program of the American Baptist Churches in the U.S.A., and the Welcoming Congregation Program within the Unitarian Universalist Association. See "Welcoming Churches: A Growing Ecumenical Movement," *Open Hands: Resources for Ministries Affirming the Diversity of Human Sexuality,* winter 1993.

2. Chapter 19 in the Book of Genesis tells the story of the destruction of Sodom and Gomorrah.

3. This part of Paul's Letter to the Romans (2:26b–27) says, "Their women exchanged natural intercourse for unnatural, and in the same way also the men, giving up natural intercourse with women, were consumed with passion for one another. Men committed shameless acts with men and received in their own persons the due penalty for their error."

CHAPTER 10: REV. DR. JACQUELYN GRANT

1. Books by Jacquelyn Grant include *White Women's Christ and Black Women's Jesus: Feminist Christology and Womanist Response* (Atlanta: Scholars Press, 1989); as editor, *Perspectives on Womanist Theology* (Atlanta: ITC Press, 1995); and as editor with Randall C. Bailey, *The Recovery of Black Presence: An Interdisciplinary Exploration: Essays in Honor of Dr. Charles B. Copher* (Nashville: Abingdon, 1995). For examples of her articles, see "Womanist Theology: Black Women's Experience as a Source for Doing Theology, with Special Reference to Christology," in James H. Cone and Gayraud S. Wilmore, eds., *Black Theology: A Documentary History, Volume II, 1980–1992* (Maryknoll, N.Y.: Orbis, 1993), 273–89; "Black Theology and the Black Woman," in James H. Cone and Gayraud S. Wilmore, eds., *Black Theology: A Documentary History, Volume I, 1966–1979,* 2d ed. revised (Maryknoll, N.Y.: Orbis, 1993), 323–38; and "The Sins of Servanthood and the Deliverance of Discipleship," in Emilie M. Townes, ed., *A Troubling in My Soul: Womanist Perspectives on Evil and Suffering* (Maryknoll, N.Y.: Orbis, 1993), 199–218.

2. See Paula Giddings, "Jacquelyn Grant: Black Women's Jesus: 'Co-Sufferer, Liberator,'" *Essence,* October 1990, 52; Leslie Scanlon, "Churches Limit the Role of Black Women," *Courier-Journal* (Louisville, Ky.), 7 November 1998, sec. B, p. 1; Barbara Reynolds, "The New Esthers Will Lead the Way," *USA Today,* 30 March 1990, sec. A, p. 13; and C. Eric Lincoln and Lawrence H. Mamiya, *The Black Church in the African American Experience* (Durham, N.C.: Duke University Press, 1990), 303.

3. "Like Father, Like Daughters," *Ebony,* July 1980, 48, 50; Shirelle Phelps, ed., *Who's Who among African Americans,* 11th ed. (Detroit: Gale, 1998).

4. Carter Heyward was among the first women to be ordained in the Episcopal Church and pioneered the development of lesbian/gay theology. She is the Howard Chandler Robbins Professor of Theology at Episcopal Divinity School and the author of *A Priest Forever: One Woman's Controversial Ordination in the Episcopal Church* (New York: Harper & Row, 1976; rev. ed., Cleveland: Pilgrim, 1999); see also Heyward, *The Redemption of God: A Theology of Mutual Relation* (Washington, D.C.: University Press of America, 1982); *Our Passion for Justice: Images of Power, Sexuality, and Liberation* (New York: Pilgrim, 1984); as editor, *God's Fierce Whimsy: Christian Feminism and Theological Education* (Cleveland: Pilgrim, 1985); *Speaking of Christ: A Lesbian Feminist Voice* (Cleveland: Pilgrim, 1989); *Touching Our Strength: The Erotic as Power and the Love of God* (San Francisco: Harper & Row, 1989); *Staying Power: Reflections on Gender, Justice, and Compassion* (Cleveland: Pilgrim, 1995); *Saving Jesus from Those Who Are Right: Rethinking What It Means to Be Christian* (Minneapolis: Fortress, 1999); and *When Boundaries Betray Us: Beyond Illusions of What Is Ethical in Therapy and Life* (Cleveland: Pilgrim, 2000).

5. See John Blake, "Gays & God: Hostility Rules among Black Congregations," *Atlanta Journal and Constitution,* 31 May 1998, sec. A, p. 19, who quotes Bailey criticizing the church's homophobia, "Christianity is a religion that says we have to be on the side of the oppressed, no matter who they are. The church is supposed to welcome those who are heavy laden. Instead the church says, 'Go away, ye who are heavy laden. There ain't no rest here.'" See also Randall C. Bailey, "Preface," in Letty M. Russell, ed., *The Church with AIDS: Renewal in the Midst of Crisis* (Louisville, Ky.: Westminster/John Knox, 1990), 7–10; "Beyond Identification: The Use of Africans in the Old Testament Poetry and Narratives," in Cain Hope Felder, ed., *Stony the Road We Trod: African American Biblical Interpretation* (Minneapolis: Fortress, 1991), 165–84; and as editor

with Grant, *The Recovery of Black Presence: An Interdisciplinary Exploration: Essays in Honor of Dr. Charles B. Copher.*

6. Renee Hill, "Who Are We for Each Other? Sexism, Sexuality, and Womanist Theology," in Cone and Wilmore, *Black Theology: A Documentary History, Volume II,* 345–50; Toinette Eugene, "How Can We Forget? An Ethic of Care for AIDS, the African American Family, and the Black Catholic Church," in Emilie M. Townes, ed., *Embracing the Spirit: Womanist Perspectives on Hope, Salvation, and Transformation* (Maryknoll, N.Y.: Orbis, 1998), 247–74; and Anita C. Hill and Leo Treadway, "Rituals of Healing: Ministry with and on Behalf of Gay and Lesbian People," in Susan Brooks Thistlethwaite and Mary Potter Engel, eds., *Lift Every Voice: Constructing Christian Theologies from the Underside* (San Francisco: Harper, 1990), 231–44.

7. For a primer on liberation theology, see Robert McAfee Brown, *Theology in a New Key: Responding to Liberation Themes* (Philadelphia: Westminster, 1978). For a brief summary of the emergence and development of Black liberation theology, see Lincoln and Mamiya, *The Black Church in the African American Experience,* 176–82.

8. The Universal Fellowship of Metropolitan Community Churches (UFMCC or MCC), the first predominantly homosexual Christian denomination, was founded by Rev. Troy Perry in 1968 in Los Angeles. Within a few years it established local churches in all major cities in the United States. See Troy D. Perry, *The Lord Is My Sheperd and He Knows I'm Gay: The Autobiography of the Reverend Troy D. Perry* (New York: Bantam, 1972); and Troy D. Perry and Thomas L. P. Swicegood, *Don't Be Afraid Anymore: The Story of Reverend Troy Perry and the Metropolitan Community Churches* (New York: St. Martin's, 1990).

9. Rev. A. Cecil Williams is senior pastor of Glide Memorial Methodist Church in San Francisco. In 1962, he pioneered the acceptance of gay people within organized religion by beginning a ministry to "castoffs," including homosexuals, in the city's Tenderloin area. A result of these efforts was the founding of the first-of-its-kind Council on Religion and the Homosexual, which established chapters in other cities and for ten years served as the main organization for educating clergy about homosexuals and meeting with the leaders and decision-making bodies of various denominations. Rev. Williams and Glide Memorial have remained models of accepting and affirming gay people. See John D'Emilio, *Sexual Politics, Sexual Communities: The Making of a Homosexual Minority in the United States, 1940–1970* (Chicago: University of Chicago Press, 1983), 101–7, 192–95, 202, 204, 214–15.

10. Kelly Brown Douglas, *Sexuality and the Black Church: A Womanist Perspective* (Maryknoll, N.Y.: Orbis, 1999), 1. Douglas quotes Hill, "Who Are We for Each Other?" in Cone and Wilmore, *Black Theology: Volume II,* 345.

11. See interview with Rev. Dr. Renee L. Hill in this volume.

CHAPTER 11: REV. EDWIN C. SANDERS II

1. A slightly longer version of this interview first appeared as "'Whosoever' Is Welcome Here: An Interview with Reverend Edwin C. Sanders II," in Eric Brandt, ed., *Dangerous Liaisons: Blacks, Gays, and the Struggle for Equality* (New York: The New Press, 1999), 142–57.

2. "We've Come Too Far to Turn Back Now," Metro (TM) Theme Song; Robert L. Holmes, *Whosoever: The Voices of Metropolitan* (Nashville: Doorway Music Company, BMI, 1998).

3. Exclusive language, for example, uses "man" and "mankind" as generic or universal terms to mean "human being" and "humanity," whereas "woman" means only "female," i.e., "man" is the human race and "woman" is a subgroup under "human." Inclusive language uses "human" and "humankind" as generic terms and "man" and "woman" when referring to members of all-male or all-female subgroups. Some religious bodies also attempt to use gender-neutral or gender-inclusive terms for God, e.g., referring to God as Father and Mother or as Parent. See Division of Education and Ministry of the National Council of Churches, *An Inclusive Language Lectionary* (New York: National Council of Churches, 1987); and Beverly Wildung Harrison, "Sexism and the Language of Christian Ethics," *Making the Connections: Essays in Feminist Social Circles,* ed. Carol S. Robb (Boston: Beacon, 1985), 22–41.

4. See, for example, Howard Thurman, *The Search for Common Ground* (Richmond, Ind.: Friends United, 1986), and *The Luminous Darkness: A Personal Interpretation of the Anatomy of Segregation and the Ground of Hope* (Richmond, Ind.: Friends United, 1965, 1989).

5. See, for example, Vincent Harding, *There Is a River: The Black Struggle for Freedom in America* (New York: Harcourt Brace Jovanovich, 1981), and *Hope and History: Why We Must Share the Story of the Movement* (Maryknoll, N.Y.: Orbis, 1990).

6. Philip Paul Hallie, *Lest Innocent Blood Be Shed: The Story of the Village of Le Chambon, and How Goodness Happened There* (New York: Harper & Row, 1979).

7. See my book, *Unrepentant, Self-Affirming, Practicing: Lesbian/Bisexual/Gay People within Organized Religion* (New York: Continuum, 1996), 189–90.

8. Edwin C. Sanders II, "New Insights and Interventions: Churches Uniting to Reach the African American Community with Health Information," *Journal of Health Care for the Poor and Underserved* 8, no. 3 (1997): 373–76.

CHAPTER 12: REV. MARJORIE BOWENS-WHEATLEY

1. Information from previous three paragraphs is available from three brochures—"The History of The Community Church of New York," "Welcome," and "Interweave"—made available by the Community Church of New York, 40 East 35th Street, New York, NY 10016. Information is also available on the Church's Web page (www.ccny.org) and by telephone (212-683-4988). For information on the Welcoming Church movement, see chapter 9, note 1.

2. Marjorie Bowens-Wheatley, "A Litany of Restoration," in Mark Morrison-Reed and Jacqui James, eds., *Been in the Storm So Long: A Meditation Manual* (Boston: Skinner House, 1991), 15.

3. Robert N. Bellah, "Fulfilling the Promise: A Recovenanting Process for the 21st Century," *Fulfilling the Promise General Assembly Handbook: Unitarian Universalism in Societal Perspective,* Unitarian Universalist Association, General Assembly, Rochester, N.Y., 27 June 1998.

4. Unitarian Universalist Association, "Minutes of the 35th UUA General Assembly," Indianapolis, Ind., June 1996.

5. Gary David Comstock, *Unrepentant, Self-Affirming, Practicing: Lesbian/Bisexual/ Gay People within Organized Religion* (New York: Continuum, 1996), 190; and Craig C. Harris, "Cut Off from Among Their People," in Joseph Beam, ed., *In the Life: A Black Anthology* (Boston: Alyson, 1986), 63–67.

6. See, for example, John Blake, "Gays & God: Hostility Rules among Black Congregations," *Atlanta Journal and Constitution,* 31 May 1998, sec. A, p. 19; and Michael Booth, "Black Church Cancels Gay Talks: Vehement Protests a Factor, Pastor Says," *Denver Post,* 17 July 1996, sec. B, p. 1.

7. Comstock, *Unrepentant, Self-Affirming, Practicing,* 2, 11–12, 13, 188–92, 221.

8. James S. Tinney, "Struggles of a Black Pentecostal," in Michael J. Smith, ed., *Black Men/White Men: A Gay Anthology* (San Francisco: Gay Sunshine, 1983), 163–72. See also James S. Tinney, "Why a Black Gay Church?" in Joseph Beam, ed., *In the Life: A Black Gay Anthology* (Boston: Alyson, 1986), 70–86; and Neil Miller, *In Search of Gay America: Women and Men in a Time of Change* (New York: Atlantic Monthly, 1989; New York: Perennial Library, 1990), 241–56.

9. This tradition or culture of acceptance is documented elsewhere. In 1929 in New York City, Reverend Adam Clayton Powell spoke of the pervasive presence of homosexual parishioners and clergy in Harlem's churches and of the support for their participation by knowing congregations. See George Chauncey, *Gay New York: Gender, Urban Culture, and the Making of the Gay Male World, 1890–1940* (New York: Basic Books, 1994), 254–56; and Adam Clayton Powell, *Against the Tide: An Autobiography* (New York: Richard R. Smith, 1938), 57–59, 206, 209–20.

10. Louise Kiernan, "A Part, & Not Apart: A Ministry to Gay, Lesbian, Bisexual, and Transgender African Americans," *The World,* September/October 1997, 21–25.

CHAPTER 13: REV. DR. JAMES A. FORBES JR.

1. Information is available on the Church's Web page (www.theriversidechurchny.org).

2. See Ari L. Goldman, "Riverside Chooses New Minister," *New York Times,* 1 February 1989, sec. B, p. 1; Ari L. Goldman, "Members Elect a New Pastor at Riverside," *New York Times,* 6 February 1989, sec. B, p. 1; Marjorie Hyer, "N.Y. Professor Elected Pastor at Riverside; Black Minister Called Eminent Preacher," *New York Times,* 6 February 1989, sec. A, p. 3; "Riverside Church in N.Y. Gets 1st Black Sr. Pastor," *Jet,* 20 February 1989, 23; "Forbes Called to Riverside," *Christian Century,* 22 February 1989, 201; "The 15 Greatest Black Preachers," *Ebony,* November 1993, 156; Larry B. Stammer, "A Call to Action for Liberals, Moderates; Politics: Old-Line Southland Clergy Are Urging a Renewed Activism as the Religious Right Gears Up for Election Day," *Los Angeles Times,* 4 May 1996, sec. B, p. 4; "Billy Graham among Top Effective Preachers," *Houston Chronicle,* 16 March 1996, 8; Kenneth L. Woodward et al., "Heard Any Good Sermons Lately?" *Newsweek,* 4 March 1996, 50; and James Forbes, *The Holy Spirit and Preaching* (Nashville: Abingdon, 1989).

3. In *Jet* magazine, see "White New York Cops Face Murder Charge in Shooting of West African Immigrant," 19 April 1999, 18; and "Prosecutor in Diallo Shooting Case Agrees with Minorities' Fears about New York Police" and "Judge Drops Charges against Protestors in Diallo Shooting," 26 April 1999, 4–5.

4. Angie and Debbie Winans, *Bold* (Detroit: Against the Flow Records, 1997). For a news report about the song, see Kate Lawson, "Duo's Song Hits a Sour Note: Younger Winans Sisters Anger Gay, Lesbian Groups by Singing 'It's Not Natural,' " *Detroit News,* 21 October 1997, sec. E, p. 1.

5. Hosted by Tavis Smiley, *BET Tonight* is Black Entertainment Television's "live,

60-minute talk/news program, seeking to give a voice to topics that are about and concerning African Americans."

6.   For a brief summary of the emergence and development of liberation theology, see C. Eric Lincoln and Lawrence H. Mamiya, *The Black Church in the African American Experience* (Durham: Duke University Press, 1990), 176–82.

7.   For examples of public appearances in which Rev. Forbes discussed homosexuality, see Gustav Spohn, "Pastor Tells Blacks to Stop Waiting for a Leader; Oppression: Conference Speaker Says Theologians and Clergy Alike Should Be Willing to Act on Societal Woes," *Los Angeles Times,* 28 October 1989, sec. B, p. 6; Ari L. Goldman, "Clerics Advised on AIDS Preaching," *New York Times,* 28 November 1989, sec. B, p. 3; and Steve Conley, "Noted Preacher Issues Challenge on Gay Rights; He Invites 'All of God's Children' to Table," *Denver Post,* 20 July 1996, sec. B, p. 6.

8.   GMHC was founded in New York City in 1981. Its mission is "to provide compassionate care to New Yorkers with AIDS, educate to keep people healthy, and advocate for fair and effective public policies," and it serves more than 7,400 clients annually with the help of over 6,600 volunteers and 169 staff members. Contact GMHC through its Web page at www.gmhc.org.

9.   See following articles under the main title, "The Louima Case," in *New York Times,* 9 June 1999: Joseph P. Fried and Blaine Harden, "The Overview," sec. A, p. 1; Joseph P. Fried, "The Aftermath," sec. B, p. 8; Vivian S. Toy, "The Career," sec. B, p. 9; David Barstow, "The Strategy," sec. B, p. 9; Somini Sengupta, "The Neighborhood," sec. B, p. 9; and Michael Cooper, "The Police," sec. B, p. 9.

10.   See "Minority Troopers Describe a Culture of Discrimination" (Associated Press), *New York Times,* 9 July 1999, sec. B, p. 2; and Roger Clegg, "Profiling by Any Other Name: Government Programs that See Race, Not Individuals, and that Treat All Social Problems as Racial Problems, Do More Harm than Good," *New Jersey Law Journal,* 5 July 1999, 23.

11.   See Ari L. Goldman, "Riverside's Pastor at Center of Turmoil," *New York Times,* 18 May 1992, sec. B, p. 1.

CHAPTER 14: REV. MSGR. RUSSELL L. DILLARD

1.   See Morris J. MacGregor, *The Emergence of a Black Catholic Community: Saint Augustine's in Washington* (Washington, D.C.: Catholic University of America Press, 1999); "D.C.'s Oldest Black Catholic Church Gets First Black Pastor," *Jet,* 4 March 1991, 30; Jacqueline Trescott, "Black Priests at a Crossroads," *Washington Post,* 8 August 1989, sec. B, p. 1; and Saint Augustine's Web page at www.saintaugustine-dc.org.

2.   National Conference of Catholic Bishops, *Always Our Children: A Pastoral Message to Parents of Homosexual Children and Suggestions for Pastoral Ministers; A Statement of the Bishops' Committee on Marriage and Family* (Washington, D.C.: United States Catholic Conference, Inc., 1997).

3.   See, for example, Courtland Milloy, "Speaking Out against the Silence," *Washington Post,* 18 January 1995, sec. D, p. 1.

CHAPTER 15: REV. DR. RENEE L. HILL

1.   See church's Web page at www.allsaints-pas.org.

2. Renee L. Hill, "Who Are We for Each Other? Sexism, Sexuality and Womanist Theology," in James H. Cone and Gayraud S. Wilmore, eds., *Black Theology: A Documentary History, Volume II, 1980–1992* (Maryknoll, N.Y.: Orbis, 1993), 345–51; "Black Theology and Black Power 1968/1998 Disrupted/Disruptive Movements," in Dwight N. Hopkins, ed., *Black Faith and Public Talk: Critical Essays on James H. Cone's Black Theology and Black Power* (Maryknoll, N.Y.: Orbis, 1999), 138–149; and with Mary Foulke, "We Are Not Your Hope for the Future: Being an Interracial Lesbian Family Living in the Present," in Robert Goss and Amy Adams Squire Strongheart, eds., *Our Families, Our Values: Snapshots of Queer Kinship* (New York: Harrington Park, 1997), 243–249.

3. See, for example, Thomas Merton, *The Seven Storey Mountain* (New York: Harcourt Brace, 1978); *No Man Is an Island* (New York: Harcourt Brace, 1978); *Bread in the Wilderness* (Collegeville, Minn.: Liturgical, 1993); *The Ascent to Truth* (New York: Harcourt Brace, 1989); *Contemplative Prayer* (New York: Image, 1971); and *Spiritual Direction and Meditation* (Collegeville, Minn.: Liturgical, 1986).

4. Hill, "Who Are We for Each Other?" in Cone and Wilmore, *Black Theology,* 345–51.

5. Kelly Brown Douglas, *Sexuality and the Black Church: A Womanist Perspective* (Maryknoll, N.Y.: Orbis, 1999), 1–2.

6. The thirty-year anniversary celebration of the 1969 Stonewall Riots that launched the gay liberation movement. For a brief discussion of the original riots, see Gary David Comstock, *Gay Theology without Apology* (Cleveland: Pilgrim, 1993), 123–26.

7. The Rev. Canon Elizabeth Kaeton is missioner and president of the Oasis, "a ministry of cultural and racial diversity in the Episcopal Diocese of Newark with all who experience prejudice and oppression because of their sexual orientation."

CHAPTER 16: REV. DR. JAMES H. CONE

1. James H. Cone, *Black Theology and Black Power* (New York: Seabury, 1969; Maryknoll, N.Y.: Orbis, 1997); *A Black Theology of Liberation* (New York: Lippincott, 1970; rev. ed., Maryknoll, N.Y.: rev. ed., Orbis, 1990); *God of the Oppressed* (New York: Seabury, 1975; rev. ed., Maryknoll, N.Y.: Orbis, 1992); *The Spirituals and the Blues: An Interpretation* (New York: Seabury, 1972; Maryknoll, N.Y.: Orbis, 1992); with Gayraud Wilmore, eds., *Black Theology: A Documentary History 1966–1979* (Maryknoll, N.Y.: Orbis, 1979) and *Black Theology: A Documentary History 1980–1992* (Maryknoll, N.Y.: Orbis, 1993); *My Soul Looks Back* (Nashville: Abingdon, 1982; Maryknoll, N.Y.: Orbis, 1986); *For My People: Black Theology and the Black Church* (Maryknoll, N.Y.: Orbis, 1984); *Martin and Malcolm and America: A Dream or a Nightmare?* (Maryknoll, N.Y.: Orbis, 1992); *Speaking the Truth: Ecumenism, Liberation, and Black Theology* (Grand Rapids: Wm. B. Eerdmans Publishing Co., 1986; Maryknoll, N.Y.: Orbis, 1999); and *Risks of Faith: The Emergence of a Black Theology of Liberation, 1968–1998* (Boston: Beacon, 1999).

2. C. Eric Lincoln and Lawrence H. Mamiya, *The Black Church in the African American Experience* (Durham, N.C.: Duke University Press, 1990), 178–79. See also Nessa Rapoport, "The Struggles of James H. Cone," *Publishers Weekly,* 15 February 1991, 30–31.

3. For a discussion and description of EATWOT, see Cone, *For My People,* 144–56.

4. Shirelle Phelps, ed., *Who's Who among African Americans,* 11th ed. (Detroit: Gale,

1998). See also "James H. Cone: Theologian, Educator, Author," *Contemporary Black Biography,* vol. 3 (Detroit: Gale Research, 1993), 40–42.

5. Daniel Spencer is currently associate professor of religion and ethics at Drake University in Des Moines, Iowa, and the author of *Gay and Gaia: Ethics, Ecology, and the Erotic* (Cleveland: Pilgrim, 1996). In my personal communication with him on 22 August 1999, he remembered that Toby Marotta's *The Politics of Homosexuality* (Boston: Houghton Mifflin, 1981) was a book that Professor Cone used and found helpful.

6. James S. Tinney was an ordained Pentecostal minister who founded the Black, gay Pentecostal Faith Temple in Washington, D.C. He was publicly excommunicated by the bishop of the Washington diocese of the Church of God in Christ. For a description of his life and work, see Neil Miller, *In Search of Gay America: Women and Men in a Time of Change* (New York: Atlantic Monthly, 1989; Perennial Library, 1990), 241–56. For examples of Tinney's writing, see "Struggles of a Black Pentecostal," in Michael J. Smith, ed., *Black Men/White Men: A Gay Anthology* (San Francisco: Gay Sunshine, 1983), 163–72; and "Why a Black Gay Church?" in Joseph Beam, ed., *In the Life: A Black Anthology* (Boston: Alyson, 1986), 70–86.

7. For a brief discussion of the Stonewall Riots, see Gary David Comstock, *Gay Theology without Apology* (Cleveland: Pilgrim, 1993), 123–26.

8. See, for example, Evelyn C. White, "Christian Right Tries to Capitalize on Anti-Gay Views," *San Francisco Chronicle,* 12 January 1994, sec. A, p. 6.

9. See Keith Boykin, *One More River to Cross: Black and Gay in America* (New York: Anchor/Doubleday, 1996), 127–128.

10. This observation and knowledge are confirmed by statistics comparing the religious beliefs and practices of white Evangelicals and Black Christians. See Pew Research Center for the People and the Press, "The Diminishing Divide . . . American Churches, American Politics," Washington, D.C., 25 June 1996, 12. See also Milton G. Sernett, "Black Religion and the Question of Evangelical Identity," in Donald W. Dayton and Robert K. Johnston, eds., *The Variety of American Evangelism* (Knoxville, Tenn.: University of Tennessee Press, 1991), 135–47.

11. Robert Dawidoff and Michael Nava, "Why Martin Luther King Jr. Is a Gay-Rights Hero: His Life and His Message Resonate beyond the Fight against Racial Prejudice," *Los Angeles Times,* 16 January 1994, sec. M, p. 5.

12. See James H. Cone, "Malcolm X: The Impact of a Cultural Revolutionary," *Christian Century,* 23 December 1992, 1189–94; and *Martin and Malcolm and America: A Dream or a Nightmare?*

CHAPTER 17: REV. DR. EMILIE M. TOWNES

1. For books, see Emilie M. Townes, *Breaking the Fine Rain of Death: African American Health Issues and a Womanist Ethic of Care* (New York: Continuum, 1998); as editor, *Embracing the Spirit: Womanist Perspectives on Hope, Salvation, and Transformation* (Maryknoll, N.Y.: Orbis, 1997); *In a Blaze of Glory: Womanist Spirituality as Social Witness* (Nashville: Abingdon, 1995); *A Troubling in My Soul: Womanist Perspectives on Evil and Suffering* (Maryknoll, N.Y.: Orbis, 1993); and *Womanist Justice, Womanist Hope* (Atlanta: Scholars Press, 1993).

2. Kelly Brown Douglas, *Sexuality and the Black Church: A Womanist Perspective* (Maryknoll, N.Y.: Orbis, 1999), 4. See also Emilie M. Townes, "The Price of the Ticket:

Racism, Sexism, Heterosexism, and the Church in Light of the AIDS Crisis," in Susan E. Davies and Eleanor H. Haney, eds., *Redefining Sexual Ethics: A Sourcebook of Essays, Stories, and Poems* (Cleveland: Pilgrim, 1991), 67–73.

3. See *The Book of Discipline of The United Methodist Church 1984*, Para. 402.2, p. 189, and Para. 404.4, p. 192; United Methodist Church, *Report of the Committee to Study Homosexuality* (Dayton, Ohio: General Council on Ministries, 1992 [from "Report on the Study of Homosexuality," *Daily Christian Advocate*, petition no. FM-10865-3000-A, 5 May 1992, 265–81]); J. Gordon Melton, ed., *The Churches Speak on Homosexuality: Official Statements from Religious Bodies and Ecumenical Organizations* (Detroit: Gale Research, 1991), 240–43; and Mearle L. Griffith and C. David Lundquist, *An Analysis of Major Issues Addressed by the 1988 General Conference and a Comparison with Beliefs and Attitudes of Local Church Members* (Dayton, Ohio: Office of Research, General Conference of Ministers, United Methodist Church, 1990), 1, 7–8, 15, 17.

The official position of the United Methodist Church as expressed in its *Book of Discipline* is that homosexuality is incompatible with Christian teaching, that it is a sin to be a practicing homosexual, that openly declared or practicing homosexuals cannot be ordained, and that church funds should not be used by any group promoting the acceptance of homosexuality.

4. The Universal Fellowship of Metropolitan Community Churches (UFMCC or MCC), the first predominantly homosexual Christian denomination, was founded by Rev. Troy Perry in 1968 in Los Angeles. Within a few years it established local churches in all major cities in the United States. See Troy D. Perry, *The Lord Is My Sheperd and He Knows I'm Gay: The Autobiography of the Reverend Troy D. Perry* (New York: Bantam, 1972); and Troy D. Perry and Thomas L. P. Swicegood, *Don't Be Afraid Anymore: The Story of Reverend Troy Perry and the Metropolitan Community Churches* (New York: St. Martin's, 1990).

5. Tex Sample was professor of church and society at Saint Paul School of Theology and is editor with Amy E. DeLong of *The Loyal Opposition: Struggling with the Church on Homosexuality* (Nashville: Abingdon, 2000) and the author of *The Spectacle of Worship in a Wired World: Electronic Culture and the Gathered People of God* (Nashville: Abingdon, 1998); *White Soul: Country Music, the Church and Working Americans* (Nashville: Abingdon, 1996); *Ministry in an Oral Culture: Living with Will Rogers, Uncle Remus, and Minnie Pearl* (Louisville, Ky.: Westminster/John Knox, 1994); *Hard Living and Mainstream Christians* (Nashville: Abingdon, 1993); *U.S. Lifestyles and Mainline Churches* (Louisville, Ky.: Westminster/John Knox, 1990); and *Blue Collar Ministry* (Valley Forge, Penn.: Judson, 1984).

6. Donna Allen is instructor of preaching and worship at Saint Paul School of Theology and also associate pastor at Gregg Tabernacle African Methodist Episcopal Church in Kansas City, Missouri.

7. Alice Walker, *In Search of Our Mothers' Gardens: Womanist Prose* (San Diego: Harcourt Brace Jovanovich, 1983), xi–xii.

8. Alice Walker, "The Only Reason You Want to Go to Heaven Is That You Have Been Driven Out of Your Mind (Off Your Land and Out of Your Lover's Arms): Clear Seeing Inherited Religion and Reclaiming the Pagan Self," *Anything We Love Can Be Saved: A Writer's Activism* (New York: Random House, 1997), 3–26.

9. Within the following denominations, efforts to help local churches declare officially that they welcome and affirm lesbian/bisexual/gay/transgendered people include:

the Reconciling Congregation Program within the United Methodist Church, the More Light Churches Network within the Presbyterian Church (U.S.A.), the Open and Affirming Program within the United Church of Christ and the Disciples of Christ, the Reconciled in Christ Program within the Evangelical Lutheran Church in America and other Lutheran denominations, the Supportive Congregation Program within Brethren/Mennonite churches, the Welcoming and Affirming Program of the American Baptist Churches in the U.S.A., and the Welcoming Congregation Program movement with the Unitarian Universalist Association. See "Welcoming Churches: A Growing Ecumenical Movement," *Open Hands: Resources for Ministries Affirming the Diversity of Human Sexuality,* Winter 1993.

10. See Fannie Barrier Williams, "The Club Movement among Colored Women of America," in Marcia Y. Riggs and Barbara Holmes, eds., *Can I Get a Witness? Prophetic Religious Voices of African American Women: An Anthology* (Maryknoll, N.Y.: Orbis, 1997), 117–31; and Angela Y. Davis, chap. 8, "Black Women and the Club Movement," *Women, Race & Class* (New York: Random House, 1981; New York: Vintage, 1983), 127–36.

11. For more information see Keith Boykin, *One More River to Cross: Black and Gay in America* (New York: Anchor/Doubleday, 1996), 127, 131–36; Larry B. Stammer, "SCLC to Honor Founder of Church for Minority Gays; Group Says that Recognition for Unity Fellowship Should Signal Mainstream Black Denominations to Recognize People Who Lead Alternative Lifestyles," *Los Angeles Times,* 16 January 1993, sec. B, p. 4; and Joyce Shelby, "Gays Discover Unity—and Spiritual Home," *New York Daily News,* 22 June 1997, 3.

12. See Don Lattin, "Liberal Protestant Group Embraces Offbeat Church," *San Francisco Chronicle,* 30 June 1995, sec. A, p. 25.

13. See Pam Belluck and Jodi Wilgoren, "Shattered Lives, A Special Report: Caring Parents, No Answers, In Columbine Killers' Past," *New York Times,* 29 June 1999, sec. A, p. 1.

14. See "Rev. Jackson Urges Worshippers to 'Turn Tragedy into Triumph,'" *Jet,* 17 January 1994, 16; and Jim Sleeper, "Psycho-Killer? The Origins of Colin Ferguson's Hate," *New Republic,* 10–17 January 1994, 17.

15. Townes, *Womanist Justice, Womanist Hope.*

16. M. Duster, ed., *Crusade for Justice: The Autobiography of Ida B. Wells* (Chicago: University of Chicago Press, 1970).

17. Dwight N. Hopkins is associate professor of theology at University of Chicago Divinity School, an ordained American Baptist minister, and the author or editor of the following books: *Introducing Black Theology of Liberation* (Maryknoll, N.Y.: Orbis, 1999); ed., *Black Faith and Public Talk: Critical Essays on James H. Cone's* Black Theology and Black Power (Maryknoll, N.Y.: Orbis, 1999); ed. with Sheila Greeve Davaney, *Changing Conversations: Religious Reflection and Cultural Analysis* (New York: Routledge, 1996); *Shoes That Fit Our Feet: Sources for a Constructive Black Theology* (Maryknoll, N.Y.: Orbis, 1993); and ed. with George Cummings, *Cut Loose Your Stammering Tongue: Black Theology in the Slave Narratives* (Maryknoll, N.Y.: Orbis, 1991).

18. Cornel West is the Alphonse Fletcher Jr. University Professor at Harvard University and the author or editor of the following books: with Roberto Mangabeira, *The Future of American Progressivism: An Initiative for Political and Economic Reform* (Boston: Beacon, 1998); with Sylvia Ann Hewlett, *The War Against Parents: What We Can Do for*

America's Beleaguered Moms and Dads (New York: Houghton Mifflin, 1998); *Restoring Hope: Conversations on the Future of Black America* (Boston: Beacon, 1997); ed. with Jack Salzman, *Struggles in the Promised Land: Towards a History of Black-Jewish Relations in the United States* (New York: Oxford University Press, 1997); ed. with George E. Curry, *The Affirmative Action Debate* (Boulder, Col.: Perseus, 1996); with Michael Lerner, *Jews & Blacks: A Dialogue on Race, Religion, and Culture in America* (New York: Plume, 1996); *Keeping Faith: Philosophy and Race in America* (New York: Routledge, 1993); *Race Matters* (Boston: Beacon, 1993); *Prophetic Thought in Postmodern Times and Prophetic Reflections: Notes on Race and Power,* vols. I-II, *Beyond Eurocentrism and Multiculturalism* (Monroe, Maine.: Common Courage, 1993); with bell hooks, *Breaking Bread: Insurgent Black Intellectual Life* (Boston: South End, 1991); *The Ethical Dimensions of Marxist Thought* (New York: Monthly Review, 1991); *The American Evasion of Philosophy: A Genealogy of Pragmatism* (Madison, Wisc.: University of Wisconsin Press, 1989); ed. with John Rajchman, *Post-Analytic Philosophy* (New York: Columbia University Press, 1985); and *Prophecy Deliverance! An Afro-American Revolutionary Christianity* (Louisville, Ky.: Westminster/John Knox, 1982).

19. In this volume see interview with Rev. Dr. James H. Cone.

CHAPTER 18: REV. DR. KELLY BROWN DOUGLAS

1. Kelly Brown Douglas, "Daring to Speak: Womanist Theology and Black Sexuality," in Emilie M. Townes, ed., *Embracing the Spirit: Womanist Perspectives on Hope, Salvation, and Transformation* (Maryknoll, N.Y.: Orbis, 1997), 234–46; "To Reflect the Image of God: A Womanist Perspective on Right Relationship" and "Teaching Womanist Theology," in Cheryl J. Sanders, ed., *Living the Intersection: Womanism and Afrocentrism in Theology* (Minneapolis: Fortress, 1995), 67–77, 147–55; "When the Subjugated Come to the Center," *Journal of Religious Thought* 52.2–53.1 (winter-spring 1995–96): 37–44; "A Womanist Looks at the Future Direction of Theological Discourse," *Anglican Theological Review* 76, no. 2 (spring 1994): 225–32; et al., special issue, "Metalogues and Dialogues: Teaching the Womanist Idea," *Journal of Feminist Studies in Religion* 8, no. 2 (fall 1992).

2. Kelly Brown Douglas, *The Black Christ,* The Bishop Henry McNeal Turner Studies in North American Black Religion, vol. 9 (Maryknoll, N.Y.: Orbis, 1994).

3. Kelly Brown Douglas, *Sexuality and the Black Church: A Womanist Perspective* (Maryknoll, N.Y.: Orbis, 1999).

4. See Bill Broadway, "A Time to Speak of AIDS; Boisterous Howard Divinity Forum Tries to Break Silence of Black Churches," *Washington Post,* 27 May 1995, sec. B, p. 7; and Religious Coalition for Reproductive Choice, *Breaking the Silence: National Black Religious Summit on Sexuality,* Washington, D.C., Howard University School of Divinity, 12–13 June 1997 (videocassette, Creative Eye, Inc., 1997).

5. James H. Cone, *Black Theology and Black Power* (New York: Seabury, 1969; Maryknoll, N.Y.: Orbis, 1997); and *A Black Theology of Liberation* (New York: Lippincott, 1970; rev. ed., Maryknoll, N.Y.: Orbis, 1990).

6. Rev. Dr. Jeremiah A. Wright Jr. is the senior pastor of Chicago's Trinity United Church of Christ, a predominantly African American congregation and the largest local congregation within the United Church of Christ. See also Jeremiah A. Wright, *Good News! Sermons of Hope for Today's Families* (Valley Forge, Pa.: Judson, 1995); *What*

Makes You Strong? Sermons of Joy and Strength from Jeremiah Wright Jr. (Valley Forge, Pa.: Judson, 1993); et al., *When Black Men Stand Up for God: Reflection on the Million Man March* (Chicago: African American Images, 1997); and *Africans Who Shaped Our Faith* (Chicago: Urban Ministries, 1995); and "Foreword," in Geneva E. Bell, *My Rose: An African American Mother's Story of AIDS* (Cleveland: Pilgrim, 1997).

CHAPTER 19: DR. M. SHAWN COPELAND

1. See Jo Sandin, "Marquette Professor Explains How Culture Was Retained: Heritage Leaped the Abyss of Slavery; Worship Tradition Continues to Shape the African American Religious Experience," *Milwaukee Journal Sentinel,* 11 November 1995, 2.

2. Elisabeth Schussler Fiorenza and M. Shawn Copeland, eds., Concilium Journal Series, *Feminist Theology in Different Contexts* (London: SCM; Maryknoll, N.Y.: Orbis, 1996); and *Violence Against Women* (London: SCM; Maryknoll, N.Y.: Orbis, 1994). For examples of articles, see M. Shawn Copeland, "Method in Emerging Black Catholic Theology," in Diana L. Hayes and Cyprian Davis, eds., *Taking Down Our Harps: Black Catholics in the United States* (Maryknoll, N.Y.: Orbis, 1998), 120–44; "Foundations for Catholic Theology in an African American Context," in Jamie T. Phelps, ed., *Black and Catholic: The Challenge and Gift of Black Folk: Contributions of African American Experience and World View to Catholic Theology* (Milwaukee: Marquette University Press, 1998), 107–47; "African American Catholics and Black Theology: An Interpretation," in Gayraud Wilmore, ed., *African American Religious Studies: An Interdisciplinary Anthology* (Durham, N.C.: Duke University Press, 1989), 228–48; and "Black and Catholic," *America,* 29 March 1980, 270–71.

3. See Shirelle Phelps, ed., *Who's Who among Black Americans,* 8th ed. (Detroit: Gale, 1994); James H. Cone, *For My People: Black Theology and the Black Church* (Maryknoll, N.Y.: Orbis, 1984), 48–51; and Copeland, "Method in Emerging Black Catholic Theology," in Hayes and Davis, *Taking Down Our Harps,* 124.

4. In *New York Times,* see Frank Rich's "Journal" column: "Summer of Matthew Shepard," 3 July 1999, sec. A, p. 11; and "Has Jerry Falwell Seen the Light," 6 November 1999, sec. A, p. 17. See also Scott Gibson, ed., *Blood & Tears: Poems for Matthew Shepard* (New York: Painted Leaf, 1999).

5. See M. Shawn Copeland, "A Genetic Study of the Idea of the Human Good in the Thought of Bernard Lonergan" (Ph.D. dissertation, Boston College, 1991); "Reconsidering the Idea of the Common Good," in Oliver F. Williams and John W. Houck, eds., *Catholic Social Thought and the New World Order: Building on One Hundred Years* (Notre Dame, Ind.: University of Notre Dame Press, 1993), 309–27; and "The Exercise of Black Theology in the United States," *Journal of Hispanic/Latino Theology* 3, no. 3 (February 1996): 5–15.

6. John Boswell, *Christianity, Social Tolerance, and Homosexuality: Gay People in Western Europe from the Beginning of the Christian Era to the Fourteenth Century* (Chicago: University of Chicago Press, 1980).

7. Audre Lorde, *A Burst of Light: Essays* (Ithaca, N.Y.: Firebrand, 1988); *Sister Outsider: Essays and Speeches* (Freedom, Calif.: Crossing, 1984); "There Is No Hierarchy of Oppressions," *Interracial Books for Children Bulletin* 14, no. 3/4 (1983): 9; *Zami: A New Spelling of My Name* (Freedom, CA: Crossing, 1982); and *The Cancer Journals* (San Francisco: Spinsters Ink, 1980).

294 Notes

8. Adrienne C. Rich, *On Lies, Secrets, and Silence: Selected Prose, 1966–1978* (New York: Norton, 1979); and *Of Woman Born: Motherhood as Experience and Institution* (New York: Norton, 1976).

9. John J. McNeill, *The Church and the Homosexual* (Kansas City: Sheed Andrews and McMeel, 1976).

10. National Conference of Catholic Bishops, *Always Our Children: A Pastoral Message to Parents of Homosexual Children and Suggestions for Pastoral Ministers; A Statement of the Bishops' Committee on Marriage and Family* (Washington, D.C.: United States Catholic Conference, Inc., 1997).

11. Henri J. M. Nouwen, *The Wounded Healer: Ministry in Contemporary Society* (Garden City, N.Y.: Image/Doubleday, 1979).

12. Margaret A. Farley, *Just Love* (New York: Continuum, 1999); *Personal Commitments: Beginning, Keeping, Changing* (New York: Harper & Row, 1986); and "An Ethic for Same-Sex Relations," in Robert Nugent, ed., *A Challenge to Love: Gay and Lesbian Catholics in the Church* (New York: Crossroad, 1989), 93–106.

13. For a brief definition, summary, and discussion of womanist theology, see C. Eric Lincoln and Lawrence H. Mamiya, *The Black Church in the African American Experience* (Durham, N.C.: Duke University Press, 1990), 301–04.

Copeland, "Method in Emerging Black Catholic Theology," in Hayes and Davis, *Taking Down Our Harps,* 131–32, writes: "Black—and red, brown, yellow—women were erased in the articulation and praxis of (white middle-class) feminist theology. Womanist perspective calls these erasures into question and projects black women's experience into Christian theology." Her other work on this subject includes "'Wading through Many Sorrows': Towards a Theology of Suffering in Womanist Perspective," in Emilie M. Townes, ed., *A Troubling in My Soul: Womanist Reflections on Evil and Suffering* (Maryknoll, N.Y.: Orbis, 1993), 109–29; "Difference as a Category in Critical Theologies for the Liberation of Women," in Schussler Fiorenza and Copeland, *Feminist Theology in Different Contexts,* 141–51; "Towards a Critical Christian Feminist Theology of Solidarity," in Mary Ann Hinsdale and Phyllis H. Kaminski, eds., *Women and Theology: The Annual Publication of the College Theology Society* (Maryknoll, N.Y.: Orbis, 1995), 3–38; and with Cheryl J. Sanders, Katie G. Cannon, Emilie M. Townes, bell hooks, and Cheryl Townsend Gilkes, "Christian Ethics and Theology in Womanist Perspective," *Journal of Feminist Studies in Religion* 5, no. 2 (fall 1989): 83–13. See also various articles by Delores S. Williams, Jacquelyn Grant, Kelly Brown Douglas, Katie G. Cannon, Toinette M. Eugene, Cheryl Townsend Gilkes, Diana L. Hayes, Cheryl J. Sanders, and Renee L. Hill in Part IV, "Womanist Theology," in James H. Cone and Gayraud S. Wilmore, eds., *Black Theology: A Documentary History, Volume II, 1980–1992* (Maryknoll, N.Y.: Orbis, 1993), 257–351. See also Ada Maria Isasi-Diaz, *Mujerista Theology: A Theology for the Twenty-First Century* (Louisville, Ky.: Westminster/John Knox, 1996); Toinette Eugene, "Appropriation and Reciprocity in Womanist/Mujerista/Feminist Work," in Lois K. Daly, ed., *Feminist Theological Ethics* (Louisville, Ky.: Westminster/John Knox, 1994), 88–94; Letty M. Russell, Katie G. Cannon, and Ada Maria Isasi-Diaz, eds., *Inheriting Our Mothers' Gardens: Feminist Theology in Third World Perspective* (Louisville, Ky.: Westminster/John Knox, 1991); and Chung Hyun Kyung, *Struggle to Be the Sun Again: Introducing Asian Women's Theology* (Maryknoll, N.Y.: Orbis, 1991).

CHAPTER 20: REV. DR. YVONNE V. DELK

1. See Rose Marie Berger, "The World as God Intends," *Sojourners,* May 1999, 18–23; Rich Hein, "Chicago Profile: Yvonne Delk," *Chicago Sun-Times,* 14 February 1992, 18; and Francis X. Clines, "Morality Mission Faces Capital Reality," *New York Times,* 7 June 1998, sec. 1, p. 18.

2. Yvonne Delk, "Singing the Lord's Song," in Marcia Y. Riggs and Barbara Holmes, eds., *Can I Get a Witness? Prophetic Religious Voices of African American Women: An Anthology* (Maryknoll, N.Y.: Orbis, 1997), 93–102; also included in Ella Pearson Mitchell, ed., *Those Preachin' Women: Sermons by Black Women Preachers* (Valley Forge, Pa.: Judson, 1985), 51–59.

For writing by Delk, see "The Unfinished Agenda: Racism," *New Conversations* 11, no. 2–3 (winter-spring 1989): 40–44; and in *Sojourners:* "A Time for Action: Building a Strategy to Dismantle Racism," March 1998, 25; "A Silver Trumpet Passed On: Jean Sindab's Place in History," January–February 1997, 20–22; "Living the Word: By What Authority?" June 1993, 34–35; and "Living by the Word: Breathing Space," May 1993, 36–38.

Available on audio and/or visual cassettes: Yvonne V. Delk, "Spirit of Truth, Set Us Free" and "Spirit of Truth: Free Us to Follow," *Iliff Week of Lectures* (Chicago: University Park United Methodist Church, January 1993); "World-Changing Words," *Preaching with Power: A Forum on Black Preaching and Theology, 11–14 March 1991* (Philadelphia: Lutheran Theological Seminary, Urban Theological Institute, 1991); *New Roads to Faith: Black Perspectives in Church Education* (New York: United Church Press, 1982); *The Church Alive: A Liberating Force in the '80s,* Mordecai W. Johnson Institute of Religion Series (Rochester, N.Y.: Colgate-Rochester Divinity School/Bexley Hall/Crozier Theological Seminary, 1981); and *Black Chronicle,* Shalom Resource Series for Joint Educational Development (New York: United Church Press, 1974).

3. See www.ucc.org, KYP: *Keeping You Posted,* January 1998; Shirelle Phelps, ed., *Who's Who among African Americans,* 11th ed. (Detroit: Gale, 1998); and Mary Cameron Frey, "YWCA Leader Luncheon Honors 8 Women," *Chicago Sun-Times,* 19 October 1994, sec. 2, p. 46.

4. Gary David Comstock, *Unrepentant, Self-Affirming, Practicing: Lesbian/Bisexual/Gay People within Organized Religion* (New York: Continuum, 1996), 191.

5. See Henri J. M. Nouwen, *The Wounded Healer: Ministry in Contemporary Society* (Garden City, N.Y.: Image/Doubleday, 1979).

6. In 1972, the Golden Gate Association of the Northern California Conference of the United Church of Christ ordained William Johnson into Christian ministry. It was the first ordination of an openly gay person in the history of the Christian church. Subsequently, Rev. Johnson founded the UCC's Gay Caucus. Currently, he is Minister for HIV/AIDS Ministries and Lesbian, Gay, Bisexual, and Transgender Concerns in the UCC's national office.

7. General Synod meets every other year and is a representative body of delegates from throughout the various denominational levels.

8. In the UCC's structural organization of National instrumentalities, regional Conferences, district Associations, and local churches, only Associations have the authority and decision-making power to ordain clergy.

9. See the Coalition's Web page at www.coalition.simplenet.com where it describes

itself as "an officially recognized interest group of the United Church of Christ" that "provides support and sanctuary to all lesbian, gay, bisexual and transgender sisters and brothers, their families and friends, . . . advocates for their full inclusion in church and society," and "brings Christ's affirming message of love and justice for all people."

10. On the UCC's Web page at www.ucc.org, see Paul H. Sherry, "Now, No Condemnation; The Rights of Gay, Lesbian, and Bisexual Persons in Society and Their Membership and Ministry in the Church: A Pastoral Letter to the United Church of Christ," November 1998.

11. One of over twenty "Groups Granted Voice without Vote" at the UCC's Twenty-First General Synod.

12. The Open and Affirming (ONA) program encourages and helps local congregations publicly declare that they welcome lesbian/bisexual/gay/transgendered people. See Web page at www.coalition.simplenet.com; and "Welcoming Churches: A Growing Ecumenical Movement," *Open Hands: Resources for Ministries Affirming the Diversity of Human Sexuality,* winter 1993.

13. Within the UCC's governing structure, there are four denominational levels: national instrumentalities, conferences, associations, and local congregations.

14. See similar view expressed in "Mr. Falwell's Progress" [editorial], *New York Times,* 26 October 1999, sec. A, p. 26.